Tactical Communication in Crisis Incidents

Interpersonal Crisis Intervention Skills When Dealing with People in Stressful Situations

Chief Ron Louie, (Ret.), MA, MPA
Portland State University
Portland Community College

Law Enforcement Code of Ethics

As a Law Enforcement Officer, my fundamental duty is to serve mankind; to safeguard lives and property; to protect the innocent against deception; the weak against oppression or intimidation, and the peaceful against violence or disorder.

Cover photos courtesy of Commander Joel Wilson, Ret. →
Cap and Badge photo courtesy of Jo Taylor, RN.
Retirement photo courtesy of CrystralVue Photography
Unless otherwise noted, all other images and photos from info@pdclipart.org (public domain)

Second Edition ISBN: 978-0-615-63669-6 (2011), Odin Ink/Portland State University, Portland, Oregon

First Edition ISBN: 978-7575-5307-3 (2008), Kendall Hunt Publishers, Dubuque, Iowa

Printed in the United States of America

This book is dedicated to my wife Jo who encouraged me to update my original 1981 crisis intervention research and publish this contemporary survey of tactical communication and crisis intervention skills, and who has supported me in so many ways throughout my law enforcement career. I also want to dedicate this book to Sergeant Mike Meloy, (Ret.) my Palo Alto, California, Police Department crisis intervention teaching partner and best friend, as well as the women and men of the Hillsboro, Oregon, Police Department whose openness to change, experimentation and learning new skills permitted me to experience and share with them the success in community policing that comes with adhering to mediation and effective communication skills in policing crises.

Officer Ron Louie & Sgt. Mike Meloy
(1943-2011), on patrol, Palo Alto,
California, 1977

Contents

About the Author

With over 33 years of law enforcement experience, Ron Louie served as the Chief of the Hillsboro, Oregon, Police Department from 1992 to his retirement in 2007. He was the Chief of the Astoria, Oregon, Police Department from 1987-1992. Prior to assuming command in Astoria, Chief Louie spent 13 years with the Palo Alto, California, Police Department, leaving there as a Lieutenant. Chief Louie joined the Palo Alto Police Department in 1974 because that was one of the few police agencies to have abolished the height requirement (he failed his hometown of San Francisco's police entrance requirement of 5'9" - Chief Louie is 5'6") and also because they paid more than what he was making as a part time Anthropology teacher.

A 1999 graduate of the FBI Executive Leadership Institute in Quantico, Virginia, he also is a 1995 graduate of the FBI National Academy, and a 1988 graduate of the Oregon Executive Development Institute (Oregon Command College).

Chief Louie has extensive teaching experience on the university and community college levels (anthropology, Asian history, social science, crisis intervention/tactical communication, hostage negotiation, critical incident management, public safety strategic planning, diversity in law enforcement, executive leadership, management and supervisory skills development) and consulting in community policing and organizational leadership in Alaska, California, New Mexico, Oregon, and Washington, D.C. He is a published author in crisis intervention/tactical communication, contemporary community policing, public safety leadership and public safety strategic planning.

Chief Louie holds a Master of Arts degree in Public Administration from California State University, Hayward, a Master of Arts degree in Anthropology from San Francisco State University, a Bachelor of Arts degree in Social Science (graduating *Magna Cum Laude*) from California State University, Hayward, and an Associate of Arts degree (with *Honors*) in Business Administration from the College of San Mateo, California.

An active participant in issues of diversity and anti-discrimination, Chief Louie served 10 years with the Oregon Committee, U.S. Civil Rights Commission, served on the Oregon Attorney General's Use of Force Task Force, the Governor's Committee on Law Enforcement Contacts (Racial Profiling Committee), State of Oregon Criminal Justice Commission, and currently is a member of the Human Rights Council of Washington County, the Pacific Institute of Ethics and Social Policy (Pacific University) and serves on the Board of Directors of Community Action of Washington County, Oregon.

In 2007, Chief Louie received the prestigious Vollum Ecumenical Ministries Humanitarian of the Year Award, the American Legion Officer of the Year Award, the Administrator of the Year Award from the Oregon Crime Prevention Association, and the Max Patterson Excellence in Youth Services Community Policing Award from the Oregon Association of Chiefs of Police.

Chief Louie is an adjunct professor of Criminal Justice at Portland State University, and Portland Community College, and Political Science at Pacific University, Forest Grove, Oregon.

The son of a Chinese immigrant and Classic Chinese Opera actor, Chief Louie was born and raised in San Francisco, dropped out of high school at age 16, joined the U.S. Marines, also at age 16, and served in Vietnam. Chief Louie and his wife Jo Anne, a Registered Nurse, live in Hillsboro, Oregon with their adult son and daughter living nearby.

Acknowledgements

I want to acknowledge editorial assistance from my wife Jo as well as police attorney Akin Blitz and former civil attorney and writer William J.P. Grace.   I want to also thank Dr. William Lewinski and the *Force Science© Institute*, Minnesota State University at Mankato, for providing   the most up-to-date research on police use of force and tactical communication. For police technical assistance, I want to thank the following police tactical communication and crisis intervention specialists: Lieutenants Richard Goerling, Michael Rouches, Henry Riemann, and Scott Hewitson and Sergeants Craig Allen, Deborah Case and Mike Done, and hostage negotiator detective Ed Vance and tactical communication instructors Officers Mike Thompson and defensive tactics instructor Officer Joe Ganete.

Sgt. Craig Allen, Dr. Bill Lewinski and Chief Ron Louie, Ret., at Force Science© Institute *Traffic Stop Study*, Hillsboro, Oregon.

Introduction

"Tactical Communications in Crisis Incidents" represents a core curriculum of essential police training. Training in interpersonal communications and training designed to develop the "emotional intelligence of police officers" is critical. Police must reflect the values of the communities they serve and protect people when confrontations between police and the emotionally disturbed or drug affected occur.

Policing in America has come a long way from the days when Chief Ron Louie started police work with Palo Alto Police Department (1974), and I began work with the Marion County Sheriff's Office (1969). The 1960's and 1970's represented an era of the Viet Nam war, protests and civil disobedience, and dangerous threats posed by the drug addicted, bikers and gangs of that day.

Now our communities expect their police to present a softer image -- gone are the long clubs (such as axe handles), helmets, ballistic clip boards, six cell Kel Lite flashlights that double as a heavy baton, and a confrontational and forceful response to civil disobedience by those who challenged authority. Our society has evolved from those of "the Greatest Generation" who were not used to questioning authority. The "Baby Boomers" have softened and gained in tolerance and openness as they have taken the place of their parents. The "Baby Boomers" have raised today's young adults who are the Gen X-Y & Z people who share a greater social conscience and higher expectation of government and, in particular, their police. Gen X-Y&Z people are more compassionate in their world view, more tolerant, understanding and accepting of others. Civil disobedience of the 1960's has given way to a society of limited resources for the institutionalized and hospitalized treatment of psychologically and psychiatrically disabled who we now mainstream in society. Police understand all too well that the goal posts have shifted; community policing and greater transparency, and the widely shared expectation that crises end well are examples of community driven changes in values and perception.

Police have long understood the need to earn and maintain community trust. To do so today, the police must be transparent; the police must show the community that they (from the rookie officer on the force to the Chief) deserve trust and support. When tragedies befall a community as a result of police action, the police must be able to demonstrate that they *"Will always do the right thing for the right reason."* In crisis situations, this often requires practiced tactical communication and response skills, flexibility, creativity and a non-impulsive use of time and space.

Society demands that the police are able to demonstrate that officers have done all that could be done to avoid a death. Within the criminal justice system and the civil judiciary, the tests to justify police actions are spelled out in legal principles set forth in law. Police are now frequently realizing that families of loved ones and communities are becoming more sensitive to issues faced by racial minorities and those challenged by mental illness. Communities are reacting with disapproval and questioning when death results from a police confrontation. The community wants to know whether the officer could have done more to avert a fatal outcome. The answer usually is "no" and that answer is often viewed as less than acceptable when the officer has not been trained in crisis intervention response techniques. When the Portland, Oregon Mayor and Police Chief mandated crisis response training for some members of the city's police force, one of the first questions the local media asked after a crisis event was whether the involved officer(s) had received the appropriate crisis response training. The ability to demonstrate that all sworn officers and police professional staff have undergone hours of training to develop communication skills needed in critical incidents and to mediate and to de-escalate will be an increasingly critical asset in a police agency's community relations tool kit.

Mastery in tactical communications is important for another reason and this may prove important in defending civil liability claims. Police departments that do not train and develop officers' communications skills may continue to be effective. However, communities will increasingly demand police competency in their response to critical events and citizens may mistrust and withhold support from those police departments which fail to demonstrate effectiveness in tactical communications strategies.

If you, the reader, are a police officer, police administrator or student of criminal justice, CONGRATULATIONS for taking the time to study tactical and "difficult" communications. By taking the subject matter of this training seriously and honing your abilities to respond to others, particularly those in distress or those who are markedly different, you embark on a process that can result in personal growth and enhanced communication skills that will serve you well both on and off duty. As this crisis response and training occurs in law enforcement agencies with greater frequency, the police profession will further enhance its ability to communicate and be in rapport with others.

Akin Blitz.
Police Labor and Employment Attorney
Portland, Oregon
ablitz@bullardlaw.com
September 2011

Akin Blitz served as a police officer in Oregon from 1969 to 1975 before serving as a provost marshal officer and judge advocate in the Marine Corps. He earned his Juris Doctor degree in 1975 at Lewis and Clark Law School, and his Master of Laws from Georgetown University Law Center in 1979. Thereafter, as an Assistant Attorney General and in private law practice, he has represented law enforcement agencies throughout Oregon and Washington, advised on policy and officer discipline matters, defended tort and civil rights litigation related to police actions, and represented the Oregon Association Chiefs of Police and the Oregon State Sheriffs' Association in a variety of matters including legislation. He serves as a commissioned officer and Legal Advisor to several principal law enforcement clients.

Chapter I: Introduction and Definitions of Crisis Intervention and Tactical Communication

This public safety-related training will review the field of *Police Crisis Intervention* and *Tactical Communication* by presenting various communication strategies and models that police employ when dealing with crisis situations and people in conflict. For the purposes of this training the following definitions will be used:

Jo Taylor, RN

> *Police Crisis intervention is narrowly defined as that situation when police officers are called to intervene in the lives of people who are experiencing an emotional or physical crisis.*

Crisis Intervention is "... the provision of emergency psychological care to victims to assist those victims in returning to an adaptive level of functioning ..." (Everly and Mitchell 1999). For police, this intervention period is usually only as long as it takes to stabilize a situation (such as a domestic dispute, or argument between neighbors) and attempt to resolve the more immediate problem that provoked the 911 call. For mental health care professionals, crisis intervention continues beyond any one particular traumatic incident in the form of on-going psychological support such as therapy or counselling. Police crisis intervention is for the short term and professional psychological intervention for the therapeutic long term.

(Cmdr. Joel Wilson)

> *Tactical communication is an inventory of specific words, phrases, non-verbal and verbal communication techniques and skills, utilized to calm and control people who are experiencing some form of personal crisis or traumatic event.*

(PhotoExpress)

> *Police Negotiator and Mediator is the primary police officer, whether specialist such as a Hostage Negotiator, or patrol officer, who is attempting to establish verbal communication with a subject who is experiencing a crisis-related situation. Mediator is the term used for professionally trained police officers and civilian specialists who mediate disputes between opposing sides, such as disputing neighbors or landlord/tenant disagreements.*

Many times the *police negotiator* title is bestowed upon the specially trained hostage negotiator however, as first responding street officers receive more of this type of crisis communication training, they become the primary person responsible not only for communicating with the person at the other end of the 911 call, but also for successfully resolving the call. With those crisis intervention calls requiring a full tactical call out, some agencies encourage delaying the initial contact with the subject until the arrival of specialized units such as Emergency Response/SWAT and Hostage Negotiators, but many experienced negotiators support first responders making contact as soon as possible (Frier 2007, 44).

Experience has shown that the more crisis-trained your first responders, the quicker crisis calls are resolved and the fewer times you need to call out specialized teams such as Hostage Negotiation and Emergency Response/SWAT. However, if it appears there will be no short term resolution, then specialized teams should be called out to coordinate the now developing critical incident (Louie 2010).

➤ **A word about terms:** Although the focus of this text will be on the public safety officer, those using tactical communication skills may range from a police officer or deputy sheriff, to the paramedic, from a trained civilian mediator to specialists trained in crisis counselling and crisis intervention; *they are all Crisis Interveners.*

Goals of Police Crisis Intervention:

- *Intervene quickly* to provide defusing support, minimize escalation and prevent violence.
- *Stabilize the scene* by separating people if it is a dispute situation, and continue to provide defusing support to individuals, while attempting to identify the causes of the dispute.
- *Mediate between disputants* or in the case of a lone person, assist by helping the person recognize and understand what has happened and attempt to minimize the emotional obstacles the person in crisis is confronting.
- *Facilitate problem solving* through active listening and mediating skills, directing those involved to seek solutions. For the lone individual such as a barricaded person refusing to surrender, facilitate problem solving by reducing these barriers and providing a sense of balance and coping.
- *Assist by helping others to accept help* and resolve their current issues. Part of this assistance could be to coordinate the provision of resources that may provide support for the person in crisis, such as social services, counselling or psychiatric treatment.

➤ Reasons for Studying Crisis Intervention & Tactical Communication

Crisis

Crisis intervention and Tactical Communication are not new concepts, nor a new practice in police work. Police officers have employed these techniques in their communities for decades. Many of these professionals learned them through on- the-job experience in resolving domestic disputes, handling disturbances, and responding to 911 emergencies. However, rather than learn them through trial-and-error, contemporary public safety professionals study these tried-and-true methods in classroom and practicum settings (such as role playing), then apply them in the field.

➤ The reasons for studying police crisis intervention and tactical communication are clear:

- ✓ To insure the safety of both police officers and those whom they contact.
- ✓ To develop skills to control people and situations and to minimize or prevent violence.
- ✓ To formulate and follow appropriate plans and strategies.
- ✓ To increase cooperation with those persons in contact with the police.
- ✓ To improve community relations.
- ✓ To minimize citizen complaints (a significant portion of citizen complaints are based on communication breakdowns between the officers and public; - *it's all about communication*).
- ✓ To increase use of referral agencies; assisting people to obtain appropriate professional guidance and help.

2

- ✓ To reduce the number of repeat calls and/or contacts.
- ✓ To enhance police communication skills. Witnesses and victims are generally more cooperative when they view you as an empathetic ally.
- ✓ Take the path of least resistance; why fight when you can *schmooze*.   According to Hillsboro Police Crisis Intervention instructor Lt. Mike Rouches, schmooze means "to converse casually, especially in order to gain an advantage, influence, or make an interpersonal connection."
- ✓ To both reinforce and demonstrate police department values of service to the community and ensure police officer competency by providing contemporary training.

> **"Crisis intervention is a type of short-term psychological intervention used to help individuals experiencing temporary extreme emotions to recognize, correct, and cope with them"**
> (Regini 2004, 1)

➢ The need for contemporary training:

"If it is known to a moral certainty that officers will confront a certain situation, and that encounter will force officers to make a choice between different alternatives … the agency must provide these officers with reasonable training to equip them to make these difficult and critical choices" (Walker v. City of New York in Reiter 2007, 1).

This legal logic is already being used (i.e., *failure to train*) by those attacking police behavior and tactics in court, reasoning that the police officers "should have been trained in other alternatives." The imperative for police departments is to invest in contemporary training with continuing up-dates.

(Cmdr. Joel Wilson)

> *Most police training focuses on tactics and weapons … with far less training time devoted to interpersonal communication skill building, although most of a police officer's time involves interpersonal verbal communication.*

> *Tactical training is critical …and saves lives…but other tactics such as crisis intervention, tactical communication, mediation and negotiation also need to be emphasized in police training.*

(Cmdr. Joel Wilson)

> **Reasons Why Crisis Intervention and Tactical Communication are Part of the Police Role:**

- ✓ The police are constantly on patrol, and can respond rapidly to crisis situations. Police patrols are a 24/7 service and are always in the field.
- ✓ Many disputes involve violence or possess the potential for violence.
- ✓ Only the police are prepared and legally authorized to handle this immediate task and its inherent risks.
- ✓ The police are the most likely to be called, whether or not they are prepared to intervene effectively.
- ✓ People are confused or do not know where to turn. To many, 911 is their only choice, or their last resort.
- ✓ The police are, or should be, aware of the available community resources for more in depth crisis intervention services; from mental health outreach to special populations like veterans, the homeless, elderly, etc.
- ✓ The pressing need for police to enhance interpersonal communication skills.
- ✓ Crisis intervention is part of the goal of community policing and enhancing the quality of life of a community.
- ✓ Citizens' expectations of police officers and public employees are greater. The public expects and deserves courtesy, fairness, and impartiality.
- ✓ The tax-paying public expects a return on their tax dollars; they expect a service when they call the police and expect them to help solve their problems.

(Cmdr. Joel Wilson)

Contemporary American police are redefining themselves more and more as problem solvers

> ## Tactical Communication & Crisis Intervention: Background and Definitions

"Crisis Intervention is an attempt to systematize the procedures involved in disturbance calls, thereby enhancing the security as well as success of the responding officers" (Louie 1981, 70). The innovative approach employed in crisis intervention revolves around the specific procedures for handling the *disturbance call* and decreasing the possibility of returning to the same scene and re-involving the police. This is not to imply that all situations can be handled or resolved by the police; the point is that many disturbance calls can be settled if handled properly (Louie 1981, 2006).

Since most police agencies train more for technical skills – such as firearms, driving and equipment proficiency – little or no attention was, and continues to be, paid to building either verbal or non-verbal tactical communication skills.

- "The irony is that many major police agencies either provide officers with no communications skills training or the time allocated is inadequate or the method of training proves to be ineffective. Surveys of agencies and academies indicate that typically less than 5% of the available instructional time is spent on communication training, despite the fact that officers will need to display communication competence during 95% of their active duties" (Butler 2007).

- The notion of crisis resolution that started to take hold in the early 1970s led more police agencies to focus on which procedures and skills will not only reduce harm to the officers, but also reduce the number of repeat calls. This novel concept prompted some police departments to focus their training programs on the theoretical subtleties of dispute resolution and mediation, and frame it in the context of an actual police 911 call or crisis.

- Police officers were trained (and still are) to "command or order" people to either behave, or be arrested. Problem solving was not seen as part of the responding officers' role.

> "Crisis Intervention training is an attempt to systematize the procedures involved in disturbance calls, thereby enhancing the security as well as success of the responding officers" (Louie 1981, 70)

> ## Combat Verbalization: Related terms describe the realm of Tactical Communication. Combat Verbalization means essentially the same as Tactical Communication; the context and words used, how one utters these words, tone of voice, and most importantly, your body language. This last and non-verbal communication is essential for effectively establishing communication with a person experiencing an emotional trauma or crisis event. "Your body language, along with your words and your tone of voice, are very important. You can diffuse most situations when these verbal skills are used effectively. In fact, an International Association of Chiefs of Police study found 99.5 percent of police contacts were resolved using only verbal tactics.

Experienced officers preferred verbal tactics for many reasons. The two most important:
The only fight you can't lose is the one

> *Police need to be trained to enhance their interpersonal communication skills*

you don't have and, the less you fight, the less you write" (Klugiewicz 2005, 38).

➢ **The Dynamics of Providing and Receiving Help:** There are psychological and cognitive limitations for a person when attempting to resolve a problem or crisis.   Even the best trained, such as airline pilots, know that, under emergency circumstances, information analysis and sharing decision making improves problem solving (Brooks 2008, 26).

For those intervening in a crisis, this information analysis and shared decision making goes beyond the immediate provocation for the 911 call and looks at the situation using a wider lens than those who are actually experiencing the crisis.   As an example, trauma nurses are trained to not just focus on an immediate and observable wound (analagous to what may have provoked the 911 call in the police example), but to look at the patient in a systemic approach, from the head down to the toes (Taylor 2011).

The more support for the individual, the better. And for those who are not crisis and emergency responder trained, intervening third parties, such as police officers, can provide the best resource management for someone experiencing a crisis. The key will be how well the police officers communicates with the people experiencing the crisis as well as the ability to look at the disturbance call scene in a more systemic perspective…not just focusing on any one particular issue.

(Cmdr. Joel Wilson)

"If the officers recognize that they cannot handle the situation, then either a referral to a more specialized agency (i.e., family counseling, drug programs, etc.) can be made or, as a last resort, the disputants can be separated and/or arrested. This latter procedure of arresting is an alternative that does not solve the problem but merely forestalls the possibility of immediate violence" (Louie 1981, 70).

The one intervening – such as a police officer – must recognize what motivates a person to accept help which may lead to resolution. This is where crisis intervention skills come into play: **tone of voice, recognizing verbal and nonverbal cues, reassurance, empathy, defusing, listening (for what is said and *not* being said), and accurately summarizing should be used to identify issues and recognize what may persuade someone to accept help.**   These tactical communication skills serve the primary purpose of helping to control people and situations. The secondary purpose is to effectively communicate with people experiencing emotional upset and distress.

The application of these skills requires practice and personal experience. The more practice (such as role playing scenarios) and practical experience (such as in the field, on a crisis or disturbance call), the greater the ability to realize when an emergency demands an immediate response.

Chapter II: Communication Theory; Listening with Understanding

> "….-the major barrier to mutual interpersonal communication is our very tendency to judge, to evaluate, to approve or disapprove, the statement of the other person, or the other group. Real communication occurs when we listen with understanding – to see the idea and attitude from the other person's point of view, to sense how it feels to them, to achieve their frame of reference in regard to the thing they are talking about" (Rogers 1961).

Although sounding more like a paradigm than a guideline, it succinctly states a primary principle of crisis intervention: ***When people perceive you are listening to them is the strategic point in time when genuine communication may be taking place.*** And starting to communicate is when one who intervenes in a crisis starts taking control of the situation through verbal and nonverbal skills and techniques. Practicing these listening skills does not compromise officer safety or third party objectivity; it just means that you are listening and trying to communicate.

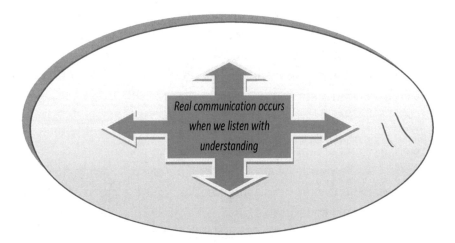

➢ What is a Crisis?

A crisis is a state: "Provoked when a person faces an obstacle to important life goals that is, for the time, insurmountable through the utilization of customary methods of problem-solving. A period of disorganization ensues, a period of upset, during which many different abortive attempts at solutions are made. Eventually some kind of adaptation is achieved which may or may not be in the best interest of that person and his fellows" (Caplan 1961, in Parker and Meier 1975, 185).

A crisis is a stressful life event that overwhelms an individual's ability to cope in the face of a perceived challenge or threat. People in crisis are off balance, disorganized, and unable to call upon their normal coping mechanisms to re-establish balance (Flannery and Everly 2000). Usually some critical or significant emotional event has triggered the crisis response -- one with no foreseeable solution. The trigger event can range from a natural disaster, calamity, or accident, to an act of personal violence, or emotional trauma such as a conflict with a loved one. The crucial issue for the crisis subject is his or her inability to cope with what is perceived, for the moment, as an *insurmountable obstacle*.

This *insurmountable obstacle* is a matter of perception that must be viewed from the perspective of the person experiencing the stress of a crisis: "How a person perceives an incident is often more important than the incident itself" (Collins 2011, 75). This is a very subtle yet critical point: when people experience a crisis, it is the unknown...the how to resolve the crisis ... that produces the stress-induced emotional and physiological impacts on the body.

> **"A person experiences stress when a demand exceeds his or her coping abilities, resulting in disturbances of cognition, emotions and behaviors that can adversely affect well-being. The body can use energy for survival or growth. It cannot do both at the same time. In protection mode, the system closes down to wall itself off from the threat"** (Collins 2011, 76).

This is the usual emotional state of mind when the police arrive at a disturbance call: **someone is facing an obstacle; feeling obstacle is insurmountable; feeling disorganized; feeling upset.** The responding officer needs to identify the following: what is the obstacle; what makes it insurmountable; why feeling disorganized; why feeling upset; i.e., are there other factors not immediately seen that may contribute to the feeling of upset?

When people are experiencing a *significant emotional event*, this may be the time when they are most susceptible to change and accepting help from an intervening third party. The one intervening, such as a police officer, must recognize what motivates a person to accept help which may contribute to a resolution. This is where crisis intervention skills (i.e., tone of voice, reassuring statements, empathy, defusing, active listening and, accurately summarizing the issues) should be used to identify issues and recognize what may persuade someone to accept help.

The utilization of these skills requires both practice and practical experience. These skills serve the primary purpose of helping to control people and situations, while the secondary purpose is to communicate effectively with people in the throes of an emotional upset.

Parker and Meier (1975, 186), point out that a crisis is an individual's *response* to a precipitating event and not the event itself. Frustration arises when the individual is unable to find a means by which a problem can be resolved.

- The role of the police officer is to guide someone to a resolution by assisting with problem solving. It is a given that police officers need to be good communicators to be effective (although many police officers are not sufficiently trained on how to effectively communicate).

8

- They need to recognize that the *immediate crisis* may be the person's reaction to not knowing what to do, or how to resolve the issue and/or problem. This is where crisis intervention skills such as defusing, tone of voice, active listening, and summarizing can help.
- Unfortunately, many police agencies train more for the technical skills (i.e., how to shoot or drive a car) rather than how to communicate with people who are under stress and in a dysfunctional state.

Crisis: facing an obstacle that seems insurmountable; feelings of disequilibrium and upset; not knowing what to do ... a crisis is to be viewed from the perspective of the person experiencing the emotional event because what may seem to be a "small crisis" to a third party, may be the catalyst for an emotional breakdown.

> ## The Nature of Crisis and Conflict: *Κρίση*

Κρίση

For public safety professionals, it is important to understand the nature of conflict when they intervene in the lives of people experiencing conflict and crisis. "Conflict is a natural phenomenon in every person's life, in fact, in nature itself. Because of society's discomfort with conflict it is seen as something that is undesirable. However, without conflict there would be no change or understanding or improvements" (Wiselogle 2010, 6).

The ancient Greeks viewed the word *crisis* (*Κρίση*) as a time "to decide or determine," and the true meaning of the word is that it represents "a turning point" (Hendrickson 2004). This definition has significant and fundamental meaning to those studying and practicing crisis intervention techniques, because the crisis event needs to be viewed as a time when people may be able to change their behaviors in such a way that they are able to overcome their respective crisis.

The task of those intervening in the lives of people experiencing crisis is to help guide them towards resolution, which is the moment in time of a "crisis turning point." Like a brick wall, people in crisis perceive they cannot overcome the crisis barrier. Interveners may need to assist those in crisis to help dismantle this barrier, brick by brick.

In reality, avoidance of conflict is not healthy because that will only keep the adrenaline levels high and lead to unhealthy results. "When the flood of adrenaline hits, your breathing becomes more rapid, your heart rate speeds up, your immune system gears up and your brain starts to malfunction, so you're operating with a survival brain instead of a reasoning brain. When you fight repeatedly and this response is triggered over and over again, your health suffers" (Fiedler 2010). Trying to avoid conflict will not reduce the tension or harmful effects of chemical changes in your body. **Conflict resolution is the best and healthiest response to conflict, *not* avoidance or violence.**

Studies have shown that people tend to deal with conflict in particular ways. Conflict between two or more people is a natural phenomenon. Since conflict elicits so many emotions, people are naturally afraid of conflict and tend to avoid such uncomfortable experiences. However, without interpersonal conflict there would be no change, either good or bad. It is important for those intervening in the lives of others, such as a police officer attempting to defuse an argument between two people, to recognize the various ways that people tend to cope with conflict. These responses are influenced by many factors, ranging from how the person has been socialized to deal with conflict, cultural conditioning, and the person's psychological mood on any particular day.

> The following examples are predicated on two opposing sides, with varying degrees of rancor and argument. Although it is problematic to agree on all the categories, there are general responses by which people react to conflict (Wiselogle 2010, Louie 2010):

- ✓ **Avoidance**
- ✓ **Accommodation**
- ✓ **Competition**
- ✓ **Compromise**
- ✓ **Collaboration**
- ✓ **Confusing and Mixing Issues**
- ✓ **Indifference**

(David Shankbone/Wikimedia Commons)

- ❑ **Avoidance** (Wiselogle 2010): **People may ignore or neglect the issue (or issues) prompting the conflict. With this type of person, it is best for the person intervening to encourage them to think about what to say and have a plan of what they want to do to help resolve the conflict** (i.e., "Tell me the best way to resolve this problem so it does not continue?"). This type of person may be too frightened to face an adversarial situation (that's why they are avoiding it in the first place). It would be helpful to let this type of person know that you are there to help defuse, and *more importantly*, control the context of the conflict. Avoidance, like Accommodation (below), will only lead to further turmoil and emotional upset. Helping this type of person can be a difficult task, especially if an antagonist is present. This is where utilizing defusing skills to calm both parties is essential. If the antagonist is not defused, then both the Avoidance and Accommodation type of person will continue to avoid the pain of a tense confrontation.

One approach may be to ask the Avoidance type of person "what is the worst thing that could happen," as well as "how would you want this situation resolved?" The more the person in crisis is able to articulate his or her response, the better, because the avoidance type of person is at least *confronting* the situation intellectually and is being urged to articulate a response by the intervener.

Your mission is to guide this person, in a conversational tone, to encourage dialogue. This conversation could be occurring while the police officers have separated disputing parties. Note that the Avoidance type of person usually will reveal more information when speaking with a third party and when the other disputant is not present. And this does not have to be a complicated situation. You could be dealing with two people having a minor dispute, say two neighbors for example. Your job as an intervener is to help guide the process. Many times, having an objective third party present creates the best environment for mediation problem solving.

❑ **Accommodation** (Wiselogle 2010)**: This type of person may just give in to appease and accommodate the demands of the antagonist. Unlike the Avoidance type of person, this individual may engage in some dialogue, but will limit the discussion through accommodation, allowing the antagonist to win.** But by allowing someone else to win, the problem or issue that provoked the conflict (and the reason for the 911 call) may still persist, and this type of person will continue to be in turmoil (Pahn 2010). Therefore, it is best to try to resolve as soon as possible otherwise, the calls for help may well continue.

In addition, the more times police are required to respond to the same disputants, the greater the probability of violence and injury. A good strategy, then, for the crisis intervener is to maneuver this type of person away from apologizing or *giving in* just to accommodate his or her adversary. Your task is to engage the person in a conversation that explores their perception of the situation or crisis; i.e., "what's your take on the best way to solve this?"

As the person talks, they at least get some distance from the easy way out. And the more this type of person reveals how he or she feels (initiated by asking: "tell me how you feel about that" or "I sense that you are angry about this situation…tell me more,") the more you can explore the differences and similarities between this person and the antagonist. **With this type of person, you want to maneuver them to acknowledge their point of view, and then convey it to the person they are arguing with** (Pahn 2010).

By comparing and contrasting, you encourage the Accommodation type of person to identify solutions beyond mere statements that are quick and easy accommodations.

A Tactical Communication approach would be to ask: "tell me what happened here today?" Once the conversation starts, encourage the person to continue talking and try *not to interrupt.* Many times police are in such a hurry to get through the 911 call that they rush the participants, thereby drastically limiting the *conversation* they want to initiate. As the participant is talking, direct the questioning, such as: "give me an idea of how you want this resolved." By doing so, you are attempting to ascertain if there are any reasonable solutions short of just *giving in and accommodating.*

- ❑ **Competition** (Wiselogle 2010): **This type of person is determined *to win* at all costs and *will* be aggressive.** He or she will attempt to dominate the contact and it is important for the crisis intervener to defuse and control this type of individual. The less you control him or her, the more you will allow this type of person to intimidate others, such as those who Accommodate and Avoid.

The Competitive type of person will continually repeat his or her point so it is important to control this repetition. The best tactic when this occurs is this: once the person continues to repeat a particular point, you "paraphrase" by restating the point, and then shift the conversation by asking the other party to tell their side of the story.

As a result, you are shifting the conversation away from the competitor-type and allowing others to take part in the conversation. This takes finesse and skill since the competitor type may constantly interrupt and even challenge others present. This type of situation is where your skills as a defuser and mediator come into play.

- ❑ **Compromise** (Wiselogle 2010): **This type of person will be more pliable since their inclination is to compromise.** However, it is important to make sure you encourage him or her to articulate their issues and not allow them to short-cut to a compromise. This is because it is important to recognize this person's goals and values as well as perception of the conflict. All too often, this type of person may just give up too soon, instead of reaching a viable solution to the conflict or crisis.

In crisis intervention, such as a dispute between two people, it is critical to make sure there is an exploration of both sides' perspectives, otherwise, the rush to an agreement, such as with the Compromise type of person, may not solve the problem, requiring the police to return time and again to the same location.

- ❑ **Collaboration** (Wiselogle 2010): This type of person is aware of mutual solutions and is usually more amenable to a joint solution. This individual is similar to the person who compromises but the collaborationist has a tendency to ignore time constraints and may go on longer than the Compromiser. Collaboration does take effort, so this personality type may become overly focused on an immediate objective, rather than seek a solution to the greater problem.

The Collaborator may also dominate a conversation, leaving less time for others to speak, so it is important to also direct this person. One example of conversational direction may be to summarize what the collaboration-type has said, even if it is offered as a solution, and then redirect the conversation to the other disputants.

- **Confusing and Mixing Issues** (Louie 2010): **This type of person responds to conflict by mingling an entire agenda of past and present grievances.** As an example, as two disputing parties, such as disputing neighbors, are separated, this type of person may loudly protest and complain about an issue that occurred sometime in the past and not necessarily even related to what provoked the current conflict. This type of person is very difficult to deal with because the crisis intervener is usually bombarded with so many issues or complaints that it may be difficult to separate the *wheat from the chaff*. This is where Active Listening skills are absolutely paramount; the crisis intervener needs to intently focus on which issues raised (usually stated with a raised voice as well) are key to solving the current conflict.

The crisis intervener needs to practice patience and active listening with those that Confuse and Mix issues because they can be very frustrating. This type of person will constantly surface *old issues* and *hidden agendas* so the one intervening needs to frequently defuse and refocus this person back to the reality at hand – the reason for the argument and the resulting 911 call.

The usual salutation and question of "what happened here today?" needs to be followed up with specific questions that are germane to the situation at hand. When inundated with a myriad of issues, the crisis intervener needs to respond with: "I hear what you are telling me about your neighbor for the past few years, but tell me about what happened here today and what can we all do to help fix this problem. I realize there are deeper issues that you have with your neighbor (you can insert friend, husband, wife, etc. here, depending on the context) so let's find a way to resolve this situation that is fair to both of you, and of course, help keep the police out of your business." Most people are uncomfortable with having the police in their homes and the latter statement motivates them to focus on the immediate problem, and keep the police out of their lives in the future.

The crisis intervener needs to practice patience with this type of person because they can be very frustrating. It is usually best to allow them a little more time to ventilate and repeat the issues. Actually, when they start to restate and repeat what they have already told you is the time to redirect the ventilation (to *short circuit,* so to speak) and have them refocus on the issue at hand instead. A good technique is to paraphrase (restate in your own words what you believe you have been told) what they have told you, confirm their feelings (how they feel about what has happened), and then direct them toward workable solutions.

The conversation may sound something like this: "Okay, as I understand it, you are frustrated over the many years your neighbor has ignored what you say are common courtesies; such as picking up the leaves and debris, making disturbing noises late at night and refusing to move the garbage cans once they have been picked up." In this latter example, you have not only summarized what the person has said, but you have also identified an emotion – frustration - which is an acknowledgment of how they may feel (i.e., a perception check). **This is a good strategy to develop rapport because the person will recognize that you have actually listened so well that you can accurately repeat what has been told to you** (*and this may be when genuine communication starts to take place*). Now you need to redirect them and refocus on the issues at hand, leaving behind the history for the moment. This history will have to be revisited and explored in a longer term mediation or counseling session.

❑ **Indifference** (Louie 2010)**: This type of person can be more difficult than all of the above because this type of person doesn't really care (at least outwardly) about resolving any issues, much less the one he or she is presently engaged in!** All of the above descriptors presuppose that the disputants have some motivation to resolve their respective issues, however, the indifferent type of person may show very little interest in even discussing the issues.

(Cmdr. Joel Wilson)

With this type of person, the best strategy is to try to determine if there is any self-interest motivation to resolve the dispute. At the least, this type of person, although not very sincere about resolution, may be willing to make peace if it means the police will leave; and will maintain the peace just to keep the police from returning.

The challenge for the crisis intervener is to identify what it will take, within reason, to get this type of person to make an agreement to end a dispute. And of course, the worst type of confrontation is between two people who really don't care to resolve their differences and even feed off the tension as a preferable state of controlled animosity.

The above discussion of how people may react to conflict is not an exhaustive list and is only intended to provide an approach strategy for the crisis intervener. The definitions may even blend among the characterizations, but by having an understanding of how people may generally react to conflict assists the crisis interveners in how they chose to focus a conflict resolution strategy.

Out of the tension of a personal crisis is the time when people may be receptive to change. This is because people in crisis do not know how to overcome obstacles they are facing. Those intervening in the lives of people experiencing crisis, such as public safety professionals, are in the best position to help people through such a crisis.

What to remember is that just as conflict may provide an opportunity for change and resolution, so does harmony emerge from all the tension generated from tautly pulled guitar strings.

> ### Skills in Responding to people in a Crisis

How public safety professionals respond may determine the success or failure of the intervention process. So, do the police shout commands or, will there be opportunities (always keeping in mind officer safety), to de-escalate and defuse a situation? **Effective crisis intervention demands that the one intervening use a *communicative voice* not a *loud authoritative voice*.**

Police Hostage Negotiators (during the early 1970s, a pioneering police sub discipline of tactical communicators) know only too well how important one's tone of voice can be when trying to communicate with a person under stress. Shouting at people does not work very well under these types of situations. ***Instead, it usually makes things worse!***

> ### "From afar, Americans are asked to pay up; Debt collection gets a polite Indian touch" (*Herald International Tribune* 2008, 2)

To reinforce that using a *communicative tone of voice* may enhance cooperation with people experiencing crisis or upset, debt collectors being outsourced to India appear to be having more positive results because of how overseas debt collectors are trained. "Collectors in India are very polite, very respectful, and they don't raise their voice." India "…trains them in unexpected skills like sympathy" which promotes empathy and understanding. Customers may get very abusive, very emotional and at the same time, very sad, and "the collector's job is to try to empathize with the consumer…and try to figure out , if they are angry, why." Speaking about why someone is in debt, "maybe it's us, maybe it's someone else, you have to hear what they have to say." Collectors who raise their voices or try *tough* tactics are warned not to do so.

> ### Communication Theory: Listening with Understanding

(Cmdr. Joel Wilson)

> *Communication begins when the intervener in a crisis starts taking control of the situation through verbal and non-verbal skills and techniques. Practicing listening skills does not compromise officer safety or third party objectivity, and simply means that you are actively listening and trying to communicate.*

"Police communications must be designed around the psychology of persuasion. Powerful verbal and nonverbal communication can work to modify a subject's behavior in such subtle ways that they are not detectable by the individual being influenced. However, officers who are not properly trained in these strategies may unwittingly use words and body language that undermine their attempt to positively influence behavior" (Butler 2007, 3).

> *When people perceive that you are listening to them is the moment when genuine communication may take place.*

➢ The Art of Conversation

 **Police officers are trained to *interrogate* from a position of power, rather than *interview* in a conversational style. And the more that they interrogate, the greater the likelihood that people will become defensive.** Interviewing in a conversational style, however, when conducted in a more cordial voice, can disarm people and thereby reduce some of the collateral stress of the situation. This is analogous to shouting versus using a non-hostile tone of voice. Interrogating versus conversational interviewing should also be recognized as a tactical communication technique choice. A decision to use this technique depends on the situation and state of mind and behavior of the people with whom the police are attempting to communicate. Unfortunately, many police see themselves as always in an interrogation mode, whether speaking with a criminal suspect or non-criminal subjects having a heated argument. Observe any veteran police detective or Hostage Negotiator and watch how skillfully they *speak with, in a conversational tone* and *not to* people in crisis or under stress. Establishing rapport is critical for cooperation and control and is part of their tactical communication skill set.

> *An interview with a suspect should not be seen as an interrogation but as an opportunity to establish rapport to provide officers with an additional tool to gain information in a non-confrontational way.*

When attempting to communicate with someone experiencing a stressful event, clues to enhancing effectiveness can be found in how police interview and interrogate criminal suspects. **The key is to approach the verbal communication as a *conversation*, not an *interrogation*** (although most certainly it is a subtle and directed interview with the intention of seeking the truth). These skills become an inventory of Tactical Communication phrases and an overall strategy of how to craft a conversation out of an adversarial (between a police officer and suspect) or stressful (between a police crisis intervener and crisis victim) meeting.

"You can use a simple conversation to persuade the truth. A conversation is more than a simple interaction. It is an opportunity to gather information that leads you to the truth. It is a process of conveying information through verbal and nonverbal gestures. The initial conversation is traditionally utilized as a rapport-building stage" (Sumpter 2008a, 14).

Although people in crisis should not be treated as *suspects*, the communication skills are shared among crisis interveners trying to solve a problem and police detectives attempting to seek the truth from a suspect. Breaking down the initial interaction into a series of stages that builds rapport, gains information and eventually weakens the suspect's stance is similar to a crisis intervener defusing an angry disputant, then attempting to communicate beyond the anger of the moment.

Many times interviewing a suspect turns into a push-pull battle for truth, especially when the suspect aggressively approaches the interview. In this case, an officer spends a lot of time trying to control the suspect and little on building rapport.

If the officer gives the suspect the *conversational floor*, he or she can subtly and subconsciously work the suspect to his or her favor by utilizing some basic tools. And the same may be true of a recalcitrant crisis subject who does not want to talk with the police.

To start, you must find something in common; *"we like those who are like ourselves"* (Sumpter2008a). Therefore, search for some sort of commonality. Look at what the subject is wearing, or tattoos, or other objects of interest. Showing interest is the key; as an example, let's say the subject has a military tattoo... you may say something like: "hey, you are a Jarhead (meaning a U.S. Marine) just like me...what outfit were you with?" If the subject responds in the affirmative, then follow through with the conversation for a while...don't be in a rush (street cops always seem to be in a rush, but detectives know they have to slow down, which is counter-intuitive to most cops). And continue the conversation with something like: "Sorry we have to meet like this...I'd rather be splitting a beer at the EM Club" (Enlisted Men's' Club). Using a mutually identifiable jargon may help facilitate rapport. In the latter example, it is a reinforcement of the military and warrior brotherhood.

> *Whatever is said, you want to set a conversational tone and lead with a familiar topic ... that's why the idioms and jargon are important to help establish a connection ... one that will be easy for the subject to engage in and not be too preoccupied with deception.*

As you progress through your conversation, you simultaneously build rapport while working to persuade the subject to tell the truth (again, the same for a suspect as well as a victim). At this initial stage of the so-called conversation, you are looking to establish "baseline behavior" (Sumpter 2008b) which is the normal verbal and nonverbal communication style and behavior of the subject. The more you engage in a conversation that is nonthreatening (and definitely not accusatory, at least not yet) the more the subject will somewhat be off guard and you will be able to observe this baseline behavior. "As the interview continues, the officer watches and notes differences in behavior. If a contradiction is noted, the topic can be revisited at a later time. An officer failing to observe normal behavior will have nothing to compare against during latter stages of the interview" (Sumpter 2008b, 14-15).

> The following police interview techniques (Miller 2011; Sumpter 2008a, 2008b) are applicable to those attempting to communicate with someone facing a crisis or experiencing an emotional event, as much as someone who is suspected of a criminal act.

Mirroring: As the subject is speaking, actively listen while *mirroring* the subject's personal communication behaviors. *Mirroring is the process of consciously modeling the suspect's behaviors, such as speech pattern, posture, and other personal and idiosyncratic gestures.* You may swear if he swears (but be subtle...don't mimic), use your hands if he uses his, and raise your voice (slightly...not the same volume as the subject's) if the subject does. You will find as rapport strengthens, the subject will begin opening posture, which is more prone to the interviewer's lead.

 **Pacing:** While mirroring the verbal interaction and looking for baseline behavior, subtly begin pacing nonverbal behavior. As the subject changes posture, subtly do the same. When the subject leans back or forward in his chair, do the same. Keep in mind that these body movements are done subtly and should be unnoticeable. This is especially true when communicating with the mentally ill and emotionally disturbed: "If someone notices you are mirroring they will take it as an insult. They will believe you are mocking them" (Miller 2011). Both mirroring and pacing send a subconscious message that brings you closer to passing what is known as the *compatibility test* between the interviewer and subject. Some studies (Miller 2011) have shown that pacing and mirroring body language helps the person being interviewed to relax.

In the case of attempting to communicate with someone experiencing stress or a crisis, although not a suspect, they may very well not want to confide in you and may be deceptive, just like the police criminal suspect.

 **Leading:** Once you have mirrored and paced the interview to a point where there is verbal and nonverbal agreement, turn the table and lead the subject in your direction. Leading is a process where you gauge the listener's cooperation from nonverbal behaviors. When the time is right, change your posture for 30 seconds to see if there is a similar change in the subject. If there is a similar change, then rapport is strong, but if not, continue with the give-and-take of a conversation and stay away from the "truth-seeking" questions (remember, you don't want to be seen as interrogating).

 **Confidence:** The most important aspect of any interview, whether suspect or crisis victim, is confidence. In the case of a suspect interview, if the suspect perceives the police interviewer as weak or not self-assured, the suspect may interpret this weakness as vulnerability and will increase deception (because the subject believes he can get away with it!). If interviewing a crisis subject, the person may see the police officer as ineffectual; how can this officer help me when he/she appears to lack command presence and confidence?

"Confidence starts with the projection and rate of your voice. The faster the rate of speech, the more interest and confidence it projects. With this, the most important aspect of communication is inflection. The raising and lowering of pitch generates acceptance or rejection. A person who knows his subject well is confident in what is said even without the words" (Sumpter 2008a, 14-15). **But don't keep the rate of speech at a faster rate**; vary the speed to accentuate points, and then slow down to give the other person time to think.

 **Speech volume and pitch:** Finally, the key to controlling speech volume and pitch is to stress the important words and phrases while effectively using a pause, which is an important aspect in displaying confidence. An officer who states "The most important part of this interview…is for you to be honest," emphasizes the interview and the word honest. Although the suspect may be far from actually telling the truth so early in the contact, the suspect will see that the interviewer is poised and confident, with a command presence that may eventually influence how the suspect responds. At the least, this projection of confidence will put the suspect in

a guarded psychological state, making it more difficult to continually be deceitful...it's easy to tell the truth and difficult to continue to lie. And it is not uncommon for people when finally "starting to tell the truth" to actually feel a sense of reduced stress and belated relief (Sumpter 2008a).

With the crisis subject, you may start with: "The most important part of our conversation is for me to listen to you so that I may understand what really happened here and perhaps be able to help you." The emphasis is on "what really happened here," which indicates that the officer wants to hear the truth, without having to insult the person by assuming he or she will not be truthful. Again, deception is just as common with people who are angry and arguing as it is with a criminal suspect; it is only in the reason and degree of deception that separates the criminal suspect from the crisis victim.

Mirroring, pacing, and leading are ways to build rapport and ways to break down an aggressive subject and prepare the subject to let down his or her guard and tell the truth (at least, some truth although it may not be a true *Perry Mason* courtroom confession).   As an interviewer progresses into these stages, the interviewer must keep in mind that as he or she is looking for changes in behavior and the suspect is doing the same (Sumpter 2008a, 2008b).

Nonverbal cues, tone and sincerity of voice, and words used can be critical to establishing rapport with a person experiencing emotional upset. When attempting to establish rapport, there is a "continuum" of how sincere a person is interpreted and received.

> ## The art and science of interviewing and questioning; using open-ended and closed-ended questions.

Using the wrong tactics when questioning people, especially witnesses

(Cmdr. Joel Wilson)

In a recent study from the Memorial University of Newfoundland analyzing the effectiveness of police interviewing skills, it was discovered that in many cases police investigators were actually "reducing the amount of information retrieved" by not only taking too much time and not allowing those being interviewed more time to respond, but also by asking questions (known as "closed-end questions") that were eliciting shorter responses from those being interviewed (Force Science News #149, 2010).

The review of 90 police-witness interviews revealed:

- On average, the officers actually talked at least 36% of the time, which is far above the recommended ratio of 20% for standard interviewing (meaning the officers should only talk approximately 20% of the time, allowing 80% of time for those being interviewed to respond). By talking *so much* the officers were actually reducing the opportunity for those being interviewed to respond and elaborate on their responses. And it is during this important *80%* that people tend to offer more information, even beyond the actual focus of the initial questions posed by the officer.

20/80

- In the study, only 6% of the questions posed by the interviewing officers were characterized as open-ended questions, meaning questions that could not be answered as a "yes" or "no" but rather encouraged the speaker to elaborate and continue talking.

- In 12% of the interviews, those being interviewed "were warned in advance about the legal consequences of providing false information," a caveat that resulted in "significantly shorter" responses. However, the more experienced detectives tended not to issue any such warning, recognizing the *chilling effect* this type of warning may have on interviews and peoples' willingness to divulge information.

The study also concluded that "detectives commonly fail to distinguish between interrogating a suspect and interviewing a cooperative witness, and generally take an approach that inhibits the free flow of information needed from witnesses."

Open-ended and Closed-ended Questions

Open-ended questions: Are intended to provoke a greater response and unsolicited statements. "Open-ended questions are foundational to cognitive interviewing, which encourages free-form narratives of recollections by interviewees and has been scientifically established to have the greatest potential for thoroughly tapping memory" (Force Science News #149, 2010). Open-ended questions encourage a more "free narrative" from the interviewee.

Closed-ended questions: Limits interviewee statements because what is being said is a very specific response to the closed-ended question, with no encouragement to elaborate or provide unsolicited information. Consequently, information will not be generated if the interviewer forgets to ask a relevant question. One explanation for close-ended questioning is the mistaken belief that such specific-oriented questions may control an interview.

Closed-ended questions should be used when the interviewer already knows what has happened and is merely attempting to confirm what is already known or can be proven. But closed-ended questions can be interpreted as antagonistic – or annoying – and may provoke the interviewee to become even more guarded and cautious, thereby increasing the likelihood of deceit.

Dr. Bill Lewinski (Force Science News #149, 2010) of the Force Science Institute describes four categories of open-ended questions that can be effective in "eliciting useful and thorough responses"

• **DESCRIPTIVE:** "Tell me what happened…."

• **CAUSAL:** "What do you think brought this about…."

• **HISTORICAL:** "Give me time-frames as to when and how this evolved…."

• **COMPARATIVE:** "Have you ever seen or experienced anything like this before…." "How did that compare…."

The Onion metaphor: And as the interviewee responds to the latter questions, the interviewer prompts greater elaboration by use of *minimal encouragers* ("um hum," "OK," "tell me more," etc.). Dr. Lewinski equates this interview strategy to peeling an onion, one layer at a time, "probing for more recollections with the same types of open-ended questions. You end up with maximum information in the witness's own words."

But with the criminal suspect as well as crisis victim, you must concentrate on subtle changes and not something that can appear demeaning. If patient, the interviewer should be prepared to work hard to build and maintain rapport during the interview. But poor rapport can lead to interviewee passivity and foster poor communication
(Lewinski in Force Science News #149, 2010).

> ## Communication Theory and Tactical Communication Techniques: Using empathy by reinforcing body language and facial expressions

Studies have revealed that words are usually only 7% effective in communication, tone of voice is usually 38% effective, and nonverbal cues and body language are usually 55% effective (Mehrabian 1971).   Reinforcing the impact of the nonverbal in effective communication, a 2009 Southern Illinois University study (Owen 2009) sought to determine what influences the perceptions of teacher professionalism and found that first impressions of teacher professionalism were based on the very same effectiveness ratios of nonverbal cues such as appearance, followed by tone of voice and finally what was said.

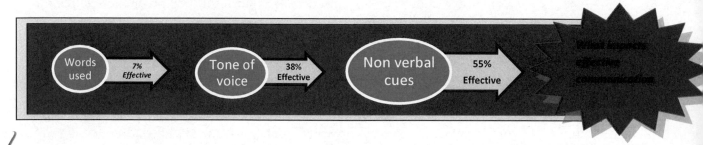

Body language signals nonverbal cues and consists of body movements, posture, gestures, and facial expressions such as eye brow, jaw and eye movements. People tend to send these non-verbal cues or messages subconsciously, although there are times, such as role playing or deliberate intention when these facial and body movements are intended to emphasize a dramatic message (such as looking angry or sad). Experts in the field of nonverbal communication contend that there is 60% at a minimum and at the most 97% of communication which is nonverbal (Borg 2008).

"The way people move their bodies tells us a lot about their feelings or intentions, and we use this information on a daily basis to communicate with each other" (BBC 2009).

- **Establishing Empathy as a continuum of perceived sincerity:**

An example of this continuum to establish empathy would be like the following scenario involving mediating police officers who have just separated arguing spouses. Comment of wife to one of the officers: "My husband just sits around all day and gets drunk."

- **Low empathic response** from the officer, using a more stern volume, expressionless face and stiff body posture: "How much does he drink?"
- **Moderate empathic response**, using a lower voice tone: "Perhaps your husband needs help."
- **High empathic response** using body and facial expressions indicating sincerity: "I can see that you are frustrated; what can we do today to try to resolve why the police were called?   I am here to try to help both you and your husband."

A *high empathic response* demonstrates that you are actively listening and there to help. "But helping someone to come to terms with their situation does not mean telling them how you would deal with it. Hearing them out and understanding what's going on will help them to calm themselves down and work the situation out for themselves. Your role as an active listener is to help the person you are talking with to recognize the source of his or her frustration. In that, you will be able to help be a part of the solution" (McHattie 2010).

The high empathic response only takes a few seconds more than the other responses but has the potential of developing a stronger communication link between the wife and officers. Communicating with these types of empathic responses may not necessarily solve a problem, but it may reduce hostility and emotion among those arguing or in conflict, and perhaps provide a more cordial atmosphere for discussing the issues at hand. However, before the *discussion phase* there needs to be a *defusing* of the situation.

Skillful use of tone and sincerity of voice with a reinforcing body language and nonverbal cues may actually become a primary defusing technique. *People may not be able to recite what was said to them, but they do recall how they felt … and they never forget it!*

> *Employing the skill to effectively communicate when people are in crisis may provide the unique opportunity to actually help people move out of the initial state of crisis and into a position of problem solving (this occurs when the person under stress recognizes there may be solutions to his/her problem).*
>
> **People may forget what you said, but they will never forget how you made them feel!**

➤ Communication Theory: Emotion Labeling
(Louie and Vance 2007)

It is vitally important to always acknowledge the emotions you are interpreting from someone who is in crisis. By surfacing your observations in the form of questions or comments, you may pry open a psychological door that has been closed. And your efforts may be rewarded by establishing an empathic connection, allowing you to push open that psychological door.

Opening such a door is usually verified by a quick response, even in defensive tones such as: "of course I am angry" or "no, I am not hurt, I am pissed," or "of course I am alone…my wife just left me.". These responses need to be quickly followed by active listening that encourages the person to open up even more. Soon, the questions and responses hopefully will develop into a dialogue that will lead to building trust.

If there is an adverse reaction from the subject, then it is easy to back off: "I didn't say you *were* angry, I said you *sound angry*." And remember timing; once you say the latter, follow-up quickly with "we are here to help you…tell us what happened here today." You want to encourage the person to continue talking, even if seemingly angry or upset. As the person continues, use subtle defusing techniques (such as *active listening* nods of the head or verbally encouraging the person to continue with *minimal encouragers*) to minimize the anger yet maintain the dialogue. **You are actually asking *clarifying questions* because these types of questions are not about what you have heard from the speaker as much as what you did not hear**…that is why you want to continue exploring emotions and feelings, because touching those sensitive topics may provoke greater depth of response that will give the interviewer more valuable information:

- ➢ **People often have many emotions, expressed all at once (so listen!).**
- ➢ **Extremely effective; can build tremendous rapport by labeling emotions the subject is feeling but has not yet recognized: "I can hear anger in your voice, and it seems like this situation has hurt you also. What can we do tonight to help you?"**
- ➢ **If possible, never let a feeling go by without labeling it; people want to have others understand how they feel.**

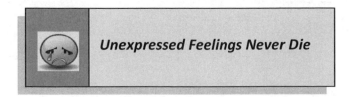

Unexpressed Feelings Never Die

> ## Communication Theory; Eye Contact to Establish Empathy

Cmdr. J. Wilson

Coupled with tone and sincerity of voice should be ***non-threatening eye contact*** (meaning don't glare or look aggressive).

- However, "direct eye contact can be threatening" as it "might provoke paranoia or aggression" (Block 2006). The intervening officer needs to quickly judge and assess if the tone of voice needs to be altered as well as the utilization of direct or indirect eye contact. But in general, direct eye contact is recommended to signal *active listening*. There may be times when utilizing empathy can be problematic, such as when dealing with people experiencing paranoia:

  ✓ "Empathy is usually good but discouraged when dealing with paranoia. Paranoia leads people to feel they are being invaded (often coupled with delusions or fears of being sexually assaulted). Getting into their experience is, therefore, threatening and might lead to escalation" (Block 2006). But for the intervening officer, generally speaking, displaying empathy is the best initial approach.

- "Patterns of eye contact are different across cultures" (Levine and Adelman 1993). From an American perspective, little or no eye contact conveys suspicion and concealment yet in many cultures around the world, direct eye contact may be considered disrespectful, especially towards someone in authority such as a police officer or government official.

> ## Communication Theory; Using Empathy to make a connection:

> ***Empathy:*** *To understand thoughts and feelings so well that you could summarize them for the person; to recognize those thoughts and feelings.*

"The key to empathy is letting the other person know that you understand and can put yourself in their position" (McHattie 2010). But word of caution: don't tell people you "know how they feel" but rather, that you can "see that you are upset" or that you "hear what you are telling me."

- **Empathy** Is an identification and understanding of another's situation, feeling and motivation for such feeling, or for doing something, or for one's behavior. This identification and understanding is not an agreement with these emotions of another person, but merely a recognition.

- **Empathy is not sympathy** (Sympathy: "An expression of pity or sorrow for the distress of other," American Heritage Dictionary 2000). Pity and sorrow are not productive and if expressed, will only be interpreted as patronizing behavior and will not enhance interpersonal communication. It is not necessary to actually "feel what they feel or know how they feel" to provide empathy.

Empathy is not about being nice
Empathizing with someone, therefore, does not mean agreeing with or necessarily liking what the person is saying or doing. It is not an agreement but rather an understanding. Many times police officers *keep their distance* because they erroneously think that if they are empathetic, they are somehow *being nice* (which may be counter to their self- image of a police officer, or what they perceive to be their role as an objective third party intervening in a crisis). Or they believe being empathetic may somehow portray them as agreeing with a disputant or agreeing with the issues. **Displaying empathy can be one of the most powerful demonstrations of understanding and will greatly enhance one's ability to communicate.**

Empathy is not the time to:
✓ Be condescending;
✓ Pretend to understand something that doesn't make sense to you;
✓ Give unsolicited advice;
✓ Respond with superficial comments that dismiss or minimize how the person feels;
✓ Jump to a conclusion before thoroughly listening to what is being said. (McHattie 2010)

(Cmdr. Joel Wilson)

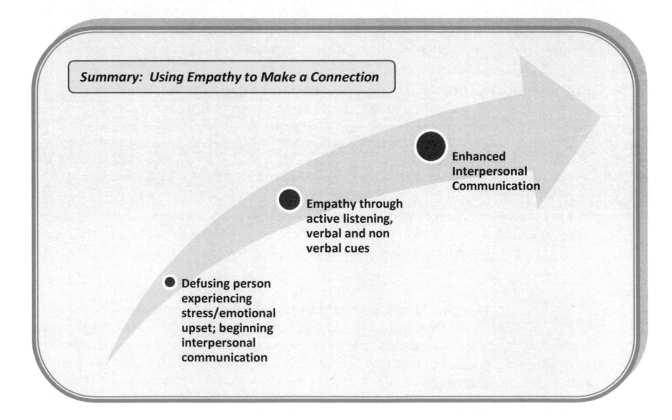

Summary: Using Empathy to Make a Connection

Enhanced Interpersonal Communication

Empathy through active listening, verbal and non verbal cues

Defusing person experiencing stress/emotional upset; beginning interpersonal communication

➤ **Communication Theory: Verbal First Aid – A Tactical Communication Technique.** "The right words, at the right time, can have a profound effect on the victim of a traumatic experience" (Acosta and Prager 2002).

 **"Verbal First Aid is based on the astounding, yet simple, idea that what we think, what we feel, and what we say and hear gets translated instantaneously into physiological processes"**
(Acosta and Prager 2002).

Verbal First Aid relates to people who are victims of physical injury such as a vehicle collision or assault. Conscious or not, the first words the responding officer utters are absolutely critical. And the same is true for the first words spoken at the scene of a disturbance call, although no one may seem physically injured – *if people are in a crisis, and upset, then this applies.*

 "When a victim is lying on the ground, the words they hear in the first crucial moments can make all the difference in the world. Whatever they hear has a tremendous impact and can affect the autonomic nervous system. What they hear will determine if that impact is helpful or harmful" (Acosta and Prager 2002).

Although unconscious, the victim can still comprehend: "This guy looks awful" vs. "I think he's going to make it" (battlefield medics and Navy corpsmen know this very well when first contacting a wounded comrade, unconscious our not: "you're going to be OK – it's the million dollar wound that will send you home; boy are you lucky!"). And the same is true when confronting someone who has experienced verbal trauma as well; what the officer says during those first critical moments can help or hurt the ability to establish rapport and eventually, control over people and the situation.

The wounded warrior: Writing about the exploits of a WWII U.S. paratrooper company in Europe, author Stephen Ambrose illustrates how the unconscious may have recollections. As fellow paratroopers looked down on the lifeless body of a comrade who had just been shot through the throat and mouth, one remarks "Aw, hell, forget him," and another says "He's gone, he's gonna die" (Ambrose 1992, 162-163). Years later the wounded paratrooper is interviewed and Ambrose recites: "He heard it all, and never forgot it, and never let the men forget it when he recovered and rejoined the company" (Ambrose 1992, 163).

The hospital patient: There are also many anecdotal reports of unresponsive and comatose patients who have awakened to report hearing loved ones or healthcare workers discussing their condition while they were seemingly unaware. One such patient who was experiencing complications from a kidney transplant, appeared unconscious and unresponsive, yet accurately related hearing his wife and family in the hall outside the hospital room discussing his funeral arrangements. This angered and disappointed the patient who exclaimed "How dare they give up on me! I never lost hope, how could they?" He ultimately survived the illness and divorced his wife (Taylor 2011).

Here is the key point: "When people are in an altered state, they take suggestions from someone in authority." When people are experiencing significant emotional or physical stress, they are also susceptible to control through non hostile authority such as a police officer recognizing the stress or injury at the moment, but also establishing rapport through tone of voice and verbal and non-verbal cues.

"Rapport is the track on which all communication runs. The rapport you have with a victim will determine how your words are internalized." As an intervening officer, it is important that not only are you a person in authority, but also one who can communicate. "Gaining rapport means that you hear them, see them, and empathize with them."

"Once you have established credibility, authority, and rapport, you can begin giving therapeutic suggestions." For police crisis intervention, the "therapeutic suggestions" become verbal control through defusing, interviewing and mediating.

> *Once the rapport starts to take seed, the officer needs to skillfully communicate with active listening and interviewing skills.*

> ## Communication Theory: Pitfalls to Avoid

Recognizing *pitfalls to avoid* (listed below) is an aspect of interpersonal communication discipline that requires the police officer to make choices of what to say and what not to say. These choices become the tactical communication strategy to apply in specific situations, depending on the state of mind and behavior of the person or persons experiencing the crisis. Therapist and police trainer Dr. Mary Zinkin (2000, 11) has developed a list of behaviors and terms to avoid when attempting to communicate with someone experiencing a stressful event.

- **Me-too-ism.** "That's nothing! Let me tell you what happened to me!" When intervening in a crisis, resist the temptation to convince those in crisis that you *feel their pain* or *know what they are going through* or that the moment in time is all about me; *empathize, don't patronize or be ego-involved!*

- **Moralizing, preaching, and being judgmental.** Suspend judgment; recognize that what is said might offend your value system but set that judgment aside so you can listen. *Put yourself in neutral.* This is where the one intervening needs to role-play, recognizing non-verbal as well as verbal cues can betray feelings of judgment. If this happens, you may lose credibility and will not be seen as objective.

- **Asking a direct question to satisfy your curiosity.** It is none of your business unless they want to divulge information. Be very careful what questions you ask; ask only those questions that will help identify and resolve, not explore too far afield. Don't become an *interrogation voyeur*!

- **Giving advice.** Resist telling people what you think is right.

- **Cheap consolation.** "It's going to be all right." This may very well be interpreted as patronizing or minimizing the issue – which is usually interpreted as insulting.

- **Arguing or disagreeing with the speaker.** If you do this, then you join in on the argument and lose your ability to help and be objective.

- **Analyzing or interpreting.** It is OK to interpret as long as you check out with others your understanding of what you think they are feeling and saying – this is called ***perception checking*** (checking out what you think the other person feels) and ***paraphrasing*** (repeating what you think the other person said or meant).

- **Ignoring obvious heavy emotions.** Don't let them turn it loose and then walk away from it – they have no way to resolve their feelings. Recognizing the emotions at hand, or reading between the lines with a *third ear*, can be a significant opening to explore further what people are trying to say.

Summary – Pitfalls to Avoid

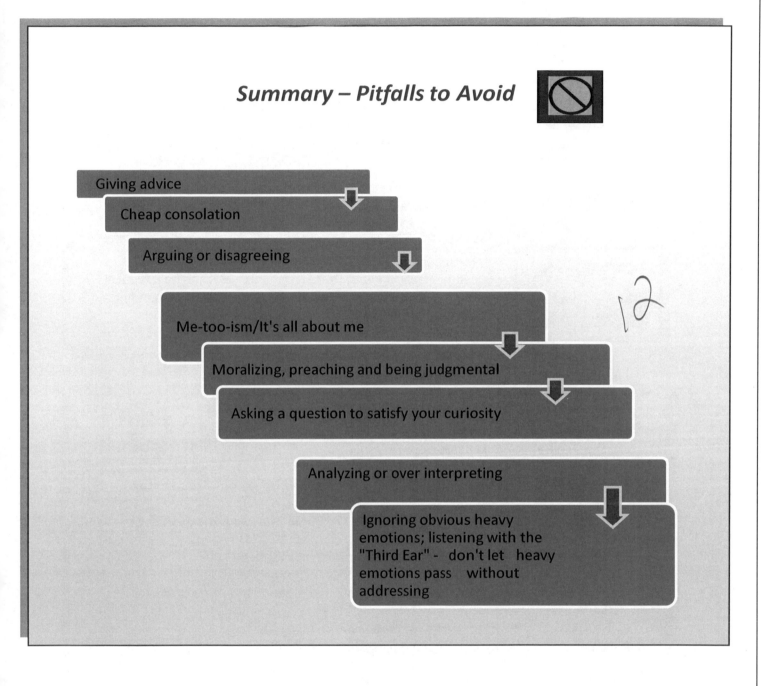

Giving advice

Cheap consolation

Arguing or disagreeing

Me-too-ism/It's all about me

Moralizing, preaching and being judgmental

Asking a question to satisfy your curiosity

Analyzing or over interpreting

Ignoring obvious heavy emotions; listening with the "Third Ear" - don't let heavy emotions pass without addressing

Chapter III: Crisis Intervention Models

There are many crisis intervention models but not all are appropriate for the short term nature of police calls. The following models are *police appropriate* and, depending upon the situation, can be applied to people or individuals experiencing crisis or emotional stress.   What the crisis intervention student needs to recognize are those common themes and techniques that reappear with regularity; the greater the frequency, the more the likelihood it is relevant to the crisis intervention process. The final model (Chapter 10) presented is a more detailed and structured model designed for police training.

> ## The Bard Crisis Intervention Model

> During the early 1970s, the New York Police Department called-in psychologist Dr. Morton Bard (1970) to help reduce the rising number of police officer injuries while responding to domestic violence calls. Dr. Bard developed a list of guidelines, listed as sequential steps for the officers to follow.

1. Prevent violence by separating the disputants.
2. Allow only one person to talk at a time.
3. Take the disputants into separate rooms.
4. Switch officers so that the stories can be checked out.
5. When listening to the stories, try to find out what each individual contributed to the conflict.
6. If one of the disputants holds himself to blame, find out in what ways the other shares the blame.
7. Ask questions so as to get the details as clear as possible.
8. Find out if there has been a previous history of this kind of behavior.
9. See if the history goes back to before the marriage; to other relationships or similar relationships in the present.
10. Give each person the opportunity to speak in detail.
11. Bring the disputants together to tell their stories to each other.
12. Again, make sure only one person speaks at a time.
13. Point out similarities and discrepancies in the stories.
14. Get a reaction from both about what the officers say they see is going on.
15. Ask what the couple plans to do in response to what has transpired and to the officers' reactions.   If they seem to understand and say they want to try to work it out, accept it.
16. If you disagree with their response, suggest that they seek other help. If necessary, make the referral.
17. While noting that there may be further difficulties, assure them that if they sit down and talk at least they can come out in the open and try to resolve it.
18. If not in the beginning, then before you leave, make sure that they know your name.

> ## Updating the 1970 Bard Model to contemporary policing

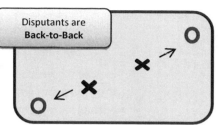

Disputants are
Back-to-Back

In step 3 ("Take the disputants into separate rooms"):

- Bard suggests that the disputants should be placed in separate rooms. The disadvantage in this procedure is that both disputants become more anxious to know what the other disputant is saying. This is also poor officer safety since the officers would be separated. *One positional tactic would be to initially position the disputants (X) such that they are not in direct eye contact, and have the officers (O) able to observe each other as well as both disputants.*

In step 4 ("Switch officers so that the stories can be checked out"):

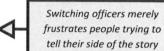

Switching officers merely frustrates people trying to tell their side of the story

- *Do not switch officers*; it is more effective to have one officer manage the discussion while the second officer assists in keeping the disputants calm, acting in the role of *Defuser*.

In steps 5 and 6 ("...try to find out in each case what each individual contributed to the conflict" and, "If one of the disputants holds himself to blame, find out in what ways the other shares the blame"):

- *The officer must be very cautious not to generate a discussion that will focus on blame or guilt*; this merely rekindles the very same passions that fuelled the argument. The officers need to maneuvre the disputants beyond the issues of blame and guilt.

Jumping to step 16 ("If you disagree with their response, suggest that they seek other help"):

- *The officer must always be wary of displaying disagreement and consequently allowing his or her personal values to become a basis for decision making.* If you suggest a course of action, and the disputants are not in agreement, then there is a tendency for the disputants to shift the responsibility of outcomes to the one who suggested the solution in the first place.

In step 18 ("If not in the beginning, then before you leave, make sure that they know your name"):

- It is very important to give your name at the *beginning* of the contact, *not* the end. And if appropriate, when you introduce yourself – always maintaining officer safety – shake hands and be cordial. If you are uncomfortable with shaking hands, then introduce yourself and politely nod; but if a hand is extended, it would be polite to extend yours as well. Understand you are performing a role as well as a service and you may not always be doing something you are comfortable with (such as trying to calm a very annoying person).

  Also, introducing yourself at the beginning of a contact can serve the dual purpose of helping to defuse someone. Let's say you are confronting an angry or argumentative person and say something like: "Hi, my name is Officer Smith (extend your hand for a handshake)...tell me what happened here today?" As the person unconsciously extends his or her hand (which is expected in many cultures) you are distracting them from their anger and breaking their emotional momentum. Once broken, however briefly, you need to be quick to engage them in a conversation that helps get some distance from their anger. ***This is where your tone of voice can help calm disputants – at the beginning of the contact.***

At the end of the contact is a good time to not only shake everyone's hand and offer encouragement, but also to leave your business card. Individual business cards are a necessity, not a luxury, and should be considered as part of an officer's equipment inventory. Belatedly, more and more police agencies are starting to recognize the need for business cards. As an example, in early 2009, the Portland, Oregon, Police Bureau finally issued cards to most of the Bureau's 900 police officers (Bernstein 2009) although neighboring agencies had been issuing them for years. By 2011, there was an expectation that Portland police officers would give their business card whenever asked...but some officers still felt that the business card was not to be given on demand. And yes, there is accountability for the police. A Multnomah County, Oregon, jury awarded a 33-year-old woman $82,000 saying they wanted to send Portland, Oregon, police a message: "Hand over a business card the next time a citizen asks for one" (Green 2011).

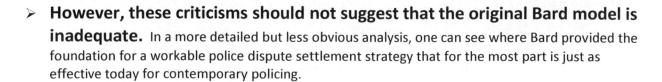

Using the business card as a distraction technique: The business card can also serve as a distraction prop. Let's say you are confronted with an angry person who is loudly pointing his finger at someone else, telling you what this person has done. But you sense that this person will continue for some time with his rant, so you pull out a business card and a pen (again, if officer safety allows this) and briefly interrupt by asking the person's name. Then you write the name on the card and as the person is still seething and peering at someone else, you show the person your card, momentarily distracting him and breaking his angry gaze as he glances down at the business card (invariably, people *will always* look at the card). As the person reaches for the card, move your body in such a way that the angry person turns slightly to look at you. Continue these small movements until the person eventually has his back to the other person he was arguing with. If the person is still too loud or both sides can be heard, step back or politely escort the person away and out of hearing distance from the other person (keeping eyes on your partner for officer safety).

Jo Taylor, RN

> **However, these criticisms should not suggest that the original Bard model is inadequate.** In a more detailed but less obvious analysis, one can see where Bard provided the foundation for a workable police dispute settlement strategy that for the most part is just as effective today for contemporary policing.

Bard identifies as a priority "to allow only one person to speak at a time." **Establishing the ground rules at the onset is critical for the crisis intervention process.** It is very important for officers to begin their crisis intervention contact with this ***primary ground rule***, saying something like:

- "OK, I can see you have something to say and my partner and I want to hear it, but we can only hear one at a time. I promise you both will have a chance to talk, so let's hear from you first, then you (looking at the other disputant) next. Now tell me what happened here today?"

Police officers are not universally trained in how to effectively communicate, so having to constantly defuse or deescalate people is very difficult (and frustrating) for the average police officer. Officers need to recognize that these techniques have the impact and consequence of helping to control a potentially volatile situation; *that's tactical communication!*

In the latter scenario, as one person starts to recite their version of what happened, the other person will no doubt become offended and defensive as he or she hears some rather unflattering comments, placing blame for the police 911 call squarely on his or her shoulders.

As this second person interrupts, the other officer, *serving now in a defusing role*, briefly nods and in a quiet and calm voice, almost whispering says:

- "You will have a chance to speak in just a minute...let's hear what this person has to say first...it doesn't mean this person is correct and you are not." This can happen simultaneously as the first person continues to talk and may happen many times during the rather emotional contact. **The officers always have to be prepared to defuse.**

Officers need to recognize that these techniques have the impact and consequence of helping to control a potentially volatile situation. **Shouting and commanding does not work as well as using an authoritative yet communicative voice**. Those officers untrained in defusing techniques have a tendency to either raise their voices or shout commands when people continue to argue or not comply with their instructions. This is understandable; most police officers would rather respond to a *bank-robbery-in-progress call* than a domestic disturbance call. However, ask any disputant and they will tell you (thereby conveniently shifting blame), that the police officers made matters worse by their behavior. Judging from many of the popular TV cop reality shows, it is easy to see how the antics of the officers, although entertaining, can exacerbate already tense situations.

> **Shouting and commanding does not work as well as using an authoritative yet communicative voice. Remember the ancient proverb: *"a soft answer turneth away"***

Using an authoritative yet communicative voice tells disputants that you are not only in charge, but you are there to help. Offering each of them an opportunity to speak is a defusing tactic. As a psychological residual, the disputants may actually be calmed by this approach, and their anxieties reduced because they are being reassured they will be heard. They will appreciate that they will be given an opportunity to give their side of the story (something which may indeed be a rare opportunity for them, especially with people in the same household.) This authoritative yet communicative voice is akin to command presence and authoritative bearing, yet it is tempered with the officer's ability to verbally and non-verbally communicate in a non-threatening manner.

➢ *Communicative tact* should be part of an officer's verbal and nonverbal communicative arsenal.

It is certainly risky to first defuse people, and then encourage them to revisit their dispute (especially since the officers now have to work so hard to keep the disputants calm). Moreover, nothing is solved by ordering people apart who will only *re-collide* once you leave the scene. Further, you do not want to return to another 911 call because your chances of injury are now increased since the disputants will be expecting you.

If one of your fellow officers on a previous shift was also at the location and warned the disputants "if we have to come back, someone is going to jail," you may have to pay the psychological price that the threats leave in the minds of the disputants. You may also let your guard down the second time because it seems to be just another routine – and familiar – call for you! It is readily apparent how these steps form the basis for a pragmatic approach to managing conflict situations. These steps should be viewed as actual phases in the crisis intervention process (covered in Chapter IX).

> *The following sections will discuss the training of crisis intervention and tactical communication techniques as well as the application of various crisis intervention models for police officer training.*

➢ **Foundation Principles for Intervening in a Crisis**

The Best model around-

Schwartz (1971:188) proposes specific procedural principles that will enable one who intervenes in a crisis – such as a public safety officer – to properly handle a crisis situation. These procedural principles are fundamental to successfully dealing with people experiencing emotional distress (and will be seen time and again in other models). Although this type of police crisis intervention training is complex, the training is designed for the first responder, hopefully making contact only one or two times (such as an initial police call with maybe a follow-up visit at a later time to ensure success) – not long term like the role of a counsellor or therapist.

Cmdr. Joel Wilson

focus on these

T2 #3

1. **Help the individual face the crisis.** Do not minimize or belittle. The responding officers need to recognize what is important to the person or people they are dealing with and recognize their own bias.

2. **Assist the individual to face the crisis in manageable doses.** This takes a *finesse skill*: Recounting all the reasons why someone is in crisis (which may be the reason for the 911 call), all at once, is not helpful. As issues unfold (through skillful defusing, interviewing and summarizing) the one intervening needs to decide which issues need to be addressed at the moment, and which cannot be handled or are too complex for what is hoped to be a single contact.

3. **Assist fact finding.** Help the individual examine the problem in a reality-based frame of reference. And although the individual may appear mentally ill, they are not stupid!

4. **Avoid false reassurance.** Everything may not turn out all right but reassurance in the individual's ability to handle the crisis is of value.

5. **Discourage projection.** Blaming of others is not of therapeutic value to the individual. For example, when two people are arguing, ignore the blaming and accusing statements; focus in the areas where the two people may eventually agree. Allowing blaming merely places the other person or side on the defensive which in turn increases the need to continually defuse.

6. **Help the individual to accept help.** Use of family or other social resources may assist in restoring equilibrium and providing support for the person in crisis. However, one must be very cautious when seeking significant others such as family members or loved ones since that may also exacerbate a situation. Police Hostage Negotiators know only too well how bringing in a significant other or loved one may lead to disaster.

7. **Assist with everyday tasks.** Part of being overwhelmed (difficulty coping) unable to handle the mundane as well as the complex. So, if you are arranging for someone to seek counselling or other help, make sure they can get to their destination. This step normally occurs toward the end of the crisis intervention process when you finally have agreements among the disputants (or an agreement with an individual). The more complicated the situation, the more the need for follow-up to ensure help was eventually received.

Summary: Foundation Principles for Intervening in a Crisis; Helping the person in crisis to accept help (Schwartz 1971)

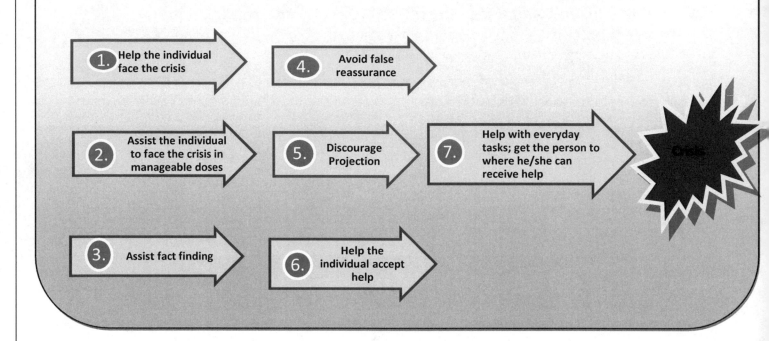

1. Help the individual face the crisis

2. Assist the individual to face the crisis in manageable doses

3. Assist fact finding

4. Avoid false reassurance

5. Discourage Projection

6. Help the individual accept help

7. Help with everyday tasks; get the person to where he/she can receive help

Crisis

➢ Communication Theory: What Motivates People to Change?

Alan Coffey (1974, 106-107) conceptualizes police crisis intervention more as *events* than actual *steps*:

People tend not to change until the pain of staying the same is greater than the fear of the risk-taking unknown.

- **Complaint**; or reason for police being called.
- **Police response**; from *code-3* to low profile or non-aggressive contact.
- **Physical danger and risk assessment**; taking basic officer safety precautions.
- **Reaction decision**; either arrest or intervene.
- **Intervention decision**; may continue with contact or seek a referral for help (depends on the complexity of the issue and what can be reasonably accomplished initially).
- **Diagnostic interview**; may also refer to other specialists at this phase as well (but not very helpful at 2 A.M. in the morning).
- **Action plan**; how to move out of the crisis (will the person or people in crisis accept some resolution).
- **Intervention methods**; from short to long term contact.

- **Case disposition**; again, successfully resolved or referral to specialists.

Alan Coffey notes that a crisis situation, such as a tense family argument, may create a "painful environment" that actually may motivate family members to seek solutions they may never have tried or considered. Usually the fear of the unknown may prevent people from discussing alternatives. However, "the pain of a crisis may exceed this fear of the unknown and, in this sense, the family crisis situation may be viewed as 'positive' – positive because it has the 'potential' to motivate the family to try something 'new' – to conceptually retool the family" to seek solutions (Coffey 1974, 105).

The arrival of the police may be strategic in terms of providing some help. Police officers trained in crisis intervention skills and techniques recognize that although there appears to be disruption and confusion when they arrive at a scene, such as a domestic dispute, they may be in the best position, as third party mediators, to help resolve issues by providing a problem-solving environment. Providing the environment to discuss the crisis, such as a police officer utilizing defusing, interviewing and mediation skills, may lead to resolution. Obviously, the more complex the issue, the less likely one intervention (such as a police officer responding to a domestic disturbance call) will truly resolve an issue that may have been brewing and festering for years.

However, it may very well be that intervention by the police officer could potentially lead to some immediate resolution, and hopefully reduce the number of times police have to continually respond to a particular family disturbance call. Further, the more complex the problem, the more the need for referral intervention and on-going support are for the family. **The more the police have to respond to the same location, the greater the probability of injury to both the responding officers and the people at the location of the police call.**

The same may be true for a person who is alone and feeling helpless. This is what police hostage negotiators look for when they are attempting to help resolve an individual's personal conflicts. Their interviewing skills are designed to discover what the issues the person in crisis is facing at the time the police were called. **It is important to identify what motivates a person to change and accept help.**

> **Dr. Christopher Cooper (2000, 10) of Chicago's St. Xavier University, is a leading authority on police mediation in the United States. He advocates Mediation Basics for police officers to follow:**

St. Xavier University

- **Explain mediation concept to participants:** It's the "not knowing what's going to happen" that keeps people at a tense emotional level. And as a defusing strategy, taking the time to explain what is going to happen while the police are there gives the disputants some breathing time – this may actually help to calm people. When people are tense, they need oxygen, including the responding officers! Practice breathing when tense.
- **Introduce parties who do not know one another:** The more personal, the better and the officers need to make sure they introduce themselves as well. And this introduction can also serve as a defusing technique since it momentarily distracts people, giving the mediating officer enough time to redirect what may have been a heated argument when the officers arrived at the scene.

> The **Primary Ground Rule** is that *only one person may speak at a time and all sides will have an opportunity to tell their story.*

- **Deliver ground rules:** One person speaks at a time – no interrupting, no profanity, no shouting, no threats or intimidating behavior, etc. **These ground rules need to be stated at the onset of the communication process and skillfully enforced throughout the contact.**
- **Advise of confidentiality:** The discussion remains confidential; try to minimize embarrassment.
- **Explain nature of agreement:** Parties remain bound; legal action may follow if unsuccessful.
- **Discuss alternatives:** This may be by arbitration; people may not be of a mind to agree on anything at the moment and may need a more structured environment such as a formal mediation program or directed decision such as arbitration.
- **Allow parties to convey their version of the incident.**
- **Give parties chance to rebut:** But not to repeat blame or guilt. Usually by the third time a statement has been repeated, it is time to move the conversation forward towards solution (summarizing what has been said up to that moment usually provides such a window to move on).
- **Ask questions, clarify issues by restating, and seek agreement on issues:** These are the essence of interviewing and mediation skills. Through active listening, the mediating officer listens to identify key issues (identified as "**issue spotting**" by Dr. Cooper) then mentally prepares to summarize in the next step.
- **Reiteration by mediating officer:** Officer clarifies the key issues and asks disputants to verify that these are the issues, then office summarizes.
- **Parties brainstorm possible solutions:** Officer encourages problem solving (but avoids suggesting solutions). Officer facilitates disputants brainstorming in an effort to generate possible solutions, listens for points of agreement, then encourages continuing conversation on these points of agreement. During this stage of the mediation process, the officer needs to listen for any comments that may suggest not only mutual agreement, but a possible solution (Dr. Cooper identifies as "**listening for a breakthrough**" that even the disputants may not immediately recognize as a solution and needs to be explored further by the officer).
- **Officer clarifies agreement, seeks verification from parties: Officer m**ay need to put in writing to formalize the agreements and reinforce ownership in the solutions.

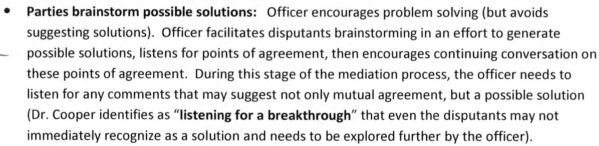

A dispute has layers - Dr. Cooper contends that with many disputes there are two layers: The **manifest** or immediately observed layer (such as issues mentioned during a dispute) and, the **underlying** (referring to deeper issues, not immediately seen or identified). "The underlying dispute is typically the 'real' matter in a dispute. It can underlie the manifest dispute and propel it" (Cooper 1999, 6-7).

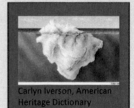

Carlyn Iverson, American Heritage Dictionary

Although not identified by Dr. Cooper, these layers can be illustrated as an iceberg, with the "manifest layer" visible and the "underlying layer" as below the sea and not immediately observable. The task of the mediating officer is to actively listen for these manifest and underlying issues, then encourage them to surface for the disputants to explore and discuss.

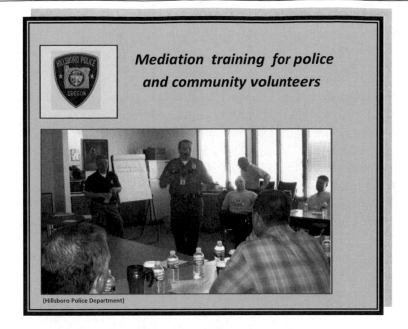

Mediation training for police and community volunteers

(Hillsboro Police Department)

➢ **In Dr. Mary Zinkin's model (2000), known as the *Collaborative Negotiation Process*, the sequential steps are an "educational process using information and resources to satisfy essential interests of disputants through an exchange of promises. Whenever you openly share goals and interests with the other and problem solve together, you are negotiating."**

This model was developed in Portland, Oregon, in partnership with Dr. Zinkin and the Hillsboro, Oregon, Police Department. All members of the department, both sworn and professional staff, participated in a 32-hour mediation training. Volunteer community members were also trained along with the departmental  members since the intent of the mediation program is to provide community volunteers to assist residents experiencing various types of conflicts (such as disputing neighbors or disagreements between customers and merchants and more recently, with parents and truant children). An additional 32 hours was provided for selected departmental members and community volunteers to serve as primary mediators. The model is predicated on two or more people willing to sit down and talk about their yet-to-be-solved problem.

The following steps outline the Collaborative Negotiation Process model:
1. **Preparation**; identify interests of disputing parties.
2. **Be willing to communicate to others**; be open to listening to others.
3. **Procedural agreements**; ground rules to create problem solving environment.
4. **Exchange of Information**; share own interests, clarify and probe others.
5. **Identify common Interests and diverse Interests;** this is a critical phase that requires identification of not only opposing interests, but common interests as well. *These common interests may lead to a solution.*
6. **Creative problem solving**; generate options stated by the disputants.
7. **Decision-making;** select mutually agreeable solutions.

These steps are translated into a face-to-face process wherein two opposing disputants, flanked by two trained mediators, meet at a neutral location to discuss their issues.

| The following is an example of how the Mediation Process works *(Zinkin 2000, Williams 1997)*: |

- **Opening statement by mediator:**
  - ✓ **Description of the mediation process;** steps of the process will be explained, clarification of issues, desired outcomes, brainstorming and selection of agreeable resolution.
  - ✓ **Qualifications of the mediator;** all mediators have met or exceed the state of Oregon requirements (32 hours of training). Clarify role of mediator; mediator assists in bringing parties to resolution but does not make decisions for disputing parties.
  - ✓ **Neutrality;** the mediator will not take sides.
  - ✓ **Confidentiality;** the conversation that takes place will not go outside the room.
  - ✓ **Voluntary;** it will be clarified that all parties are there through their willingness to participate.
  - ✓ **Note taking** (not to document or keep a record, just to keep track of the discussion); all notes taken will be destroyed.

- **The discussion process:**
  - ✓ **Presentation and summary of the information**, then allow parties to tell their stories.
  - ✓ **Clarification of the issues by the Mediator** to get the parties to recognize one another.
  - ✓ **The Mediator identifies issues and concerns**, and then draws out the issues from the parties.
  - ✓ **Expression of conflict and emotions,** then how the dispute/problem affects the parties.
  - ✓ **Communicate needs**, interests and what does each party need to do to change the tense situation.
  - ✓ **Reframing the issues**; mediator presents the problem back to the parties and states progress made.

- **Mediation skills demonstrated by the mediators:**
  - ✓ **Ventilation;** providing the opportunity, in a safe environment, to outwardly express emotions.
  - ✓ **Clarification;** questioning and asking questions that makes clear to all parties what the issues and outcomes are, reframed back to the parties.
  - ✓ **Identification of Issues/concerns/problems;** fuller understanding, validation of respective feelings and positions, and letting each party hear and understand the nature of each other's concerns.
  - ✓ **Discussion/problem solving;** brainstorming, and interest based negotiations (meaning, finding solutions that meet the interests of both parties).
  - ✓ **Agreements/understandings;** restate agreements, and questions regarding agreements, and ask all parties for confirmation of agreement.
  - ✓ **Closure;** acknowledge the hard work and thank parties for participating.

The purpose of the mediation training is to allow first responding officers and police professional staff (even those at the front counter of a police station or over the police telephone) to resolve disputes in the field. The allied purpose is to allow more in depth problem solving, in a more structured environment, for disputing parties to be managed by trained civilian volunteers.

➢ Types of Officer Responses to these Tactical Communication and Crisis Intervention Models – Three examples:

The methods employed by police officers when confronted with a disturbance call are ultimately reflected in their role perceptions as law enforcement professionals (Louie 1981).

1. *One type of officer may perceive his or her role as a basic "keeper of the peace" and thereby consider disturbance calls as a violation of the law, irrespective of the circumstances surrounding the nature of the disturbance.*

    -   This type of officer does not perceive his or her role as a *social worker* and is not concerned with solving the particular problem that generated the 911 call.

    -   A typical response by this type of officer would be to enter the disturbance scene (i.e., a home in a family dispute, or in a store with an argument between a merchant and a customer), separate the disputants and then advise the disputants they are in violation of the law and must cease, otherwise they will be arrested. The officer will usually warn the disputants that if he or she must return to the scene, an arrest will be made. This type of officer is attempting to *solve* the problem by the use of fear and authority. Since the reasons for the argument have not been explored or resolved, it is probable that the officer will have to return (now the potential of danger for the officers and disputants has increased.)

2. *A Second type of officer will respond to the scene, and as an example, in the case of a drunken husband, become somewhat involved by escorting or arranging for the husband to stay in a motel or home of a friend.*

    -   This officer's primary concern is to avert violence. Since the husband is perceived as the antagonist, the officer merely removes the husband from the scene. Again, the nature of the problem may not be discussed and the use of fear and authority may be employed by the officer. Since nothing has been resolved, then there is a greater likelihood that there will be successive 911 calls to this address.

3. *A Third type of officer in the same situation may employ the crisis intervention model in the hopes of achieving a resolution to the problem. This type of officer perceives his or her role as mediator (but not as a social worker) performing, in essence, a service that will hopefully keep the police from continuing to respond to repeat calls at the same address (the bane of all police and sheriff departments across the country).*

    -   This officer will spend more time at the scene and will have to become involved as a mediator. Note for supervisors: these calls generally take more time and supervisors need to understand that it may not be in anyone's best interest to pressure the officer to conclude quickly just to take the next call in the queue. If the reason for the 911 call can be resolved, then perhaps the police will not have to return time and time again – in the long run, a much more effective way to deal with limited patrol officer availability.

- This type of officer may even find it necessary to refer the family to an agency specializing in counseling or alcoholism. Or perhaps, the drinking was a symptom of an even greater problem such as unemployment or chronic illness.

- The officer may elect to refer the husband (or wife) to a social service or employment agency. In the case of a military veteran (a fast growing population), a referral to the county or state veterans' affairs office may be made. If employee benefits are involved, the spouse may be directed to an Employee Assistance Program for alcohol or family counseling. The officer must ensure that details such as costs and procedures for the referral are understood (this is where a Community Resources and Referral Guide can be helpful).

- The third type of officer may dislike disturbance calls just as much as the first and second officers, but finds it more beneficial and effective to address the problem, rather than allow it to fester and possibly end in tragedy.

> **View barriers as comprised of bricks, to be removed one at a time:**
Since people perceive a crisis as one or more barriers, such as a brick wall, which is impeding them, if the officers are able to help them overcome or minimize these barriers, such that they are able to adapt, overcome or hop over such barriers, then people may be motivated to face their problems and issues. Even removing one brick of the barrier wall may help to demonstrate that barriers can be overcome.

 As an example, let us say one portion of an argument between a couple is over a $1900 hospital emergency room visit (let's say the drunken husband fell down and injured himself), thereby provoking a 911 call and Emergency Room visit, as the couple are arguing over mounting bills. Perhaps the officer can provide a phone number for the couple to call to arrange a reasonable monthly payment plan and even qualify for a sliding scale bill that will greatly reduce the $1900 (it is not uncommon for hospitals to allow for $50 per month to help pay off a bill as well as provide applications for sliding fees and State assistance).

By showing a possible solution to this immediate issue, the officer is able to help minimize the fear and frustration the couple are facing and this may open the door for more in-depth problem solving (such as surfacing Dr. Cooper's *underlying issues*). As people see problems confronted and solved, then they start to realize they may be able to take control of what was first thought of as an out-of-control dilemma. When people are in crisis, it is appropriate to address their issues in manageable doses, and it is also appropriate to help them resolve their issues, also in manageable doses. At the least, the couple may now view the officer as someone truly there to help them, which will enhance rapport building.

Chapter IV: Police Officer Cross Cultural Communication; Language Barriers

The dynamics of tactical communication and crisis intervention must include recognition of the changing community demographics officers are experiencing on a daily basis. Aside from traditional interpersonal communication training, officers need to recognize the changing diversity of their community as well as changing workforce.

The changing demographics throughout America, plus the growth of multicultural communities, coupled with the limited number of bilingual officers, seriously impacts effective communication within these communities, resulting from language and communication barriers – *it's a matter of officer safety.*

> **Dimensions of Diversity**. **There are basically two dimensions of diversity: Primary and Secondary.** A Primary Dimension is a core characteristic that a person is born with which remains with the individual in all stages of his or her life. A **Secondary Dimension** comprises characteristics a person acquires as the result of a choice he or she has made, or a choice someone else made for him or her (Loden 1996).

These dimensions of diversity influence how a person perceives reality, adopts and reflects values, and subsequently influences how a person communicates with others. **By understanding how a person is influenced by these dimensions may help in recognizing biases and prejudices. And the more one understands his or her respective biases and prejudices, the more equipped he or she is to recognize** *emotional intelligence*, **which in turn influences how he/she communicates with others.**

Primary Dimensions of Diversity includes:
- ✓ Age
- ✓ Ethnicity
- ✓ Gender
- ✓ Mental/physical abilities and characteristic
- ✓ Race
- ✓ Sexual orientation

Secondary Dimensions of Diversity includes:
- ✓ Communication style
- ✓ Education
- ✓ Family status
- ✓ Military experience
- ✓ Organizational role and level
- ✓ Religion
- ✓ First language
- ✓ Geographic location
- ✓ Income
- ✓ Work experience
- ✓ Work style

What is Diversity? The term *Diversity* is used to describe a vast range of similarities and differences that have become factors requiring attention in living and working together. The term is often applied to the communication and training interventions in an organization that seek to deal with the interface of people who are different from each other. Basically, diversity represents all the ways that we are the same or different (Shusta et al, 2007).

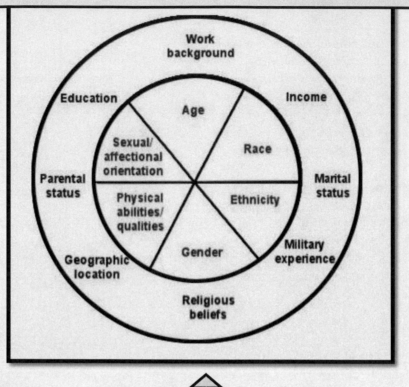

The Diversity Wheel facilitates understanding of a broad range of Primary and Secondary Dimensions of Diversity *(Shusta el al, 2007)*

Diversity Wheel example from *Diversity Infusion Project*, Elon, University, North Carolina (2011)

The following sections will briefly explore suggestions on how to communicate with diverse populations

➢ **Tips for Communicating When English is a Second Language** (Shusta, et al, 2007)

  ✓ Speak slowly and enunciate clearly.
  ✓ Face the person and speak directly even when using a translator.
  ✓ Avoid concentrated eye contact if the other speaker is not making direct eye contact (and do not jump to the conclusion that avoiding eye contact may indicate deceit... it may be cultural and the person may just be frightened to be speaking with a police officer).

- ✓ Do not use jargon, slang, idioms such as "gonna," "gotta," "wanna" "perp" "suspect" etc.
- ✓ Avoid complex verb tenses (e.g., "If I would have known, I might have been able to provide assistance").
- ✓ Repeat key issues and questions in different ways.
- ✓ Avoid asking questions that can be answered by *yes or no*; rather, ask questions so that the answer can show understanding.
- ✓ Use short, simple sentences; pause between sentences.
- ✓ Use visual cues such as gestures, demonstrations and brief written phrases.
- ✓ Use active rather than passive verbs (e.g., "I expect your attention" [active] rather than "Your attention is expected" [passive]).
- ✓ Have materials duplicated in bilingual format (such as departmental Community Resources Guide).
- ✓ Pause frequently and give breaks. Monitor your speed when you speak...Slow Down!
- ✓ Use only one idea per sentence.
- ✓ Respect the silence that non-native speakers of English need to formulate and mentally translate their sentences.
- ✓ Check comprehension by having the other speaker repeat material or instructions, and summarize frequently.
- ✓ Encourage and provide positive feedback on the person's ability to communicate.
- ✓ Listen even more attentively than you do when communicating with a native speaker of English.
- ✓ Be patient! Every first generation of immigrants struggles with the acquisition of English.
- ✓ Use paraphrasing (saying what you understood in your own words) with both the ESL speaker and if available, the translator.

Do Not Speak Louder...it will not help – Duh!

> ## Attitudes toward people speaking English as a second language (Shusta et al., 2007)
- ✓ Not reliable for determining immigration status.
- ✓ Officers feel uncomfortable when people speak their native language with others and perceive they are being deceitful if not speaking English.
- ✓ Be very careful with children translating, especially if there are complicated terms and issues (Louie 2007).
- ✓ Find someone else to translate (and even then, be careful and tentative on what information you received; Louie 2007).

> ## Key Cross-Cultural Areas in Communication for Officers to Consider
(Shusta et al., 2007)

Officers have traditionally used styles of communication and language that at one time were acceptable. Now, because of diverse groups within the police agency and within our cities, the unspoken rules about appropriate and inappropriate communication are changing. Officers' perceptions of a cultural group may be skewed by the populations they encounter and will be enhanced when they are aware of:

- ✓ Perceptions that all possess;
- ✓ Cultural filters;

> *Through interpersonal communication, officers have tremendous power to influence the behavior and responses of the people they contact. A lack of knowledge of the dynamics of cross-cultural communication will diminish this power and improved communication with all citizens will result in safer interactions for officers and the people contacted.*

➤ Proxemics – Distance

Officers need to recognize acceptable distances (known variously as: *personal space, interpersonal distance, comfort zone* and *body bubble*) when they are attempting to communicate with people, especially those experiencing stress (Hall 2007) and they also need to recognize how their personal distance, or interpersonal space, impacts others. This interpersonal space can be visualized as an *invisible bubble or zone of interpersonal space* or distance that is dependent upon relationships and that if violated, such as someone standing too close, will not only cause discomfort but may adversely impact interpersonal communication. These distances can be categorized as following:

- *Intimate Distance*: 0-18 inches (clinging child; loved one). This distance ranges from touching to approximately 18 inches and is reserved for loved ones, close friends and even pets.
- *Personal Distance*: 18 inches to 4 feet (good friends). This distance starts around 18 inches, or arm's length, up to 4 feet.
- *Social Distance*: 4 feet to 12 feet (impersonal business or *Field Interrogation distance*). This distance is reserved primarily for strangers or people one is not familiar with.
- *Public Distance*: 12 feet plus (Public politician; close is 12-25 feet; far is 24 feet plus). This distance is for public events such as speeches and ceremonies. (Engleberg 2006).
- *Police Distance:* greater than arm's length, with sufficient space to quickly grab a baton or gun (Louie 2010). To some, this distance appears *standoffish* but is in reality good officer safety.
- However, if officer safety permits, it's OK to stand closer.

The Cultural Context of Conversational Distance:

"Culture styles are important too. A Japanese employer and employee usually stand farther apart while talking than their American counterparts. Latin Americans and Arabs tend to stand closer than Americans do when talking" (Levine and Adelman, 1993). Understanding the nature of communication distance is important because if violated (such as speaking too closely) the response may be interpreted as aggressive or at the least, discomforting, thereby making effective communication difficult.

Although those who are introverted may need more space, even if an American, generally speaking social distance is determined by culture. And people are generally more comfortable with people within their own cultural norms, because there is a mutually shared and similar (culturally acceptable) body language.

"One research study demonstrated that when British graduate students imitated some Arab patterns of nonverbal behavior (making increased eye contact, smiling, and directly facing their Arab partners), the Arabs felt that these students were more likeable and trustworthy than most of the other British students" (Levine and Adelman, 1993).

When one person's nonverbal language matches that of another, there is increased comfort. In nonverbal communication across cultures there are similarities and differences. Whether we choose to emphasize the former or the latter, the *silent language* is much louder than it first appears.

High-and-Low Context Communication

Aside from the obvious tone of voice and rate of speech, more subtle differences in cross cultural communication occur at different and less obvious levels. These differences are known as *High* and *Low Context* communication (Shusta, et al., 2007) and police officers may encounter these types of responses as they attempt to communicate with people from various cultures.

- **Higher Context communication tendencies:**
  - ✓ Tendency to avoid saying *no*;
  - ✓ Tendency to avoid conflict;
  - ✓ Difficulty answering *yes* and *no* and either/or questions (tendency to see in many shades of grey);
  - ✓ Concerned about saving face in self and others;
  - ✓ Focus on the wider context of interaction;
  - ✓ Preference for getting to the point indirectly.

Some American and British business people describe the above as typical when dealing with business people from the People's Republic of China (Louie 2007). Commenting on the American style of negotiation in China: "The root cause (is) a failure on the American side to understand the much broader context of Chinese culture and values, a problem that too often leaves Western negotiators both flummoxed and flailing" (Graham and Lam 2003).

 "Chinese negotiators are more concerned with the means than the end, with the process more than the goal. The best compromises are derived only through the ritual back-and-forth of haggling. This process cannot be cut short. And compromise allows the two sides to hold equally valid positions. The challenge of mutual understanding is great; American and Chinese approaches often appear incompatible" (Graham and Lam 2003). This could be the context for an American police officer attempting to resolve a dispute between people communicating in a "higher context" mode.

In this land mine-laden landscape of cross cultural communication, rather than train first responders as Anthropologists, it is best to fall back on the common courtesies of interpersonal communication that are emphasized in this training. So, although the police officer may appear too direct (i.e., lower context norms) in communication with someone more accustomed to higher context norms, **it is best to concentrate on the actual delivery of the verbal and non-verbal messages.**

> *The more the officer is aware of appropriate voice tone and rate of speech, reinforced with appropriate non-verbal body and facial expressions, the more likely the officer will be successful at communicating with someone from a different cultural experience.*

- **Lower Context communication tendencies:**
  - ✓ *Yes* equals *yes* and *no* equals *no*;
  - ✓ Ease with direct communication and responding directly to conflict;
  - ✓ Focus more on words and what is verbalized (do not tend to *read between the lines*).

Preference for getting right to the point. And some business people from the People's Republic of China may consider the above to be a too abrupt and rude delivery - *"let's eat some great food and talk about business tomorrow"* (Louie 2007).

 ➤ **Your Voice and Rate of Speech in the United States** (Shusta, et al., 2007).
Are you easy to listen to? Are your words easily understood? Many times police officers speak at such a fast rate that they are not easily understood, whether speaking to someone in crisis, suffering from mental illness or...someone who speaks English as a second language.

 Rate of average speech in the United States varies from a high of 180-250 words per minute in the West, Northwest and Midwest to a slower rate in the Southern portion of the country. But irrespective of geography, police officers need to speak at a slower rate when attempting to communicate with people experiencing stress.

➤ **Thinking is faster than speaking** (Louie 2007b)
As a person is speaking, a listener processes quicker. So while someone is speaking from a slower 100 to perhaps 250 words per minute, the one listening can *think* at a much faster rate (perhaps as high as 400 words per minute). This word per minute disparity gives an active listener time to formulate a response. This is why it is important to carefully listen to what is being said, and then process how to respond, understanding that the response needs to acknowledge that you are listening!

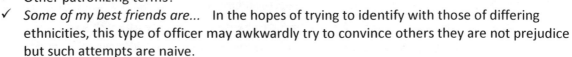

> *People want to be heard and understood, no matter what language they are speaking. If an officer is able to respond with an understanding of what is being said, it will become a starting point for dialogue, notwithstanding the broken English.*

➤ **Using Language or Style to Become** *"Just Like one of them"* (Shusta, et al., 2007). It is not uncommon to still hear officers awkwardly attempt to communicate with those of other ethnicities by mimicking their speech idioms. All this does is to convey discomfort, insincerity or phoniness. With this type of officer, all credibility is lost and those present will only wish to expedite his or her exit.

- **Some examples of these patronizing terms and phrases**:
  - ✓ *Bro, jive, my man;*
  - ✓ *Home boy* or *homey;*
  - ✓ *Chief* to Native American;
  - ✓ Other patronizing terms?
  - ✓ *Some of my best friends are...* In the hopes of trying to identify with those of differing ethnicities, this type of officer may awkwardly try to convince others they are not prejudice but such attempts are naive.

➤ **Walking on Eggshells** (Shusta, et al., 2007). The opposite of the latter is the type of officer so fearful of offending that he or she does the following:
- Overcompensating in order to not offend;
- Being too sensitive;
- Inability to be one's normal self;
- Appearing insincere and not authentic.

> **"You People,"** (Shusta, et al., 2007). Although not necessarily intended by the speaker, there are times using the term "you people" to refer to others may be interpreted as bigoted speech. The mainstream population does not perceive these terms as prejudicial however, from the perspective of ethnic minorities, they have frequently heard their respective ethnic groups referred to as *those people*. This phrase should be avoided. And in the tense context of attempting to diffuse people who are arguing, the police officer may actually exacerbate the situation by using the *you people* reference...so try to avoid this phrase.

> **"You are treating me this way because I'm ...."** (Shusta, et al., 2007). On the other hand, police officers may have the defensive verbal grenade of *"you are treating me this way because I am ...."* thrown at them. The best response for the police officer is to use what are called *verbal judo deflectors*, which acknowledge what has been said but moves on and does not let the conversation become defensive for the police officer. These verbal deflectors do not ignore the statements heard but allow the officer not to get sucked-in on trying to prove he or she is not prejudiced (which places the officer in a defensive position and shifts some power to the accuser). The late Dr. George Thompson (1993) of verbal judo fame, believes that statements made to the officer should not be ignored, and that silence can make matters worse. He contends that it is better to acknowledge the sentiment (however true or not) but then move on with the conversation. These types of responses are non-judgmental and are readily available in the police officer's tactical communication arsenal. Here are some examples:

- "I appreciate what you are saying but I am here because someone called 911."
- "I hear what you're saying, but I am here because someone called the police."

It is most important to *always be yourself* and try not to act like someone you are not. The more natural you communicate, the more spontaneous and comfortable you will be, and that's how you will be seen by others. People the world over will understand if you are trying to be sincere, however awkward it may be for you – such as attempting to communicate with someone from a different culture.

Chapter V: Specific Populations when Dealing with People in Crisis

These following sections will briefly explore behaviors that first responders may observe when responding to 911-disturbance calls. Suggestions on how to attempt interpersonal communication will be discussed.

➤ **Intoxicated people: Well-timed, well-crafted distractions can help curb violence associated with intoxication** (Giancola 2007)

"According to a psychological theory called the *attention-allocation model*, **drunkenness narrows a person's field of attention so he or she 'can really only focus on one thing at a time'.** In hostile situations, drunks who are inclined toward violence tend to focus on provocative, aggression-facilitating stimuli ..." (Giancola 2007, 1).

Acute alcohol consumption is often related to aggressive behavior and alcohol is involved in about 50% of violent crimes (Giancola 2007, 1). For the crisis intervener, having background information, such as "how does he/she act when drunk" may indicate what to expect. Use this critical information to preplan your response as you are nearing the 911 call (Louie 2007c). "Alcohol doesn't make you do different things; it just allows what is already inside you to come out. It takes the brakes off" (Giancola 2007).

Conversely, "...both alcohol and drugs can 'disinhibit a person from coherent thinking'" (McElvain 2007, 1).   Knowing this background information can better prepare the responding officers to preplan and understand that their communication style will have to be clear, concise and a somewhat slower *speech speed* than normal conversation. The officer who speaks quickly (meaning a quicker, 250+ words per minute), shouts commands, and is not clear and precise with what he/she is saying, will not be as effective in controlling those under the influence; and the same can be said with someone experiencing an emotional episode (Louie 2008).

(istockphoto)

When drunk, subjects have "less cognitive space (in their attention capacity) to house and process hostile cues" (Giancola 2007, 2). So, the degree of distraction is important: "If the attempted diversion is too mild, it won't attract enough of the subject's attention. If it's too intense or confusing, it 'might engender more aggression due to frustration'" (Giancola 2007, 2).

Dr. Bill Lewinski (2007, 2) of the Force Science Institute concurs that distraction can be a valuable tool in curbing aggression: "On the street, it can work not only with drunks but with sober people who are emotionally upset. If you can capture their attention and pull them away from whatever is stoking their agitation, you may be able to get them to work with you instead of blowing up on you."

Current research indicates that subjects under the influence of drugs "were 3 times more likely to be shot or shot at by officers than those who weren't; intoxicated suspects are 3.4 times more likely than those who were sober; and people with previous arrests for violent crimes, 3.7 times more likely than those without that history" and "citizens with prior violent criminal arrest records and who are under the influence of an intoxicant provide the strongest association with police shootings" (McElvain 2007, 1).

> ## Other illnesses, injuries and medical conditions may mimic alcoholic symptoms.

First responders need to be aware that various illnesses, injuries and medical conditions can "produce symptoms that closely resemble intoxicated behavior in a human being. Insulin reactions, diabetic conditions, stroke, mental illnesses, and closed head wounds, among other things, all can result in behavior that mimics intoxication" (Garner 2006, 48).

The following list, although not exhaustive, describes observable physical conditions and behaviors that may mimic alcoholic symptoms:

(istockphoto)

- ✓ Loud, boisterous behavior and profane language;
- ✓ Clothing soiled and unkempt;
- ✓ Bloodshot eyes;
- ✓ Dilated or pinpoint pupils of the eyes;
- ✓ Strong smell of alcoholic beverage on clothes or breath;
- ✓ Belligerent behavior or unreasonably passive behavior;
- ✓ Slurred speech;
- ✓ Poor motor skills and balance;
- ✓ Displays of emotional extremes such as laughing or crying;
- ✓ Reporting hallucinations or delusions;
- ✓ Inability to perform fine motor skills;
- ✓ Difficulty in following instructions.

➢ Overview of Mental Illness

There is a growing public demand throughout the country for training police about how to respond differently to those with mental illness: "...mentally disturbed people are being dealt with as lethally dangerous criminals, even though in every case unarmed, essentially by those presumably professionally trained to serve and protect"   (Gabel 2007, A6).

The following headlines can be found in newspapers everywhere:

"Mentally ill are not criminals" | "Police need greater understanding of the mentally ill" | "Mentally ill people in crisis"

"Call for training to help cops deal with mentally ill" | "Force used to subdue threatening person questioned" | "Man killed by police possibly mentally ill"

"Clues to mental illness of man they chased and died in police custody" | "Death of mentally ill man spurs need for police training" | "Police training seems to ensure fatal outcomes"

Need for more police training in how to respond to the mentally ill

Unfortunately, many police agencies have been told over the years that they need specialized crisis intervention and how to handle the mentally ill training, however, it usually takes media headlines to push police agencies in the right direction to improve training (Louie 1990). Even a supportive general public recognizes that police need to distinguish those with mental illness behaviors from those with criminal-related behaviors – and to treat them differently.

> The current increase in mental illness awareness and crisis intervention training at the Oregon Department of Public Safety Standards and Training police academy, prompted by the state legislature and signed by the Governor, is another indication of the growing importance of increased crisis intervention training for police (Louie 2007c).

"Mandatory Mental Illness Recognition Training: Requires the Oregon Department of Public Safety Standards and Training to require at least 24 hours of training in mental illness recognition, using a crisis intervention training model for basic certification as a police officer." (OACP Legislative Report 2007).

> **Some sobering mental illness statistics** (National Institute of Mental Health in Case 2007):

(photoexpress)

More and more we all are beginning to realize how many Americans suffer from some form of mental illness. Worse yet, a greater percentage of our prison population suffer from mental illness. Yet police officers on the street continue to be trained in traditional, criminal suspect-related *arrest and control tactics* with little distinction between who is a criminal subject and who is a mentally ill subject, although observable behavior is the first indicator (Louie 2007c).

- An estimated 26.2% of adult Americans suffer from a diagnosable mental disorder in a given year. This translates into approximately 78.6 million people – more than 1 out of 4 people!
- Approximately 6%, or over 18 million people suffer serious mental illness with symptoms severe enough to affect their daily functioning .
- Six percent of the US population is affected by serious mental illness yet 16% of the jail and prison population has a serious mental illness .

> **An example of mental illness impacts on criminal justice system** (Criminal Justice Mental Health Consensus Project in Case 2007). Greater scrutiny is now being focused on the tremendous costs associated with incarcerating the mentally ill. The following are but a few examples of how costly this can be:

- Average length of stay at Riker's Island (New York City's largest jail) is 42 days; it is 215 days for an inmate with serious mental illness.
- King County, WA officials identified 20 subjects who had been repeatedly hospitalized, jailed or detoxed during a one year period at a cost of over $1.1 million.
- Seventy-two percent of people with mental illness were re-arrested within 36 months of release from the Lucas County, Ohio jail.

> Police officers on the street may not be able to impact the above statistics, but they can enhance the skills it takes to deal with this ever increasing population.

> **Mental Health defined:** "A state of emotional and psychological well-being in which an individual is able to use his or her cognitive and emotional capabilities, function in society, and meet the ordinary demands of everyday life" (Merriam-Webster Dictionary in Case 2007, 16).

- Mental Illness or Mental Disorder; **too much to define!** Starting with the A's ... acute stress disorder| Agoraphobia| alcohol and substance abuse| alcohol and substance dependence| Amphetamine Related Disorder| Anxiety disorder| Antisocial personality disorder| Autism| Avoidant personality disorder ... all the way through the T's and V's... Tourette syndrome| Transient tic disorder| Transvestic Fetishism| Trichotillomania| Vaginismus ...

  With so much to define, it is best for the responding police officers to focus on the observable behavior and handle accordingly (which means, preserve and protect life first, then defuse and control, then crisis resolution or custody – the ER staff or psychiatric staff can sort out the rest).

> ## "Calming a Storm," Psych nurses form alliances with patients to forestall violence (Domrose 2007, 18)

> *"People with mental illness become violent when they are either frightened or frustrated."*

Psychiatric nurse Cathyrn Domrose (2007) provides a glimpse into the world of the mentally ill and how to communicate with someone experiencing an emotional crisis. She says to look for "highly negative behavior" such as ideas that the *world is cutting them down* or statements that *no one is on their side*. This is an indication of something huge inside of them. A predictor of violence may be "... grimacing, teeth clenching, and taking an imposing stance. Most important is the person's energy level. If a patient ... is pacing, opening and closing fists or clearly agitated" (Domrose 2007). One suggestion is to ask: "Can we stop for just a second. Because I'm seeing something that worries me." This may redirect the person to acknowledge his or her feelings, which may be an opportunity to try to defuse.

"Many people use anger to release their feelings because it is more socially acceptable than crying. When patients do become violent, psychiatric nurses try to give them as much space as possible, while continuing to assess and calm them" (Domrose 2007, 18).

Domrose suggests the following when attempting to communicate with those experiencing emotional behavior or mental illness symptoms:

✓ "Treat people with respect and dignity, no matter how sick they are." It is important not to challenge, not to control...we want to make an alliance with the patient."

✓ Be assertive but not commanding, emphasizing consequences for ones' behavior. As an example: "Instead of telling someone 'you need to lower your voice,' say something like 'you need to lower your voice, and if you lower your voice, I will listen to you and try to help you, but I can't help you unless you lower your voice'" (Domrose 2007, 18).

✓ The most dangerous are subjects under the influence of drugs or alcohol and have no inhibitions about their behavior. For these people, "rationale" approaches will not work.

✓ With people that may need to be restrained, it is best to start (if this does not compromise officer safety) as "least restrictive" as reasonable. If this doesn't work, then physically restrain, although this may increase an individual's fear and anxiety.

✓ "Most mentally ill patients are grateful to find someone on their side who can offer relief from terrifying thoughts or hallucinations." Using empathy and communication with listening skills should be the best initial strategy. "Many people with mental illness, even those with severe psychotic symptoms, will back down once they understand their feelings are being acknowledged and respected" (Domrose 2007).

The following sections will identify descriptors of diagnosed mental disorders that first responders frequently confront, as well as assorted medications that the officers may discover.

➤ **Major Psychiatric Disorders:** *Major Depression, Generalized Anxiety, Disorder, Bipolar Disorder and Schizophrenia* (Case 2007).

- **Symptoms and behaviors the officers in the field may confront:**
  - ✓ Slurred speech (or could be intoxication)?
  - ✓ Prior stroke?
  - ✓ Diabetic crisis?
  - ✓ Speech impediment?
  - ✓ Medication?

- **Psychotic Disorders:** Schizophrenia, Schizoaffective, Delusional Disorder.
- **Mood Disorders:** Major Depression, Bi Polar Disorder, Anxiety Disorders. Phobias, PTSD, Panic Disorder, Obsessive-Compulsive Disorder.
- **Memory & Cognitive:** Autism, Alzheimer's Disease Disorders, Personality Disorders-Antisocial, Histrionic, Passive-Aggressive, Narcissistic.

➤ **Recognize signs or symptoms that may indicate mental illness is a factor in the incident** (Case 2007):
  - ✓ Severe changes in behavior;
  - ✓ Unusual or bizarre mannerisms;
  - ✓ Hostility or distrust;
  - ✓ One-sided conversations;
  - ✓ Confused or nonsensical verbal communications;
  - ✓ Inappropriate dress;
  - ✓ Mentally ill people who use alcohol or drugs are five times as likely to be violent (MacArthur Violence Risk Assessment Study in Case 2007);
  - ✓ Tremors (may appear to be *tweaking*);
  - ✓ Extreme lethargy (may appear to be *on the nod*);
  - ✓ Confusion (may appear to be intoxicated).

we left off.

When confronting someone who appears to be exhibiting mental illness symptoms and behaviors, and if not a compromise to officer safety (meaning you have time on your side and no one is in imminent danger): stabilize the scene...isolate the person ... *but you may not want to physically control just yet* (Louie 2007c).

 And Slow Everything Down!

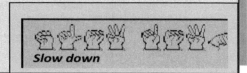
Slow down

➤ **Command Presence, but Low-Key Approach if officer safety permits** (Case 2007, Louie 2007c):
  - ✓ **Do *downplay the badge*** - many times a police officer's authority does not impress or motivate mentally ill people to comply; officers need to alter how they communicate in these types of situations.
  - ✓ **Do use your first name** when introducing yourself and explain that you are there to help.

- ✓ **Don't yell!** Speak calmly and use short simple instructions (many times police officers not only yell and shout commands, they also use vague and confusing terms such as: "don't make me….," or, "if you don't stop you are going to piss me off …" *To someone experiencing mental illness, these general and vague phrases only confuse and confound*).
- ✓ **Don't look "combative"**; keep an open, non-defensive stance with your gun side away.
- ✓ **Do keep your hands open, visible** – try not to look threatening.
- ✓ **Avoid staring or projecting aggressive facial expressions**; practice proactive non-verbal communication.
- ✓ **Stand at an angle to protect weapon side but again, try not to appear combative**.
- ✓ **Avoid interrupting** the person and going into an interview mode by asking questions…listen! Very important to allow the person to talk; people want to be heard.
- ✓ **Do speak as softly as possible**.
- ✓ **Do use short, simple sentences**.
- ✓ **Do ask open ended questions**: "What is your name?" "You seem to be upset. ..why is that?" "Are you taking any medications?" "What can I do today to help you?"

➤ **Don't act or talk as though the person is not there!** Sometimes when police officers recognize they are dealing with "someone crazy," they tend to ignore them – usually because of the bizarre behavior they are witnessing – not realizing they may be inciting even greater frustration from the subject as they utter disparaging remarks; ***they may be crazy, but they are not stupid*** (Louie 2007c).

➤ **If not a compromise to officer safety, part of *stabilizing the scene* may be to take no aggressive or controlling action on the subject, but merely to observe, and isolate.**

If this approach is working, then attempt to communicate in non-aggressive tones and non-threatening or non-demanding words. If the subject's behavior becomes dangerous to self or others, then the officers may need to employ control and arrest techniques (Louie 2007c). "Many times, I've watched in amazement while (psychiatric) staff members stood serenely in the presence of an angry, physically agitated, and often delusional individual, calming him or her merely by remaining connected when the intuitive action would be to retreat to safety" (Rogers 2007, A7).

➤ **If you have to touch or "go hands-on":**

(Cmdr Joel Wilson)

Try your absolute best to minimize the trauma the person will be experiencing while being taken into custody. This is a very frightening experience that will influence how this person responds to the next police contact. This is why many mentally ill subjects flee when they see the police or when they perceive they are going to be taken into custody (Louie 2007c).

- • Calmly explain any touching prior to going hands-on;
- • Leave the door open for a safe, effective contact for the next officer;
- • If time and officer safety is on your side, don't be in a hurry to control and take into custody. If not a compromise to officer safety, sit down and talk more, or let the subject continue to vent (Louie 2007c).

Authority to take a person who may be in danger into custody:
Although the following legal definition is from the state of Oregon, the language is generally the same throughout the country: *"A peace officer may take into custody a person who the officer has probable cause to believe is dangerous to self or to any other person and is in need of immediate care, custody or treatment for mental illness"* (Oregon Revised Statutes 426.228).

> ➤ **What officers may confront:** *Major Depression -* **Some Quick Facts**
(Case 2007)

(Dreamstime)

- ✓ Present in people of all ages, races and income;
- ✓ Median age of onset is 32 years old;
- ✓ One in 10 men will be affected by depression in their lives;
- ✓ One in 5 women − usually before they are 40 years old;
- ✓ Five percent will commit suicide;
- ✓ Suicide rate is 30 times greater than the general population;
- ✓ Loss of interest in usual activities including work and sex;
- ✓ Sleep disturbances − insomnia or oversleeping;
- ✓ A sense of hopelessness;
- ✓ Persistent sad, anxious or empty mood− cannot be *cheered-up*;
- ✓ Appetite disturbance−weight changes;
- ✓ Decreased energy and fatigue;
- ✓ Difficulty concentrating and making decisions (**this explains why an officer shouting commands is not very effective − many people experiencing severe depression look almost bewildered at the officers which in turn provokes the officers to shout even louder**; Louie 2007c);
- ✓ A sense and expression of pessimism;
- ✓ Hypochondria behavior;
- ✓ Insight/judgment; many individuals with the above symptoms may not characterize themselves as *depressed.*

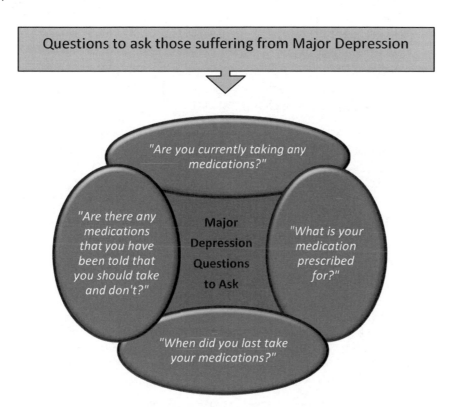

Questions to ask those suffering from Major Depression

"Are you currently taking any medications?"

"Are there any medications that you have been told that you should take and don't?"

Major Depression Questions to Ask

"What is your medication prescribed for?"

"When did you last take your medications?"

- • **Major Depression − some common anti-depressant drugs that may be found at the scene** (Case 2007): Prozac; Zolof; Paxil; Wellbutrin; Desipramine; Remeron; Effexor.

> ### What the officers may confront: *Bipolar Disorder* (Case 2007)

> "Bipolar disorder, which usually develops in the late teens or early 20s, is marked by severe shifts in mood, or alternating mood cycles of mania and depression"
> (Scott 2008, 26)

- ✓ Typically develops in late adolescence or early adulthood;
- ✓ May take years to diagnose;
- ✓ Symptoms may mimic alcohol or drug abuse;
- ✓ Ten to twenty percent rate of completed suicides;
- ✓ Seventy percent can respond well to proper medical treatment;
- ✓ Elevated mood and easily distracted;
- ✓ Talkative with racing or disconnected thoughts;
- ✓ Inflated self-esteem or grandiosity;
- ✓ Decreased need for sleep (feels rested after 3 hours of sleep);
- ✓ Increased risk taking; impulsive crimes; this is where many police officers meet the mentally ill – on a 911 call, thinking they are dealing with a criminal (Louie 2007c);
- ✓ Increase in goal-directed activity (socially, at work or at school);
- ✓ Sexual indiscretions or hyper-sexuality;
- ✓ Unrestrained buying sprees;
- ✓ Unrealistic belief in abilities;
- ✓ **Hypersensitive to noise, light and stress ...** *including a shouting police officer*;
- ✓ Hallucinations - psychotic stage (again, a common first contact with police officers);
- ✓ Seeking over-stimulation;
- ✓ Lack of sensitivity to heat, cold, hunger, pain and injury...**This is why many police pain compliance techniques are ineffective** (Louie 2007c).

> *When police are loudly ordering a subject to comply or lie down, many times the subject becomes more agitated with each and every octave spike in the police officer's voice* (Louie 2007c)

- • **Bipolar Mood Stabilizers – what may be found at the scene** (Case 2007): Lithium; Depakote;Tegretol; Neurontin;Topamax.

> ### What officers may confront: *Schizophrenia.*

> "Schizophrenia is a group of severe brain disorders in which people interpret reality abnormally. Schizophrenia may result in some combination of hallucinations, delusions and disordered thinking and behavior. The ability of people with schizophrenia to function normally and to care for themselves tends to deteriorate over time" (Mayo Clinic 2010).

- **Myths about Schizophrenia** (Case 2007):
  - ✓ People with Schizophrenia have split personality (*Dr. Jekyll-Mr. Hyde*) – not true; although the word does mean *split mind*, it refers to a disruption of the usual balance of emotions and thinking (Mayo Clinic 2010).
  - ✓ People with Schizophrenia are more violent than other people- ***not true*** .

- **Truths about Schizophrenia:**
  - ✓ Affects men and women with equal frequency;
  - ✓ Most cases develop between ages 16 and 30.
  - ✓ "Schizophrenia usually emerges in men in the late teens and early 20s, and in women in the mid-20s and early 30s. Its symptoms are classified into positive and negative categorizations, the positive including hallucinations and delusions, the negative a decreased ability to maintain cognitive and social behavior" (Scott 2008, 26).

- **Schizophrenia behaviors that may be observed or reported** (Case 2007):
  - ✓ Ritualistic movement or patterns;
  - ✓ Bizarre gestures and body positions;
  - ✓ Obsessions and compulsions;
  - ✓ Parroting what others are saying;
  - ✓ Odd speech patterns –incoherent;
  - ✓ No attention to hygiene;
  - ✓ Delusions; and beliefs that cannot be corrected by reason;
  - ✓ Hallucinations; voices, visual apparitions, bizarre interpretations of taste, touch, smell.

- **Anti-psychotic drugs that may be found at the scene** (Case 2007): Resperidal and/or Seroquel, Zuprexa, and Abilify.

➢ *Post-Traumatic Stress Disorder* (PTSD)

> Post-traumatic stress disorder (PTSD) is a severe anxiety disorder that can develop after exposure to any event that results in psychological trauma. This event may involve the threat of death to oneself or to someone else, or to one's own or someone else's physical, sexual, or psychological integrity, overwhelming the individual's ability to cope (Mayo Clinic 2011).

It's not just the war veteran; many critical events can trigger PTSD (Case 2007):

(istockphoto)

- ✓ Childhood abuse;
- ✓ Violent assaults (physical/sexual);
- ✓ Surviving a terrorist attack;
- ✓ Combatant experience of warfare;
- ✓ Natural catastrophe;
- ✓ Close brush with death.

> **PTSD Symptoms** (Case 2007): People experiencing PTSD re-experience the original trauma, typically through flashbacks or nightmares
> ✓ Insomnia;
> ✓ Aggressiveness;
> ✓ Anger;
> ✓ Hyper-vigilance;
> ✓ General restlessness;
> ✓ Avoidance of stimuli associated with the particular trauma;
> ✓ Emotional detachment;
> ✓ Flashbacks of incident;
> ✓ Nightmares.

- **PTSD Statistics** (Case 2007)

    ✓ In a VA study of 168,528 Iraqi veterans, 20% were diagnosed with psychological disorders, including 10% with PTSD;
    ✓ Only 23-40% sought professional help;
    ✓ About 30% of Vietnam vets have suffered from PTSD at some point after their return.

➢ **Recognizing PTSD as a legitimate mental illness** (Louie 2008).
Unfortunately, a recent Idaho Police Academy class insensitively used as their class motto: "Don't suffer from PTSD, go out and cause it" (Yahoo News 2007). Not only does this mock those with PTSD, it suggests that some police (rookies at the least) are not only insensitive, but that the public cannot expect fair treatment from the police when they deal with the mentally ill or emotionally distraught.

Public perception is negatively reinforced when the media routinely covers stories of the police responding to a mentally ill call, resulting in tragedy. From the police perspective, they contend they are responding to officer safety issues at the scene. From the perspective of family members and mental health advocates, the contention is that the police continue to respond to every police call as a criminal case, not taking into account the unique responses demanded when attempting to handle a crisis intervention call.

> What comes into question is how police are specifically trained to handle crisis intervention calls as distinguished from criminal-related calls. The following will showcase some examples of how police agencies are attempting to improve and enhance their response to the mentally ill and emotionally distraught.

- ➤ **Some Examples of Police and Community Responses to the Mentally Ill, People in Crisis, and Special Populations such as Military Veterans:**

- **The Memphis Model**: In 1994 the Memphis Police Department pioneered the use of a Crisis Intervention Team (CIT) with a specialized group of officers trained in crisis intervention and mental health intervention skills, working closely with the mental health community. The CIT teams work throughout the city, on different shifts, and are called in to handle mental health-related calls. (City of Memphis 2011; Korn 2008)

- **Portland Police Bureau:** In 2008, the Portland, Oregon, Police Bureau required all patrol officers to be taught crisis intervention techniques to better prepare them for handling mental health-related calls (Korn 2008). Currently the Portland program encompasses three dimensions:

  1. **Mandatory crisis intervention training for all officers**, providing a crisis intervention skill foundation for all first responders.

  2. **A one-car mobile crisis unit**, now limited to four days a week in Central Precinct, that pairs an officer with a mental health worker to identify people who come into frequent contact with police and intervene before a crisis. A patrol officer is assigned to ride with a mental health worker from Project Respond "to identify people with whom police have had frequent contact and are suffering from a mental illness. The idea is to have the mobile unit make sure these people are getting the services they need and are receiving medication if prescribed. The officer and mental health worker would also check in with case workers." The unit is "designed to make sure people suffering from mental illness in the community are getting the appropriate care they need before a crisis erupts and police are called to respond, Reese said" (Bernstein Jan. 18, 2011).

Associated Press

Here is an excerpt from a typical mobile crisis patrol contact: After the 7 a.m. roll call briefing at Central Precinct, Officer Christopher Burley and mental health counselor Del Webb go out on patrol. "Since April, the crisis unit has identified 60 people with mental illness, in some cases compounded by drug and alcohol problems. Some hear voices, wander into traffic or threaten neighbors. All live, to a degree, behind mental barricades, and are at risk of a bad, mad, sad ending involving police." During these contacts, the mobile crisis team takes note of the specific needs of those they are contacting, such as shoes, clothing and social needs such as health care appointments, even missing disability checks.

As Officer Burley and partner Del Webb approach a homeless camp under a bridge, they approach one of the homeless men: "These visitors aren't here to evict or scold. They actually want to know how he's doing. 'Pretty good,' he says, 'but I can't get the courts of our country to recognize that I'm a sovereign human being.' Long shtick short. Even though it's 38 degrees, he can't be persuaded to abandon his post under the bridge. (Something about upholding the memory and honor of his father.) Officer Burley, a former math and physics teacher with a megawatt grin, and Webb, a mental health counselor, hear many harangues in a day's work. They've learned how to interrupt -- kindly. Pre-crisis contact: But they don't badger. It doesn't help. As part of the Portland Police Bureau's mobile crisis unit, their job is to gently insinuate themselves in the lives -- and monologues -- of the mentally ill" (Bernstein, Jan. 18, 2011).

3. **The police bureau's hostage negotiation team** is the third piece; a specialty team with extensive crisis intervention and hostage negotiation training to help out on calls involving armed or suicidal people.

*   **Multnomah County, Oregon grant to study police encounters with mentally ill**.
    "Many interactions with police end well. But police get involved with mentally ill people so often that it's not surprising some encounters turn bad. Multnomah County and four other U.S. counties are trying to figure out just what makes these problems so common and what can be done to prevent them. Each county got a grant from the Bazelon Center for Mental Health Law, a Washington, D.C.-based nonprofit that works to improve policy toward people with mental illness" (Dworkin July 8, 2010).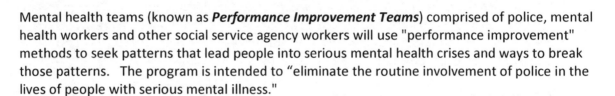

    Mental health teams (known as *Performance Improvement Teams*) comprised of police, mental health workers and other social service agency workers will use "performance improvement" methods to seek patterns that lead people into serious mental health crises and ways to break those patterns.   The program is intended to "eliminate the routine involvement of police in the lives of people with serious mental illness."

    The starting point for analysis will be to look at police encounters with the mentally ill and "see what the mental health system failed to do."   The team will evaluate police contacts with the mentally ill and try to identify what could have been done before the police contact to help the people and what programs (such as addiction and counseling services) may have been ...or should have been...providing services (Dworkin July 8, 2010).

*   **Hillsboro, Oregon, Police Department Mediation Program:**
    Starting in 1996, all 147 officers and professional staff in the Hillsboro Police Department have been required to take a minimum of 32 hours of mediation training, with selected departmental members and community volunteers taking an additional 32 hours of advanced training. Since 2006, the entire police department has completed the training, with new employees participating in annual retraining sessions. This benchmark signifies that the Hillsboro police department will be the only police department in the US with 100 percent of its officers trained in mediation (Oregonian 2006). The mediation training not only assists the officers and professional staff in handling disputing neighbors and code enforcement issues, but also in how to communicate with people experiencing crisis, such as the mentally ill and emotionally distraught. All Hillsboro police Hostage Negotiators are required to complete the advanced training and are called out on crisis calls that patrol officers are unable to resolve quickly.

    "Problem-solving often means recognizing people's emotions -- the rage inside the man who must drag himself to work each day after another sleepless night because of his neighbor's barking dog. Cops don't pay attention to those feelings. They just say, 'If you don't stop (threatening your neighbor) you'll have to go to jail" (Oregonian 2006). Mediation takes more time, which can be difficult for a busy officer. "It takes several hours to really mediate an issue," Lt. Richard Goerling said. "We don't have that kind of time out in the field. We kind of do mini-mediations." In 2005-06, Hillsboro officers mediated 69 cases on site, Mediation Program Coordinator Patti Williams said, and referred more complicated cases to the mediation program" (Oregonian 2006).

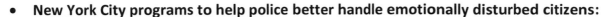

- **New York City programs to help police better handle emotionally disturbed citizens:**

  - ✓ **A task force recommended training New York Police Department dispatchers,** who handle roughly 90,000 calls annually regarding the emotionally disturbed, to ask better questions so that the officers responding have more information. The task force also called for the creation of a location database with call histories involving the mentally ill so that specially trained emergency-service officers can be dispatched more expeditiously.

  - ✓ **Another proposal is to establish Mental Health Care Monitoring Teams in New York City,** which would help coordinate and track the care of high-need clients. According to the New York Daily News, $13 million will be spent to create a sophisticated tracking system that will improve the continuity of mental-health care, identify when individuals requiring care cease treatment and speed up interventions for high-risk people when, for example, they stop taking anti-psychotic medications (Newsweek, July 31, 2008).

- **Clackamas County, Oregon, to assign crisis expert to patrol with deputies.**

(Photo by Michael Lloyd/The Oregonian)

"Janice Hancock now accompanies Clackamas County patrol officers, like sheriff's Deputy Jonathan Campbell (background), on calls to assess mentally ill people and refer them to programs, projects, counseling and housing, as needed. The sheriff's office soon will provide the mental health professional with her own car, so she can go where she can do the most good" (Bella 2010).

- **Washington County, Oregon, Sheriff's Office partnering with mental health specialists and Licensed Clinical Social Workers to ride with deputies in the field.**

These mental health specialists will be participating in routine patrols as well as consultation on specific cases.

- **Portland, Oregon, Mental Health Agency intervenes to provide help and support for mentally ill.**

(Photo by C. Onstott/ Portland Tribune)

The intent of this program is to not only save money, but to avoid conflicts with the police. "Central City Concern's Community Engagement Program seeks out the chronically homeless and mentally ill in hopes of connecting them with social services and possibly heading off encounters with police. Here, case manager Terri Everson talks with a client during a routine home visit at the Golden West Hotel" (Korn 2011).

- **Portland, Oregon, to develop mental health center to evaluate those at risk**.

Portland police and other emergency service providers will have a new place to bring mentally ill people in crisis besides the county jail or local hospitals.

"Multnomah County, the city of Portland and the nonprofit Central City Concern reached a final deal Thursday, June 17, 2010, to build and operate a mental health intake center above the Hooper "sobering center" east of the Burnside Bridge, 20 N.E. Martin Luther King Jr. Blvd. Groundbreaking for the new Crisis Assessment and Treatment Center is planned in August, with completion expected about six months later. The $5.3 million facility will feature professional and peer counselors who can work with mentally ill people experiencing breakdowns or other crises, and 16 beds where they can be lodged in a safe, dormitory-style setting" (Law 2010).

➤ Current Military Veteran statistics; harbinger of the future?

Military alcohol dependency on the rise, jumping from a 1998 ratio of 7.2 per 1,000 to a 1999 high of 11.4 per 1,000 (Snider 2009). **Alcohol treatment programs for the military on the rise:** "The rate of Army soldiers enrolled in treatment programs for alcohol dependency or abuse has nearly doubled since 2003 – a sign of the stress of repeated deployments in Iraq and Afghanistan, according to Army statistics and interviews" (Zoroya 2009a).

"…Marines who screen positive for drug or alcohol problems increased 12% from 2005 to 2008, according to Marine Corps statistics. In addition, there were 1,060 drunken-driving cases involving Marines during the first seven months of fiscal 2009, which began in October, compared with 1,430 cases in all of fiscal 2008" (Zoroya 2009b, A1).

Military use of pain-relief prescriptions on the rise: "Narcotic pain-relief prescriptions for injured U.S. troops have jumped from 30,000 a month to 50,000 since the Iraq war began, raising concerns about the drug's potential abuse and addiction" (Zoroya 2010).

360,000 Veterans may have brain injuries. "Pentagon officials estimated for the first time Wednesday that up to 360,000 Iraq and Afghanistan veterans may have suffered brain injuries. Among them are 45,000 to 90,000 veterans whose symptoms persist and warrant specialized care" (Zoroya 2009a).

An example of Oregon police agencies seeking partnerships with FBI, military services health practitioners and veterans' organizations to understand returning combat veterans' issues - hopefully *before* the 911 crisis call.

Post Traumatic Stress & the Returning Veteran
July 28-29, 2009
Improving our leadership of veterans employed in public safety

This two-day conference is designed for community stakeholders and public safety leaders to increase awareness of issues unique to the returning combat veteran. The focus will be on returning veterans employed in public safety with the goal to enhance our ability to lead these dedicated professionals as they return to their civilian careers in police, fire, medical, communications and other public safety fields. Experts from a variety of disciplines will present information and form a foundation for ongoing dialogue, process improvement, and policy development.

Hillsboro

Example of law enforcement partnerships with academic community (Pacific University, Forest Grove, Oregon).

FIRST RESPONDERS AND THE COMBAT VET

COURSE OVERVIEW: This course will provide basic information on POST 9/11 military life, Middle East and the life of our soldiers; deployment to civilian life, PTSD and Traumatic Brain Injuries (TBI), Basic Communication Skills for Vets in crisis, and information on local and regional resources for Vets.

June 17th, 2011

HOURS: 8:30 AM TO 5:00 PM (30 MINUTE LUNCH BREAK)

LOCATION: WASHINGTON COUNTY SHERIFF'S OFFICE, 215 SW ADAMS AVENUE, HILLBORO OREGON 97123

INSTRUCTORS: Variety of local and regional veteran and Psychology experts

DISCUSSION TOPICS: Military 101, PTSD and TBI (traumatic brain injuries), Tactical Communication techniques, local veterans support programs, and Washington County Veterans Court.

COST: $0 FOR WASHINGTON COUNTY LAW ENFORCEMENT AGENCIES

REGISTER BY CONTACTING: JOYCE PHILLIPS AT WCSO TRAINING UNIT 503-846-2791

Dress/supplies and equipment: This is a classroom discussion and the dress will be business casual. You will only need pen and paper for note taking.

> Example of IACP-sponsored conference focusing on issues regarding returning war vets and their employment in the law enforcement professions.

Employing Returning Combat Veterans as Police Officers

Supporting the integration or reintegration of military personnel into federal, state, local, and tribal law enforcement (November 2008)

> The following section will review various definitions of diagnosed mental illnesses that first responders are likely to confront at the 911 call.

> ➢ **What the officers may confront:** *Autism* (AELE Law Journal, July 2009)

> *Autism is characterized as a brain development disorder that results in impairment of interpersonal communication and social interaction.*

New evidence shows that the brains of adults with autism are " wired differently" (or conversely, have "faulty brain connections") from people without the disorder, and this abnormal pattern of connectivity may be responsible for the social impairments that are characteristic of autism (Science Daily 2008).

This study shows that these brain regions are failing to work together efficiently," said Natalia Kleinhans, a research assistant professor of radiology and lead author of the paper published in the journal Brain. "Our work seems to indicate that the brain pathways of people with autism are not completely disconnected, but they are not as strong as in people without autism" (Science Daily 2008).

Autistic individuals frequently engage in restricted and repetitive behavior. They are often most comfortable with routines—sometimes very rigidly, becoming easily upset by a new situation, the presence of an unknown person, loud noise, or unanticipated surprises. (**This is why police officers should not attempt to restrict these repetitive behaviors unless they are a officer safety issue.**)

Often, their response may be a *meltdown*, acting out, ritualistic behavior, inappropriate verbal statements, or other actions that may be viewed by some, mistakenly, as an indication of hostility, criminal intent, alcohol or drug intoxication, etc.

Some autistic persons have difficulty making and maintaining eye contact with others. A police officer may mistakenly interpret this as suspicious, having something to hide, or defiance, when in reality it is not being able to or not knowing how to respond appropriately, or even fear from what, to many, would be a routine social encounter. The result has sometimes, unfortunately, been rapid escalation of the encounter, with ensuing injury or death.

- **Autism affects how people see faces:** "Recognizing human faces is so basic that even newborns are drawn to the shape. But not everyone sees faces the same way. The brains of autistic people process faces differently, a University of Washington study found. The scientists showed pictures of faces and houses to 40 adults, 19 of them high-functioning adults with an IQ of at least 85 and an autism spectrum disorder. A kind of MRI showed activity in the brain when people saw the photos. The 19 autistic adults had much less brain activity connecting the fusiform face area, a brain region that helps identify faces, and two other brain regions, the left amygdala and the posterior cingulate" (Dworkin 2008). This study shows that the brains of people with autism function "differently" when looking at faces. This could be a possible explanation "why people with autism are often socially awkward or inclined to avoid ordinary social contact" (Dworkin 2008).

For those confronting Autism-affected people on the street, what are the implications? Does this imply that sounds (tone of voice, volume, etc.) will have a greater impact than non-verbal facial expressions? Are there some words that can be used that may have a calming or defusing impact?

- **Autism occurs in 2-6 of every 1000 people and is four times more prevalent in boys than girls. Autism can create difficulties with** (Case 2007):
  - ✓ Verbal and non-verbal communication;
  - ✓ Social interactions;
  - ✓ Leisure or play activities;
  - ✓ Physical manifestations;
  - ✓ Sensory sensitivity may produce a fight or flight reaction.

- **Autistic Behaviors that may be seen or reported** (Case 2007):
  - ✓ Inappropriate toy play;
  - ✓ Difficulty with changes in routine;
  - ✓ Sensitivity to noises;
  - ✓ Inappropriate laughter or crying;
  - ✓ Lack of awareness of danger;
  - ✓ Hyperactivity or passiveness;
  - ✓ Poor speech or lack of speech;
  - ✓ Sensitivity to touch;
  - ✓ Inability to relate to others;
  - ✓ Strange attachments to objects.
  - ✓ Lack of eye contact.

*Temper tantrums and impulsive behavior are an expected response to fear, confusion, or frustration as an effort to stop the stimuli **(and the stimuli may be a police officer shouting commands).***

- **How to respond** (Case 2007):
  - ✓ Allow for delayed response from questions or commands;
  - ✓ Slow everything down! (Louie 2007c)
  - ✓ Be aware of subject's self-protective response to lights, sounds, touch, orders and police K9's;
  - ✓ If not a compromise to officer safety, turn off sirens and overhead lights;
  - ✓ Look for presence of medical alert tags;
  - ✓ Avoid stopping repetitive behavior unless self-injurious or risk of injury to others.
  - ✓ Tell the person that you are not going to hurt them (if not a compromise to officer safety, show your open hands in a non-threatening manner).
  - ✓ Speak calmly and as quietly as possible in short, direct phrases (again, ***Do Not Shout!***).
  - ✓ Research suggests that **using more communicative and direct form of words** (known as "alpha commands"), the more autistic children may comply (Houlihan 2006).

Many times those suffering from autism will repeatedly move their hands in what appears to be nervous or lack of purpose and random movement. Out of frustration, police officers may reach out and grab the person's hand to prevent this behavior. ***But if not a danger or compromise to officer safety, allow for the hand and body movements because grabbing and holding will only incite greater resistance and possibly a violent reaction.***

> **The same can be applied to adults:** the more threatening you are in tone and behavior, the more not only autistic, but the general population as well, will respond in kind — **frightened, aggressive and uncooperative. Use direct and unambiguous words, slow down the rate of speech, and maintain a friendly tone** (Louie 2007c). Notify the jail of the person's suspected autism (or any other suspected mental diagnosis) in order to reduce the risk of problems with other inmates.

> "People with autism have difficulty interpreting body language, which makes it difficult for them to understand other people's emotions. The research used animated clips of figures made up of dots showing emotions which the participants with autism had trouble identifying correctly. We use others' body movements and postures, as well as people's faces and voices, to gauge their feelings. People with autism are less able to use these cues to make accurate judgments about how others are feeling" (BBC News 2009).

Body language and Autism

An example of a statewide training bulletin to serve as a guide for those responding to those diagnosed with Autism and unfortunately, now a 911 call...

This guide from the Illinois Attorney General's Office recommends the following practical suggestions when handling those believed to be autistic (AELA 2009). **Although there may be some redundancy in the following recommendations, the more the repetition with the above information, the greater the validation for accuracy with the following:**

While each person with autism is different, common characteristics include:
- Limited or no ability to speak;
- Lack of eye contact;
- Insistence on sameness ;
- Obsessive attachment to objects;
- Self-stimulating behavior including hand flapping, body rocking, or attachment to objects;
- Inappropriate behavior, such as laughing during a serious situation;
- No fear of danger;
- Over- or under-sensitivity to pain;
- Tantrums or escalated behavior for no apparent reason;
- Preference to be alone.

Responding to a call: To ensure the safety of all individuals involved, police officers responding to a situation involving someone with autism should:
- Make sure the person is unarmed and maintain a safe distance;
- Model the behavior you want the person to display;
- Use a quiet non-threatening voice;
- Use simple language;
- Avoid touching, if possible;
- Allow for delayed response;
- Turn off lights and sirens, if possible;
- Talk to people who know the person with autism, such as caregivers;
- Allow an agitated individual with autism to calm down without your intervention, if possible, and give them extra personal space.

Restraint: If you must restrain a person with autism, consider the following tips to maintain safety for both yourself and the person being arrested:
- People with autism may have a difficult time supporting their airways during restraint due to underdeveloped chest muscles. Officers should turn the person on their side to ensure normal breathing.
- Keep in mind that many people with autism are prone to seizures.
- Be prepared for resistance. People with autism may not understand the futility of struggling even when they are restrained.
- Speak and act in a calm manner to encourage de-escalation.

Interviews: Whether you are interviewing a person with autism as a victim, witness, or offender, you should use the following tips to ensure a successful interview:
- Allow plenty of time.
- Avoid leading questions.
- Develop an understanding of the person's communication style before asking more critical questions.
- Plan questioning based on ability level.
- Do not take a lack of eye contact, the changing of subjects, or answers that are vague, evasive, or blunt as evidence of guilt.
- Ask questions that rely on narrative responses. "Yes" or "no" responses could be unreliable.

> ## What may be confronted: *Psychosis, Hallucinations, and Delusions.*

Psychosis means "abnormal condition of the mind," and is a generic psychiatric term for a mental state often described as involving a "loss of contact with reality." People suffering from psychosis are described as "psychotic." Psychosis is given to the more severe forms of psychiatric disorder, during which hallucinations and delusions and impaired insight may occur. People experiencing psychosis may report hallucinations or delusional beliefs, and may exhibit personality changes and thought disorder. Depending on its severity, this may be accompanied by unusual or bizarre behavior, as well as difficulty with social interaction and impairment in carrying out the daily life activities.

A hallucination is a "sensory perception that has the compelling sense of reality of a true perception but that occurs without external stimulation of the relevant sensory organ."

A delusion is "a false belief based on incorrect inference about external reality that is firmly sustained despite what almost everyone else believes and despite what constitutes incontrovertible and obvious proof or evidence to the contrary."

Delirium, an abnormal change in a patient's level of consciousness, may result from a variety of toxic, structural or metabolic causes. Delirious patients may have waxing and waning of consciousness, may be agitated or lethargic, and frequently have disturbed sleep.
(Case 2007; Lawrence 2007; Thompson 2007)

- **What may be observed:**
  - ✓ Sensory perception in the absence of external stimuli;
  - ✓ Voices heard are perceived as distinct from the person's own thoughts;
  - ✓ Often experienced as threatening and critical;
  - ✓ Person appears preoccupied and unaware of surroundings;
  - ✓ Talks to him/herself;
  - ✓ Difficulty understanding or following conversations;
  - ✓ Misinterprets words and actions of others.

- **How to respond** (Case 2007):
  - ✓ Do not pretend that you also experience the hallucination!
  - ✓ Do ask about the hallucination –what they hear, see, etc.;
  - ✓ Do tell the person, "I don't hear the voices but I believe you do"; "I cannot see what you are seeing, but I believe you can; I would like to help you."
  - ✓ Establish trust;
  - ✓ Calm presence; the more agitated the officer appears, the more agitated the subject will be –
  - ✓ raising voice and shouting commands will not be effective;
  - ✓ Assure them that you want to help;
  - ✓ Allow them the time and space to respond (remember: *Slow Everything Down!*);
  - ✓ Assure them that you want to help.

SLOW

> *Delusions, Psychosis and Hallucinations*

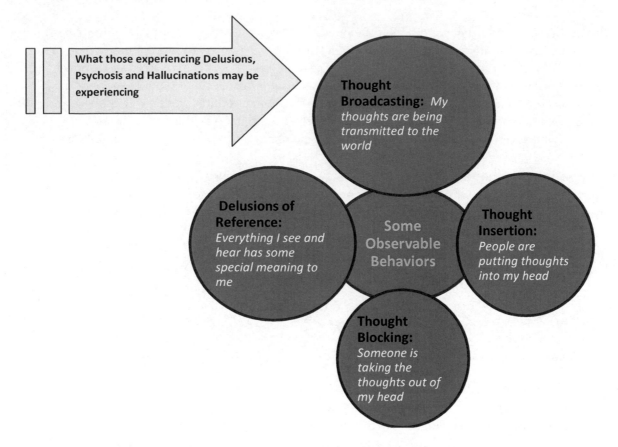

> *Excited Delirium:* **The Law Enforcement Officer's Role in Effectively Dealing with Mentally Ill Persons and Reducing In-Custody Deaths and Injuries**
(Lawrence 2006, Thompson 2007, Las Vegas Police ED Training Series 2005)

What is Delirium/Excited Delirium (ED)? Delirium itself is not a disease, but rather a clinical syndrome, or set of symptoms, which result from an underlying disease or new problem with medication (i.e., the thinking process: "Where am I?" "Who are you?" "What day is it?" etc.). Simplified: Delirium is the manifestation of early brain or mental dysfunction, for any reason (Thompson 2007). Delirium is commonly used to refer to drowsiness or disorientation, however, the medical usage also involves other symptoms, including: the inability to focus attention, sleeplessness, severe agitation and irritability. "The result of a neurochemical imbalance in the brain" (Lawrence 2007).

- **Medical Definitions for ED.** There are several medical definitions for delirium, all of which share some common core features:
  - ✓ Disturbance of consciousness (a reduced clarity of awareness of the environment or surroundings, with reduced ability to focus, sustain, or shift attention);
  - ✓ A change in cognition (i.e., memory impairment) or a perceptual disturbance;
  - ✓ Onset of hours to days and a tendency to fluctuate (Thompson 2007).

- **Causes of Delirium.** Delirium may be caused by severe physical or mental illness, or any process which interferes with the normal metabolism or function of the brain. Fever, poisons (including toxic drug reactions), brain surgery, general surgery, severe lack of food or water, drug and severe alcohol withdrawal are all known to cause delirium (Thompson 2007).

- **ED-like Symptoms.** There may be other medical conditions that mimic ED behavior but since that cannot be determined at the scene, responding officers need to quickly determine if they need to "contain-and-attempt-to-calm" or more quickly provide medical assistance (Lawrence 2006).

Chris Lawrence of the Canadian Police Research Center suggests that "...unless an apparent ED subject is presenting a direct threat to officers ... he should be regarded more as a medical problem than a police problem. The best (an officer) can do when faced with ED-like symptoms is make getting medical assistance to the scene a top priority. And that needs to be the core component of any training or policies designed to address the ED problem" (Lawrence 2006, 1).

> **It should come as no surprise that delirium can more easily present itself in those with underlying or chronic brain dysfunction** (Lawrence 2006)

- **Excited Delirium: *What Does it Look Like?*** The delirious person is likely to manifest an acute behavioral disturbance. These individuals can appear normal until they are questioned, challenged or confronted. When confronted or frightened, these individuals can become oppositional, defiant, angry, paranoid and aggressive. Further confrontation, threats and use of force will almost certainly result in further aggression and even violence (Thompson 2007).

> **Attempting to restrain and control these individuals can be difficult because they frequently possess unusual strength, pain insensitivity and instinctive resistance to any use of force. Experience in the field indicates that as many as 5 to 8 people may be required to restrain one delirious adult** *(Thompson 2007)*

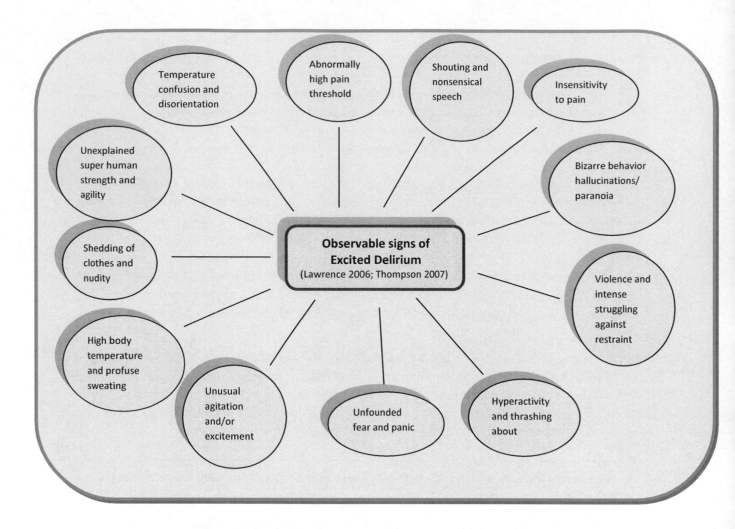

The center of the diagram reads:

Observable signs of Excited Delirium
(Lawrence 2006; Thompson 2007)

Surrounding circles:
- Temperature confusion and disorientation
- Abnormally high pain threshold
- Shouting and nonsensical speech
- Insensitivity to pain
- Unexplained super human strength and agility
- Bizarre behavior hallucinations/ paranoia
- Shedding of clothes and nudity
- Violence and intense struggling against restraint
- High body temperature and profuse sweating
- Unusual agitation and/or excitement
- Unfounded fear and panic
- Hyperactivity and thrashing about

- **Excited Delirium; A Serious Medical Emergency.** When the police are called to someone expressing ED-like symptoms – bizarre and violent behavior - it is a situation requiring them to control and take the person into custody. But this type of call is also a medical emergency and needs to be handled as such, once safety and control as been achieved (Lawrence 2007).

- **Mimicking behavior: Pay attention to statements made, or information obtained from others!**
  - ✓ <u>Graham vs. Conner</u> (1989)**,** a landmark court case, illustrates an example of a Diabetic, experiencing low blood sugar levels, whose aggressive behavior appeared to be those of someone experiencing ED.   "In that case, the subject 'advised officers that he needed sugar' to counteract his medical problem. Pay attention to people who make this kind of statement. Fruit juice or candy may indeed improve their situation" (Lawrence 2006, 2).

- **Other ED-mimicking medical emergencies reported:**
  - ✓ Hyperthermia (abnormally high body temperature) that may be a side effect from medication for bladder or gastrointestinal problems; diabetes; head injury; delirium tremens (commonly known as "the DT's" or alcohol withdrawal); overactive thyroid (Lawrence 2006).

> **Suggested ED Response Guidelines** (Thompson 2007):

Upon arrival on scene, if the subject is exhibiting signs of Excited Delirium, EMS shall be requested immediately. The EMS response time will depend on what the officer observes (i.e. the subject is bleeding from a serious injury, or simply rambling incoherently with no apparent physical injuries).

✓ As many cover officers as possible should be requested; level of response may vary, depending on how imminent the threat to public safety is.

✓ The primary officer should attempt to establish a rapport with the subject, from a distance, until cover arrives. As with all encounters, never sacrifice officer safety when dealing with ED subjects and never attempt to take the subject into custody single-handedly.

✓ Once cover officers are on scene, the focus should be to establish a perimeter around the subject and to develop a tactical plan for taking the subject into custody.

✓ Remember, getting the subject into the hands of medical personnel is paramount with ED.

✓ As with all custody situations, the goal should be to take the subject into custody with the least amount of harm to everyone involved.

✓ Subjects may have abnormally high pain threshold and *super-human* strength.

Examples of ED Response Guidelines from Canada to California

 ED Response Guidelines from the Canadian Police Research Center
(Lawrence 2006, 1-5)

✓ Dispatchers and officers should be trained to summon medical help immediately upon detecting any symptoms in a subject that resemble ED.

✓ Get multiple officers to the scene; multi-officer control tactics will probably be necessary.

✓ If safe to do so, initiate restraint techniques when EMS personnel are present, so that medical attention and transport to a treatment facility can be started promptly thereafter.

✓ Question family members, other witnesses or the subject himself (if coherent) regarding evidence that might be related to either ED or non-ED conditions (mentioned above).

✓ In designing training or policies, don't set expectations for officers' responses too high. Under pressure to *do something* some agencies are trying to construct detailed policies and better training programs that, in fact, may not be realistic.

ED Response Guidelines from San Jose PD, California
(Lewinski 2007, 1-5)

✓ Attempt to talk the person down. Because of the subject's mental state, statements and questions may need to be repeated several times. The person may also be fearful and extremely confused so officers should be patient.

✓ If the subject is contained and does not appear to pose an immediate threat, there is no rush. It may take some time for the subject to calm down.

✓ Attempt to have the individual sit down, which may have a calming effect.

✓ Refrain from maintaining constant eye contact, as this may be interpreted as threatening.

✓ If the subject is armed or combative or otherwise poses an immediate threat, officers shall employ "reasonable and necessary" force to protect themselves and others and take the person into custody. To the extent practical, try to minimize the intensity and duration of any resistance and avoid engaging in a prolonged struggle. It may be possible to limit resistance by using several officers simultaneously to restrain the subject quickly.

✓ If a relative or someone else who has rapport with the individual can safely participate, enlist their help in trying to gain compliance.

✓ Once in-custody and the scene is safe, EMS personnel should be called from the staging areas. "Some ED subjects have gone into cardiac arrest shortly after a struggle so the person's breathing shall be monitored at all times and the person's position adjusted to maximize the ability to breathe" (San Jose Police Department ED Response Guidelines in Lewinski 2007).

✓ The subject should be transported by ambulance to an emergency medical facility for evaluation and treatment.

✓ Some police critics have insisted that ED is nothing more than a convenient concept *manufactured* by law enforcement to cover-up brutality and exonerate authorities when a suspect is roughly arrested or dies in custody. There is current research (Force Science News, 2009b) identifying ED as a "unique syndrome" and not manufactured.

ED
It's now official: In a move strongly supportive of law enforcement, a special investigative task force of the American College of Emergency Physicians (ACEP) has formally declared that the violent and sometimes lethal phenomenon known as excited delirium" really does exist (Force Science News, 2009b)

"The ACEP group affirms in a recent White Paper that ED is 'a unique syndrome' that may not be identified in autopsies but that can be recognized in the field by a distinctive group of clinical and behavioral characteristics. The report makes clear that the psycho-physiological meltdown known as ED is not always fatal. Indeed, given an appropriate collaboration by responding officers and EMS personnel, the condition might be amenable to early therapeutic intervention," the document speculates" (Force Science News, 2009b).

The study found that many ED cases had a "high mortality rate" as well as association with cocaine abuse and other illicit stimulant drugs of abuse such as meth and PCP. The study estimates that approximately 250 ED subjects die each year in the US, which is approximately 8 to 14% of those experiencing ED symptoms. However, the study also concludes that "despite circumstantial relationships with stimulant drug abuse, psychiatric disease, psychiatric drug withdrawal, and underlying metabolic disorders, science has not yet determined how these factors lead to excited delirium or why only some cases end in death" (Force Science News, 2009b). Many ED cases are associated with not only "acute drug intoxication" but often a history of mental illness (especially paranoia).

For those ED individuals in contact with the police, there is frequently a physical struggle and use of electrical control devices such as the Taser and then a "sudden and unexpected death, and an autopsy which fails to reveal a definite cause of death from trauma or natural disease," (Force Science News, 2009b).

- **Some of the behaviors identified with ED subjects in the study were:**
    - ✓ Hyper-aggressive and "bizarre behavior";
    - ✓ impervious to pain;
    - ✓ combative;
    - ✓ tirelessly resistant,
    - ✓ sweating,
    - ✓ breathing rapidly,
    - ✓ agitated,
    - ✓ unusually strong,
    - ✓ inappropriately clothed (many were nude when police made contact);
    - ✓ abnormally high body temperature; and,
    - ✓ rapid heart rate (Force Science News 2009b).

(istockphoto)

Unfortunately, crisis intervention and tactical communication techniques may not be effective with ED subjects since they are reported to be *not rational* and unable to engage in a conversation. Since most ED subjects were unaware of their surroundings and lacked "rational thoughts for safety" and appeared to be delusional, it is apparent that the best response for the police is to contain and subdue, then transport for medical evaluation.

> **At this time (2009), the White Paper concludes there is "insufficient data...to determine whether fatal ED is preventable, or whether there is a point of no return after which the patient will die regardless of advanced life support interventions."**

➢ Use of the Taser – Effective or not with ED subjects?

Although the focus of this training guide is to present crisis intervention and tactical communication techniques and skills, mention needs to be made of the police use of force and the use of less lethal equipment such as the Taser since many disturbance and crisis calls involve less lethal equipment.

> *For in-service public safety personnel, their respective departments' policies and procedures will take precedent over guidelines discussed here.*

Various police agencies contend that the use of a Taser "...has proven effective when dealing with subjects exhibiting ED" (Thompson 2007). **However, a Taser may not be effective on ED subjects because pain compliance does not work.** What may be effective is not the pain compliance aspect of a Taser but rather, that very short time period immediately after Taser application while the subject is recovering from the shock of the Taser. Some police agencies recommend that the temporary immobilization period is when police should apply restraints on an ED subject:

- "A single Taser deployment should be used. The 5 second 'window of opportunity' is crucial when dealing with subjects exhibiting ED. Remember, the goal is to get the subject into custody and into the hands of medical personnel as soon as possible, **not to attempt to gain compliance**, which is futile in these incidents" (Thompson 2007, 20).

> ➢ **Use of the Taser; there also is the controversy over the use of the Taser.**

> "Although we have all seen the headlines, 'Man dies after being tased by police.' There is still no conclusive evidence that the Taser, in and of itself, has been the primary cause of death in a police incident involving its use."
> (Thompson 2007, 20).

The use of a Taser continues to be controversial, especially when police are seen as using the Taser "to make people comply" as opposed to stopping people who are a serious threat.

ACLU report criticizes police use of stun guns: "The American Civil Liberties Union says Ashland police improperly used a Taser five of the six times they have deployed the electric stun device since 2004." In response to an internal review, Ashland (Oregon) Police Chief Terry Holderness "...will limit Taser use to when an officer is seriously threatened. Previously, it was allowed if a suspect put up 'active resistance.'" (Associated Press, Sept. 14, 2007).

- The position of the ACLU (Fidanque, 2007, 1) is that they recommend "...much tighter restrictions on the use of CEDs (conducted energy devices such as Tasers); and, better officer training in techniques to de-escalate tense situations."

- The primary issue with the ACLU is that police use Tasers "to make people to comply" when other methods and techniques (control holds, batons, irritant sprays, etc.) should be used because the Taser is seen (by the ACLU and other civil rights groups) as potentially lethal (Fidanque, 2007, 1). The Ashland, Oregon, Police Department's policy change to allow Taser use only when an officer is "seriously threatened" is a compromise that allows the use of the Taser, but only for more serious and injury-threatening confrontations.

> **Ongoing research does suggest that multiple applications of the Taser, such as on a subject experiencing E.D., may increase the risk of death while in police custody, due to the energy exerted by the subject as he tenses up during muscle contractions**
> (Thompson 2007).

- Officers should avoid standing around while the subject is in custody, and instead should monitor the subject's condition until medical personnel can take over.

- Once the subject is placed on the gurney, officers and medical personnel should employ the use of available restraints to secure the subjects arms and legs to the side rails.

- In all Excited Delirium incidents, the primary officer will stay with the subject at all times. This includes accompanying the subject, inside the ambulance, while he/she is being transported to the medical facility on a *Police Officer Hold* (POH).

> *As with all mental illness or emotionally disturbed calls, officers need to recognize how their behavior and tactics employed may exacerbate an already tense situation*
> (Louie 2007c)

> **Federal court restricts Taser use by police**: This Ninth Circuit ruling, allowing an officer to be held liable for injuries a man suffered after being *Tasered*; sets a precedent that may force agencies to revisit their policies (Rubin and Winton 2009).

A federal appeals court has ruled that a California police officer can be held liable for injuries suffered by an unarmed man whom he Tasered during a traffic stop. The decision, if allowed to stand, would set a rigorous legal precedent for when police are permitted to use the devices and would force some law enforcement agencies throughout the state -- and presumably the nation -- to tighten their policies governing Taser use, experts said.

- Michael Gennaco, an expert in police conduct issues who has conducted internal reviews of Taser use for the Los Angeles County Sheriff's Department and other agencies, said the ruling by the U.S. 9th Circuit Court of Appeals prohibits officers from deploying Tasers in a host of scenarios and **largely limits their use to situations in which a person poses an obvious danger**. "This decision talks about the need for an immediate threat. Some departments allow Tasers in cases of passive resistance, such as protesters who won't move," he said. Tasering for "passive resistance is out the door now with this decision. Even resistance by tensing or bracing may not qualify" (Gennaco in Rubin and Winton, 2009, 1).

The weapons, which resemble handguns, can be fired from about 20 feet away and project two dart-like electrodes. The electrodes send an electrical charge coursing through the target -- a shock that temporarily paralyzes the person's muscles and causes extreme pain. Almost all of the stun guns used by law enforcement agencies in the United States are manufactured by Taser International.

Though stun guns have been in use for about three decades, the number of police departments issuing them to officers has proliferated in the last 10 years. Advocates tout the weapons as a less-than-lethal alternative to firearms and say they help resolve dangerous face-to-face confrontations with combative suspects. But several controversial Taser incidents, some involving fatalities, have led to widespread debate over when police should be allowed to deploy the devices.

Last year, a National Institute of Justice study found that the weapons were employed safely in the vast majority of cases, but concluded that more research is needed to determine the health effects of shocking small children and the elderly, among other groups.

> ## What we need to know more about In-custody deaths (Thompson 2007):

 "Once in custody, never place the subject in the face down position. Roll the subject onto his/her side or into a seated position if possible, so as not to restrict breathing.   Past incidents and ongoing research suggests that restricted breathing, also known as Restraint Asphyxia or Positional Asphyxia, is often the cause of in-custody deaths" (Thompson 2007).

Why? It is the right thing to do to protect all citizens.   It is also because officers and agencies across the nation are facing increased scrutiny regarding their roles in these incidents. The liability cost to defend these cases is high, and as more studies and information develops, the chance of being implicated in in-custody deaths increases.   Current statistics show that approximately 50 to 125 people die from restraint-related deaths each year in the U.S.   Most are related to being taken into custody, during violent encounters with police.

Chapter VI: Responding to the Suicidal

For active duty public safety professionals, their respective departmental policy guidelines and general orders shall be their primary authority for how to respond to suicide-in-progress and suicide calls.

The following information should be considered as general guidelines for responding to those threatening suicide. This material is not intended to be an all-inclusive study of the dynamics of suicide but rather as training points for responding police officers and public safety professionals. This material is also not intended to replace specialized training skills development such as *hostage negotiation* or *how to handle the suicidal* courses.

> ## The Suicide Call – The Basic Stages

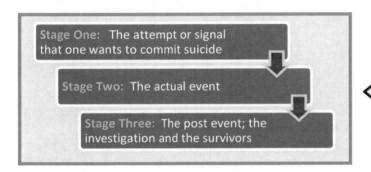

Stage One: The attempt or signal that one wants to commit suicide

Stage Two: The actual event

Stage Three: The post event; the investigation and the survivors

The suicide call can be viewed as a 3-stage evolution, initiated by the call, then the response to the scene, concluding with the resolution of the event (either a surrender of the attempted suicide subject or completed act, followed by the investigation and communication with the survivors of the suicide or attempted suicide).

> ## Strategy when attempting to communicate with a suicidal person (Vance & Louie 2007):

- **Be honest, establish rapport;** but be aware of *transference* ("the process whereby emotions are passed on or displaced from one person to another" whereby one person starts to identify with the suicidal person). Communicate compassion and empathy but recognize you may be susceptible to losing your professional objectivity as you *relate* to the person you are trying to help.

- **Respond to guilt manipulation**: "It would be sad if you did that, however, it is your choice." *The more one can articulate the fantasy of suicide, the more serious the person may be about committing suicide.*

- **Responding to the Suicidal - You may be frank and straightforward:**
  - ✓ "Are you going to commit suicide?"
  - ✓ "Are you having thoughts about killing yourself?"
  - ✓ "Do you have a plan for committing suicide?"
  - ✓ "What are you planning to do?"
  - ✓ "How long have you been planning it?"

I want to die

- ✓ "Have you ever tried to kill yourself before?" "What happened?"
- ✓ "Have you ever had thoughts about killing yourself before?" "When?" "What stopped you?"
- ✓ "Do you want to hurt yourself?"
- ✓ "What happened today to make you want to do this?"
- ✓ "Do you want to hurt anyone else? Who? Why?
- ✓ "I don't want you to hurt yourself: What can I do for you?"

(Dr. M. Reece)

Most suicidal persons appear willing to discuss their suicide; just give them time to build up a rapport with you. So, don't be afraid to talk about it – you won't give anyone ideas they have not already thought about.

➢ **This is where your communication skills are the most vital to establish a trusting connection. But you must beware of appearing transparent, superficial or patronizing:**

- **Try to determine the underlying cause;** i.e., recent family loss, job pressure, recent failures at work or other relationships, etc.
- **Do not give advice**; they have already heard enough from others. This is where you lose that *equal connection* with the other person and now appear to be talking down, patronizing or otherwise appear to not understand the person's feelings.
- **Suicidal individuals are often fearful and even feel guilty about having suicidal thoughts.**
- **Do not patronize**; always measure your tone of voice, words used, etc.
- **Practice Active Listening Skills**; this is where you start to bridge the communication gap.
- **Do not be judgmental**; they have already gone through judgmental phases with others.
- **Try to determine if a referral will be helpful.** Which referral is relevant; how realistic is the referral (meaning, is it local, reasonable cost, etc.). Is the referral agency or person available for timely follow through?
- **Avoid projection**; don't blame others. And if you join in on the person's projection, you will immediately be interpreted as patronizing.
- **Be careful if you allow others to become involved.** If the suicidal person requests a specific individual, find out why he or she wants that person brought to the scene. It may be for revenge, to punish someone, or to say good-by. Try to determine how others – spouse, friend, etc. – may escalate the situation.
- **While trying to establish rapport, allow the person to make small decisions**; let them regain decision making, no matter how small (i.e., "are you hungry, what do you want to eat, when," etc.).
- **Do you have a Community Resource & Referral Guide** that lists what is locally available to help someone in need?

Talk openly about how final death is: *"Death is forever. Suicide is a permanent solution to a temporary problem."*

An emerging problem; the returning war veteran:
Notwithstanding the more common police confrontations with people experiencing mental illness and having suicidal motivations, there also is the need to focus on the specific population of the returning war veteran, as well as those veterans of past conflicts experiencing PTSD. "The casualties of war that are not often talked about are military members who die of self-inflicted wounds. According to the U.S. Department of Veterans Affairs (VA), suicide is the 11th most frequent cause of death for military veterans in America" (Vets News 2008, 11).

"For many in the military, counseling can be a bad word – as it might be seen as a sign of weakness" yet thousands of service members are returning with disabling injuries and mental health disorders that put them at higher risk. The number of suicides committed by U.S. service members after arriving home from a combat zone is not only double the total among troops still serving in those same combat areas, but double that of the general population" (Vet News 2008, 11).

➤ Some disturbing facts regarding returning war veterans; Nationwide and the Northwest:

 "A report from the Oregon Department of Human Services (DHS), 'Violent Deaths in Oregon found that suicide remains the leading cause of violent death. In 2005, it was reported that 28 percent (153 of 771) of all Oregon suicides were among veterans. Of those, 148 were male" (Vet News 2008, 11).

- "A study by the VA's Health Services Research Division suggests that younger military members may be at the greatest risk of taking their own lives. The study focus on 807,694 depressed veterans of the VA health care system from 1999 to 2004 and suggests that more resources are needed to reduce suicide in this age group" (Vet News 2008, 11).

- According to VA records, more than 100,000 veterans are now seeking help for mental health issues and an astounding 52,000 of this number for PTSD (Vet News 2008, 11).

- "Young women who've served in the military face a suicide risk triple that of non-veterans. Among veterans age 18 to 34, the suicide rate was 1 in 7,465, compared with 1 in 22,763 among non-veterans. Suicide rates were 78 percent higher among female veterans age 35 to 44, and 58 percent higher among those age 45 to 64" (Rojas-Burke 2010).

Military members under the age of 40 are three times more likely to be diagnosed with PTSD or depression than their older counterparts.

> ## Risk factors suggested by Oregon Department of Veterans' Affairs:
> ✓ Talking about wanting to hurt or kill oneself;
> ✓ Trying to get pills, guns, or other ways to harm oneself;
> ✓ Talking or writing about death, dying, or suicide;
> ✓ Feelings of hopelessness;
> ✓ Rage, uncontrolled anger, seeking revenge;
> ✓ Acting in a reckless or risky way;
> ✓ Feeling trapped, like there's no way out;
> ✓ Feeling or saying there's no reason for living.

Resources for Veterans in the Pacific Northwest:
✓ VA Suicide Hotline, 800-273-8255; Northwest Human Services Suicide Prevention Hotline, 800-273-8255.S
✓ Sexual Assault: What Every Service Member Should Know, Dept. of Veteran Affairs, 800-775-1998.
✓ Suicide Prevention: Men and Women Veterans – Know the Warning signs of Suicide, Dept. of Veteran Affairs, 1-800-273-8255.
✓ Suicide Prevention for Veterans and Their Families and Friends; Dept. of Veteran Affairs, www.mental health.va.gov.
✓ National Suicide Prevention Lifeline: After an Attempt; U.S. Dept. of Health and Human Services, www.suicidepreventionlifeline.org.

> ## Responding to the Suicidal

> The following listing of behaviors and recommendations comes from several sources and should be presented by a trained Hostage Negotiator or Tactical Communication/Crisis Intervention training specialist

- **Pre-incident behavior** *(Vance and Louie 2007):*
    - ✓ History of domestic or criminal violence;
    - ✓ Recent breakup or a threat of dissolution of a significant relationship;
    - ✓ Recent violence, history or threats of violence, especially when a deadly weapon is involved;
    - ✓ A life threatening illness, especially if diagnosed within the last 24 hours;
    - ✓ Giving away money and / or personal possessions;
    - ✓ Prior suicide attempts using method and means indicating they want attention but different methods means very serious;
    - ✓ Drastic mood swings may signify a bipolar disorder. Determine if the subject is on or off medication;
    - ✓ Did the subject deliberately commit a criminal act to elicit a police response?
    - ✓ Did the subject set a deadline for his/her death?

> ## Violent Deaths Findings – some Oregon findings:

The number of violent deaths in 2005 declined slightly from 2004 (771 to 748 deaths).   The reduction was primarily in the number of undetermined deaths, which declined from 92 to 71. Here are some statistics:

- Gunshot wound was the most common cause of death, accounting for nearly 54 percent of violent deaths, followed by poisoning (21 percent) and hanging (13 percent).
- While suicide rates were highest among older adults, the largest number of suicide deaths occurred among Oregonians aged 25–64 (2005 statistics).   Among males, the rate of death by suicide in these age groups ranged from 21.5–35.9 per 100,000. Among females, the suicide rate ranged from 5.6–15.7 per 100,000.
- The suicide rate among Oregon's male veterans was significantly higher than nonveteran males. The age-adjusted rates of suicide among Oregon veteran males and non-veteran males for 2000–2005 were 46.05 per 100,000 and 22.09 per 100,000 respectively.
- Suicide remains a serious public health problem in Oregon. With 543 deaths, suicide accounted for 74 percent of violent deaths in 2005.
- The older adult suicide rate was 25.5 per 100,000, which was 78 percent higher than the national average of 14.3 per 100,000 in 2004. Mental and physical health problems among older adults were frequently reported circumstances.

> ## *Suicide by Inches*: Law Enforcement Officers Committing Suicide.

Funeral for police officer who killed himself (Baltimore Sun, Feb. 12, 2009)

"In a typical year, an estimated 400 of the 870,000 Law Enforcement Officers in the U.S. take their own lives. The stuff you run into can emotionally bury you unless you take care of yourself" (Dr. Bill Lewinski in Force Science News #101, 2008)

POLICE

But many more are committing what the legendary psychiatrist Karl Menninger called "**suicide by inches**."   This refers to more gradual behaviors of self-destruction; like excessive spending in an effort to buy happiness, excessive drinking, compulsive adultery as means of escape, or addictively overworking at the cost of relationships with spouse and kids."

> **Threatening Suicide Incident Behavior; use the CPR acronym**
> (Vance 2006)
> - **Current plan:** Think about strategy and tactics while responding to the scene. Mental planning is critical while responding to the crisis call. The more one thinks about how to respond, the better prepared he or she has once arrived.
> - **Prior behavior:** What is known about the subject? Information is critical since prior knowledge can be helpful in deciding how to handle someone in crisis (such as prior calls and behavior; how does the person act when drunk, etc.)
> - **Resources:** What resources are available during the incident and post-incident? Resource allocation can also be critical. At a recent police call in the Northwest, the responding supervisor failed to appropriately detail resources and control information, with deadly results (Bernstein 2010).

> ## Suicidal Behavior; Is the subject engaging in behaviors that escalate the tension such as:
> ✓ Demanding that police kill him/her;
> ✓ Non-compliance with police orders and directions;
> ✓ Advancing on or taunting the officers;
> ✓ Forcing a confrontation; exiting the building with a hostage or brandishing a weapon;
> ✓ Weapon or explosive device tied to the subject (Vance and Louie 2007).

> ## Suicide in America: Suicide on the Increase for Middle-Aged Whites (Elias 2008)
> The nation's suicide rates have been increasing annually between 1999 and 2005, especially among middle-aged whites.   Yearly increase:
> - All ages and genders: **.7%**
>   White men ages 40-64: **3%**
>   White women ages 40-64: **4%**
> - Suicide rates in the USA are up after more than a decade of dropping, and middle-aged whites primarily account for the increase.
> - The rate for whites 40 to 64 years old jumped 19% for women and 16% for men from 1999 to 2005, say researchers from the Bloomberg School of Public Health at Johns Hopkins University. Their analysis was published online in the American Journal of Preventive Medicine.

> ## Suggested Negotiating Team Activities, Behavior and Strategies for those Threatening Suicide (Honig 2001; Hutson et.al.,1998; Monahan 1992; Strentz, 1991; and, Vance 2007):
> ✓ Put your badge in your pocket as you change roles from cop to counselor;
> ✓ Insure containment and isolate the individual;
> ✓ Identify any weapons involved;
> ✓ Obtain as much pre-incident intelligence on behavior as possible;
> ✓ Consider the initial use of less lethal equipment as a diversion. Have a clear plan to apprehend after diversion;
> ✓ Assess the violence and suicide potential.

➢ **Negotiating techniques with those threatening suicide** (Vance and Louie 2007)

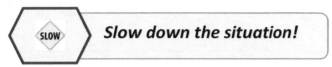

Slow down the situation!

✓ Attempt to establish and maintain rapport;
✓ Do not lie, unless you absolutely must to preserve human life;
✓ Listen and be empathetic;
✓ Ask if the person is thinking about hurting or killing himself/herself;
✓ Convey that you are trying to help;
✓ Practice active listening;
✓ Evaluate the tactical plan; is it likely to be effective?
✓ How much time and planning was done prior to the 911 call?

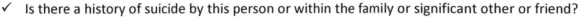
Slow down

✓ Is there a history of suicide by this person or within the family or significant other or friend?
✓ Does this person or the community have resources available to assist? Have any been used?
✓ Concentrate on offering hope, not a solution;
✓ Buy time: "Why now? You can kill yourself tomorrow. If you die today, you eliminate any and all other options."

• **Post Incident considerations – The Aftermath** (Vance and Louie 2007; Thompson 2007):
  The incident is still a police case; expect and prepare for an investigation in cases where someone is injured or killed. If there are allegations of police misconduct, such as "excessive use of force," or "civil rights violations," expect and prepare for State or Federal investigations.

  Recognize the need for a critical incident stress debriefing for all of those involved, and don't forget the dispatchers as well as non- police such as emergency medical technicians or paramedics.

  Police officers reacting to the aftermath of *Suicide by Cop* will often display symptoms of post-traumatic stress which can potentially affect their ability to perform their duties. Police officers are also victims in these cases. Among the many symptoms reported are hyper vigilance, fear, anger, sleeplessness, recurrent nightmares and depression (Pyers 2001).

➢ **A very different type of officer survival: Suggestions from a *victim officer*** (Thompson 2007).

Police officers, having gone through an intense traumatic event, will experience many psychological and physiological symptoms previously mentioned. It is how they manage those symptoms that will help one survive.

• **Moving Forward:** Talk … to spouse, pastor, family members, friends, co-workers, etc. They care about and want to support you so let them! Get professional help. Forget the stigma! If you are fortunate to have one in your agency, embrace the help of the department's Traumatic Incident Support Team. This is about taking care of oneself mentally and physically and moving forward.

- **Do these things now:** Read about police involved in traumatic events and how they survived. *Train to be a Warrior*, be able to survive whatever comes, both physically and mentally. Talk about the reality of the job with loved ones, so they can be ready to help you survive when it happens.

> **Responding to Suicide Summary:** Whether you are attempting to handle a suicide-in-progress incident, or dealing with the survivors of suicide, the skills highlighted in the training bulletin all revolve around communication skills. These communication skills are in one sense fundamental, but as they are applied to a police call, they become a very complex vocabulary that the first responder (in accordance with departmental policies and procedures) needs to balance with both verbal and non-verbal skills.

➤ *Suicide-by-Cop* (SBC)

 Many 911 disturbance calls tragically become *suicide- by-cop* calls and the responding officers need to be prepared.   Suicide-by- Cop incidents refer to an event in which an individual engages in behaviors that pose an apparent risk of serious injury or death to themselves or others, with the intent to necessitate the use of deadly force by Law Enforcement personnel (Honig, 2001).

- **Suicide – Definitions** (Thompson 2007; Vance 2007):

> **Suicide:** The act of voluntarily or intentionally taking one's own life.
>
> **Suicide-by- Cop:** A suicide method in which someone acts in a threatening way towards a law enforcement officer, eliciting a lethal response. A police colloquialism for a form of victim-precipitated homicide in which a suicidal individual engages in calculated, life-threatening and criminal behavior, in order to compel police to use deadly force.
>
> **Police Assisted Suicide:** A term used by some researchers to describe a suicide wherein the suicidal subject completes the act "with the assistance" of a police officer. This definition seems to suggest that the officer somehow willingly "assisted" the perpetrator with ending his life.
>
> **Victim Precipitated Homicide:** Another definition used by some to describe Suicide by Cop, whereas the perpetrator is in control of taking his/her own life, by means of using another to facilitate their own demise.

➤ Suicide-by-Cop Statistics and Current Research Regarding Lethality
(Force Science News 2009a; Vance 2007; Thompson 2007)

 A recent eight-year study of 707 shootings throughout the U.S. and Canada of **SBC** incidents *reveals a significant increase* in these types of critical incidents. The study also revealed that they differ from regular officer-involved-shootings (**OIS**), and establishes that they create exceptional threats to civilian bystanders, responding officers, and the subjects themselves.   "The single most important finding in this research is its officer-safety implications, the head author, Dr. Kris Mohandie said."   "These suicidal individuals do, in fact, pose a lethal risk to

other people--especially law enforcement--in their quest to die. Officers and the public need very much to be aware of this" (Mohandie in Force Science News 2009a). This study identifies SBC incidents as posing "a greater risk of homicide or at least violence toward others, than a nonsuicidal individual." The greater risk emerges from the motivation of the SBC suspects because of the "high degree of desperation, hopelessness, impulsivity, self-destructiveness, and acting out" (Force Science News 2009a).

> ***For the police negotiator, it is imperative to understand the psychology of SBC subjects and that they present a substantial risk to others, and there is a one-in-three chance of someone other than the SBC subject being injured or killed during an incident*** (Force Science News 2009a).

 As indentified in the study, a *normal* suspect involved in a shooting incident usually surrenders or *gives up his agenda* when it appears he is unable to escape and reacts with surprise and fears for his life, especially when police rounds are fired at him. This type of suspect has a will to live and recognizes the futility of a police standoff. However, the SBC type of suspect continues with provacative and threatening behavior "perhaps consciously realizing that his desire to die...is momentarily within his grasp" (Force Science News 2009a). ***This may be why more rounds are fired by police at SBC suspects.***

- **Here are some of the study's findings:**
    - ✓ **Ninety eight percent** of the subjects "demonstrated a behavioral threat," such as pointing or gesturing with a weapon at another person or attempting to shoot someone during the incident.
    - ✓ **Ninety percent** "aggressed against the police" and nearly half "harmed or attempted to harm civilians."
    - ✓ **About 50%** of the subjects who had a firearm actually fired it at the police. "The fact that these subjects 'are more likely to shoot at officers and harm civilians..., draw more fire from officers, are more likely to die, appear to be more threatening to others, and are more likely to be armed than regular **OIS** subjects' speaks to their enhanced threat level, the study notes" (Force Science News 2009a).

Officer
Involved
Shootings

Important background notes for those attempting to communicate with SBC subjects (Force Science News 2009a):

✓ **80%** - More than 8 out of 10 had "reportedly experienced recent behavioral changes."

✓ **75%** - Nearly three-fourths were entangled in relationship problems.

✓ **66%** - More than two-thirds "were struggling with spiritual issues/conflicts."

✓ **61%** - Sixty-one percent of the **SBC** subjects talked about their suicidal ideation during the incident," with the vast majority speaking specifically about the notion of suicide by cop to responding officers.

✓ **50%** - Nearly half the time SBC subjects say nothing about suicide to anybody before the incident. This can lead surviving relatives to regard officers' reports of suicidal remarks with skepticism and distrust. To enhance officer credibility, it is important to start the audio recording process quickly (Force Science News 2009a).

The researchers also noted that subjects "sometimes expressed strong Catholic beliefs about sin and suicide, as example stating that 'I'll get the cops to shoot me so I can still go to heaven.   Others held concepts about God, the devil, and demonic possession of 'delusional proportions.'"

2011: What we can predict is that 1 in 3 officer-involved shootings in the future will most likely be Suicide-By-Cop (SBC)

SBC Core Conclusion: *Significant Increase in SBC incidents.*
- During 1990s, 13% of all Officer involved Shootings (OIS) were Suicide by Cop (SBC).
- But by 2009, 36% of 707 cases were attempted or completed SBC incidents.

We can predict that fewer than 1 in 5 SBC incidents will be planned

Incident Context: Up to 2009, of the 20% subjects who "feigned" having a firearm, nearly half of them reached their hands in their waistbands to simulate grabbing for a weapon.
- Of those armed with a firearm, 86% were loaded. **Only 8% of SBC cases started out as "suicidal subject" calls. More often, officers responded initially to a domestic violence or family disturbance type of call.**

Most (81% up to 2009) will apparently be "spontaneous"

Research indicates that: Rather than laying a specific plan in advance, "a subject may just be primed for self-destruction because his life is not going well. In muddling along, he does something that draws police attention and this becomes the last straw, the final peg that comes out of his board of stability. He says, 'Fuck it, I'm outta here,' " and proceeds to provoke the SBC."

- SBC subjects "were more likely to be psychotic, to have experienced recent behavioral changes, to have spiritual issues and relationship problems, and to be divorced or separated. They were less likely to be on parole or probation or to be known gang members."
- SBC subjects present a substantial risk to others and there is a one-in-three chance of someone other than the SBC subject being injured or killed during an incident.
- From the International Association of Chiefs of Police: **Agencies must have an effective crisis intervention program that helps officers de-escalate confrontations; and, police need to maintain a strong, personal collaboration with mental health professionals, consumers, their families and advocates.**

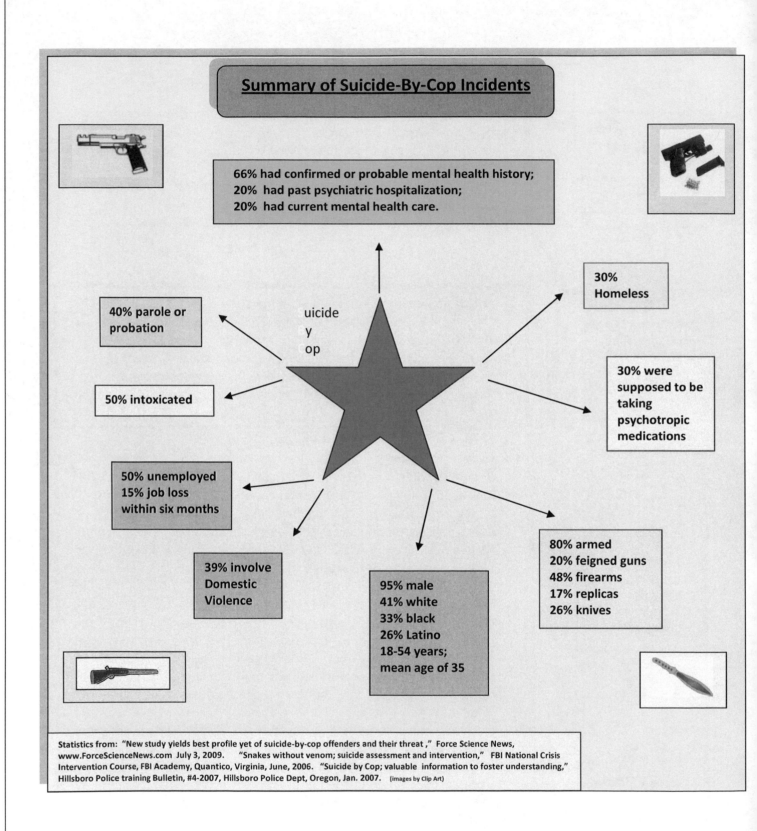

Summary of Suicide-By-Cop Incidents

66% had confirmed or probable mental health history;
20% had past psychiatric hospitalization;
20% had current mental health care.

uicide
y
op

40% parole or probation

50% intoxicated

50% unemployed
15% job loss
within six months

39% involve
Domestic
Violence

95% male
41% white
33% black
26% Latino
18-54 years;
mean age of 35

30% Homeless

30% were supposed to be taking psychotropic medications

80% armed
20% feigned guns
48% firearms
17% replicas
26% knives

Statistics from: "New study yields best profile yet of suicide-by-cop offenders and their threat ," Force Science News, www.ForceScienceNews.com July 3, 2009.   "Snakes without venom; suicide assessment and intervention," FBI National Crisis Intervention Course, FBI Academy, Quantico, Virginia, June, 2006. "Suicide by Cop; valuable information to foster understanding," Hillsboro Police training Bulletin, #4-2007, Hillsboro Police Dept, Oregon, Jan. 2007.   (Images by Clip Art)

- **Why Suicide-by-Cop?**

Suicidal people may choose suicide-by- cop because they are feeling despondent and hopeless, but for whatever reason, they don't want to take their own life directly. Such people may not harbor anger towards the police and view them as providing one final service for them (Thompson 2007).

Another type of person who chooses SBC, who may not be particularly angry, is someone who is legitimately mentally ill. They may dislike law enforcement officers because they may have been hospitalized by them against their will. However, in the past they may feel positively toward law enforcement after their medications are re-stabilized (Thompson 2007). And for those who survive Suicide by Cop incidents, many end up apologizing to the police for their behavior (Louie 2007a).

Victims want to ensure their death. They single out police officers because not only are they equipped with firearms, but they also have extensive training to react to potentially life-threatening situations with accurate and deadly force (Lewan 1992).

By forcing the police to kill them, victims may avoid the stigma and social taboos associated with suicide (Thompson 2007). They're not always pre-planned; sometimes SBC happens at the spur of the moment, especially if guns are available. A depressed person may be pushed over the edge by the loss of a job, relationship, or some other setback in life (Thompson 2007).

Suicidal individuals, in their desperation to escape their emotional pain, will use a variety of instruments such as guns, ropes, pills, knives, etc., … and in some cases, an unsuspecting law enforcement officer to end their lives (Pyers 2001).

- **Victim or Perpetrator?** (Thompson 2007):

  ✓ Remember, a crime is being committed by a suspect or perpetrator in all SBC incidents. There are many victims in the aftermath of these incidents: family members, friends, co-workers, and of course, the police officer, his/her family, and agency.
  ✓ According to a ten year Los Angeles Sheriff's Department study, there has been a significant increase in SBC cases. The data suggests that about 25% of all officer- involved shootings in 1997 could be classified as suicide-by-cop. This almost doubled the 1987 rate (Huston, et al., 1998). Unfortunately, Los Angeles County is not alone; other studies have revealed similar statistics (FBI 2006 Suicide Assessment and Intervention Course in Vance 2006).

➤ **Snakes with and without venom** (Vance 2006)

It is very important to separate suicidal people from those who are engaged in SBC. Although each of these individuals is engaged in suicide, their methods are quite different. To understand the difference, consider the analogy of encountering two snakes. One snake is venom-less. The other is poisonous.

- The **suicidal** person is the ***venom-less snake***. The bite of this snake will require some medical attention and perhaps a tetanus shot. The police officer who negotiates with a suicidal person and is unable to prevent him or her from taking their own life, may require some counseling, and may suffer from Post Traumatic Stress Disorder, a very treatable malady.

- The SBC person is the ***poisonous snake***. The police officer who negotiates with the suicidal person who is intent on suicide-by-cop is dealing with the deadly snake. This snake is intent on biting the officer to insure he, she, or their peers, will kill it. Thus, in addition to the above treatment, some many, or most of the officers involved in this scenario may require surgery or the services of the county coroner, not a pleasant picture. "This is a very deadly business" (SA Thomas Strentz, FBI, retired, in Vance 2006).

Web resources and references for suicide and suicide-by-cop (Thompson 2007):
- American Association of Suicidology: www.suicidology.org
- American Foundation For Suicide Prevention: www.afsp.org
- National Alliance for the Mentally Ill: www.nami.org
- San Francisco Suicide Prevention: www.sfsucide.org/index2.html
- Suicide Awareness Voices of Education (SA/VE): www.save.org
- Surgeon General of the United States: www.surgeongeneral.gov
- The Suicide Information and Education Centre, Calgary, Alberta, Canada: www.suicideinfo.ca
- Valencia-Stincelli, Rebecca. (1998). Suicide by cop. Interviews and. Interrogations

---

Oregon Suicide Prevention Resources (Rollins 2008; B1):
- National Hopeline Network: 503-784-2433
- National Suicide Prevention Lifeline: 800-273-8255
- Portland and Multnomah County Crisis Lines: 503-988-4888; 800-716-9769
- Washington County's 24-hour Crisis Intervention line: 503-291-9111
- Vancouver/Clark County Crisis Line: 360-696-9560; 800-626-8137
- Crisis lines for other parts of Oregon: www.orgon.gov/DHS/ph/ipe/ysp/cntymap.shtml
- Oregon Partnership HelpLine (for crisis and substance abuse, alcohol treatment referral line): 800-923-4357
- Oregon Partnership YouthLine (a peer-to-peer crisis line, under adult supervision, for youths): 877-553-8336

➤ Survivors of Suicide

(Miss. Dept. Mental Health)

First responders need to understand the dynamics of *survivors of suicide*. These people are extremely vulnerable and special communication skills need to be utilized.   "The tragedy of suicide cannot be compared to any other crisis; it is separate and distinct from other cases of death. Adding to the grief of such a loss is the taboo our society places on the very subject of suicide. As a result, the survivors' feelings of isolation, shame, and guilt are very often intensified" (CPOA 1983).

It is estimated that for each suicide death, between four to six people are left bereaved. Survivors are not limited to family members and may include significant others, roommates, close friends, co-workers, etc. These people frequently come in contact with police during and after suicidal events and the police need to be prepared to deal with them with the same compassion and communication skill as they do in the most extreme of crisis situations. Many times police treat the survivors of suicide as supplements to their reports, thinking the "suicide is over so only need to finish the report" mentality (CPOA 1983).

➢ Responding to the Suicide Survivors

"Suicide survivorship differs from any other death survivorship in that the bereavement caused is exacerbated by the accompanying social stigma and loss of self-esteem introduced by the survivors' inability to have prevented the death" (Hatton and Valente 1981 in CPOA 1983, 1).

- "There is often identification with the deceased. This may involve the survivor assuming traits or taking on symptoms exhibited by the deceased. Tragically, it may also involve copying the suicidal behavior itself" (Schuyler 1973 in CPOA 1983, 1).
- "Not uncommon is the event of the surviving spouse later attempting or committing suicide. Those who do not act in that way later admit to the experience or a tremendous inner struggle with such thoughts and behavior" (Danto 1973 in CPOA 1983, 1).
- Survivors of suicide are susceptible and vulnerable. They may identify with the self-destructive behavior of the 'person they lost' and may themselves exhibit suicidal behaviors (Schuyler 1973). This is an expression of their grief – ranging from responding to their own guilt, an "inner struggle with such thoughts and behavior to longing to be with the one they lost" (Danto 1973 in CPOA 1983, 1).
- To this person, the world is no longer relevant and the survivor may very well see the same "demons" as the one lost (this can range from the general "societal ills" to specific people). The survivor may also try to find someone else responsible for the tragedy and loss.

➢ Procedures for Communicating with Survivors of Suicide – Most are in shock or even hysterical; the most severe form of bereavement may be expressed
(CPOA 1983)

The manner of notification is of extreme importance and, understandably, of equally extreme discomfort to the officer. Many survivors have reported a very cold, unemotional and uncaring verbal death notification, with a quick and abrupt departure.

Even if the body is not present, just telling someone a loved one is dead and where they can see the body is only part of the information they need to convey.   One needs to "deliver" this message with caring and compassion – literally role playing how they would like someone to speak with their loved one.

> *You will be remembered for the rest of the survivors' lives. They may not recall your name, however, they will be able to describe your actions and how you made them feel, in explicit detail.*

Some physical reactions that may be anticipated are: fainting, vomiting, lack of bladder or bowel control, disbelief, confusion, anger, repulsion, fright, and maybe even outwardly appearing calm or expressing relief. (When a mother was told of her adult son's "suicide- by-cop" incident, her first response was an almost matter- of-fact statement to police of, "well, it was just a matter of time." Her grief satisfied, days later she filed a lawsuit against the police; Louie 2007c.) Police need to be aware of these possible reactions and be sensitive to the needs of the survivors.

Many survivors, after being informed of the tragedy, may be unable to remember simple information such as phone numbers, even names of people. This is a time when they are most vulnerable and in need of assistance. Police and Fire Chaplains can be invaluable at this point.

Anger is also commonly expressed by the survivors. "Denial, angry denial...directed at the doctors and the police, the medical examiners and the undertakers, against anyone other than the person death had robbed them of" (CPOA 1983, 2).

"There are always two parties to a death; the person who dies and the survivors who are bereaved. The sting of death is less sharp for the person who dies than it is for the bereaved survivor. This... is the capital fact about the relationship between living and dying. There are two parties to the suffering that death inflicts; and in the apportionment of this suffering, the survivor takes the brunt" (CPOA 1983, 4).

> **The responding officer is in the critical position of helping the survivor of suicide cope and live on.**

- ➢ **Responding to the Suicidal – Speaking with the Family Survivors** (Vance & Louie 2007)

  - **Speak directly about the suicide;** don't avoid the issue or speak in disguised or convoluted terms. "Be sensitively direct" (Louie 2007a).

  - **There is not a good or easy way to communicate that someone has ... committed suicide.** The words are not as important as the manner in which they are expressed by the police officer. Remember, people may even forget what you said, but they will never forget how you made them feel (Louie 2007a)!

  - **One technique that has been reported as helpful by both survivors and police officers in the notification process is called "groundling."** In this situation, *groundling* would involve physical contact between the officer and the survivor – such as a gentle touch on the shoulder or conversely, not "freezing up" as the shocked survivor embraces the officer. This is where the art and science of being a compassionate police officer is ultimately tested (Vance 2007).

  - **Survivors frequently comment on how helpful and understanding the police were, noting that concern and caring was conveyed by the officer.** If the body is still on scene with the survivor, the utmost reverence and respect needs to be expressed and demonstrated by the officers. This is what the survivors see and always remember. The officers always need to be aware of their own emotional defenses such as "cop humor" or behavior that is incongruent with the situation (Louie 2007a). Imagine how reverently we handle our war dead; be as reverent and respectful of the deceased at the scene.

- **Don't be overly protective of the survivors.** Sometimes in our attempt to protect the survivors, we may inadvertently and unintentionally cause them more pain. Often survivors wish to touch or just see their loved one to say good-by. If this is not going to interfere with the investigation and the survivor asks, there is no real reason not to allow it. Survivors have reported that the grief and healing process starts at this point in time (Vance 2007).

- **One practical – and greatly appreciated – response would be how the officer assists the family or survivors with the need to clean the death scene.** Even a simple referral to a cleaning service, with the offer to make the call, is appreciated and demonstrates caring; always have a Community Resource & Referral Guide with up-dated information (Louie 2007a).

- **Practice Active Listening**; allow the person to talk, cry, hug and even ramble somewhat – be patient. "Many bereaved people are surprised and frightened by the sheer intensity of their emotions and imaginings after bereavement. Reassurance that they are not going mad, that such feelings are perfectly natural, and that crying does not mean a 'nervous breakdown' can be given explicitly, and especially be an attitude that shows that the helper is not alarmed, frightened, or even surprised" (CPOA 1983, 3).

- **Be aware of your own feelings**; while you may feel moved, you may come across to the survivor as cold and indifferent. "Police officers themselves do not emphasize the emotional stresses in their work. Danger is so integral that explicit recognition of fear might induce emotional barriers to work performance. In addition, police officers routinely observe the consequences of death on family members. Although most officers are profoundly affected by this exposure many develop a difficulty in empathizing with the reaction of family members" (CPOA 1983, 3).

➢ Responding to the Suicidal – If a suicide note is left

If it does not compromise the investigation, be sure to leave a copy of the note.
Copy it down – don't just read it aloud. People are in shock and may forget.
And survivors need to know what "exactly" was written – as painful as that may be.
If the officer is unable to leave a copy or doesn't have the information, provide that to them at a later time or let them know how they can get a copy (CPOA 1983).

> *Understand that some survivors may read the words for the rest of their lives...*

Responding to the Suicidal – "What can I do to help you right now?" "Is there anyone I can call or contact that you want with you right now?" "If you leave the house today (i.e., to go to the hospital, or mortuary, etc.) do you need a neighbor or someone else to help you; to help you take care of your pet...children?"

Most survivors are in shock, and they are ill-prepared to think about how you can be of assistance, especially at that very moment of notification.

Try to provide basic help, such as child care, pet care, arranging for transportation, etc. Seek out the helpful neighbor or close friend living nearby. Sometimes survivors will start thinking of family members or loved ones far away – in another state or country – and you may need to help contact these people. The simple act of dialing the phone may cause some to "panic or freeze" because their mind is racing with so many thoughts and emotions.

 Next, don't always assume that there is a religious affiliation, but if there is, try to find out who to call. This is where Police and Fire chaplains are invaluable.

As with any victim of a tragedy and crisis, ask if you can call someone for them. Try to assess other needs while at the scene: transportation, notifying trusted neighbors or co-workers, arranging *pet care*, etc.

 *Understand that the pet of a deceased becomes a living memory for the survivors – something now very precious to them.*

If you are unable to remain, it is absolutely critical to have someone the survivor trusts to be present for comfort. Make sure the person who is available to comfort can get there – even if it takes a squad car to transport.

Determine if other resources are available; from clergy to community-based groups that can assist. As an example, if the deceased – or survivor – is a member of an organization such as a veterans' group or service organization, ask if you can call them to come over and help. If your agency has internal support people (i.e., chaplains, Crisis Response Team, etc.), and if appropriate, call them in to assist.

Chapter VII: Police Officer Emotional Intelligence, Developing a Teflon Character, and Being Prepared Mentally and Physically

> **"You acknowledge Emotional Intelligence to enhance awareness of self and to avoid posturing and language that riles and agitates those you are entrusted to help"** (Lt. Mike Rouches, Tactical Communication Instructor)

Officers need to recognize their *Emotional Intelligence* (Saville 2006). This is the "...ability to interpret, understand, and manage one's own and others' emotions." Emotional intelligence is a measure of: self-control, conflict management and empathy. Officers become more aware of those emotional triggers that provoke a negative or aggressive response, such as when a disputant challenges the officers or insults them. "Becoming more aware of emotional triggers that can instigate an angry violent response, such as when officers are called 'pigs'" (Saville 2006:39). This basically is the ability of an officer to understand and manage personal emotions while in the midst of trying to help solve someone else's problems.

> ➤ **Police Officer *Emotional Intelligence*, Developing a *Teflon Character*, and Being Prepared Mentally as Well as Physically**

> **Emotional Intelligence is a measure of self-control, conflict management and empathy**

Maintaining a healthy emotional intelligence allows a person to manage the stress, and the emotional triggers that are intended to provoke a negative response, he or she is facing (such as a traumatic 911 call). "There are many ways to adapt and keep stress in check. People who believe they are in control of their stress are far more successful than those who see themselves as victims of the situation or stressful events. Therefore, the principal way to handle stress is to train the mind" Collins 2011, 76).

- "Law enforcement officers are human. As such, we all carry around personal 'baggage' and sometimes preconceived ideas about others – this is normal. This baggage we carry around is sometimes influenced by experiences from the past, upbringing/values, strong opinions, political views, and other factors" (Goerling et al., 2007, 12).

- "One of the biggest traps we fall into is putting our meanings and our perceptions onto others. That is, expecting or assuming that others feel the same way we do about a given person or circumstance. As police officers, we'll never be able to convince everyone to feel, act, or view things as we do; nor is that our responsibility. Expect people to disagree with you – it's not personal" (Goerling et al., 2007, 15).

Trying to remain neutral and at the same time trying to not become impatient are some of the greatest challenges for officers intervening in peoples' crises. Officers in the field are under continual pressure to move from one police call to the next, thereby contributing to impatience. And the more impatient the officer appears, the more difficult it will be to effectively communicate with disputants. *Officers usually don't pay very much attention to how they are perceived by others because if they did, there would be fewer miscommunications between officers and citizens.*

Trying to remain neutral and not appear to be impatient takes purposeful practice and recognition. Taking a cue from Nurses, those who are able to "… remain calm have learned to modify their own stress responses and have found adaptation models that keep their bodies from stress overload. One approach is to go to a quiet place four times a day for five minutes each time. While in that quiet place, focus on counting the breath as it goes in and out, 1-2, 1-2, or repeat the words in-out, in-out for five minutes. The mind's awareness moves to the present, leaving thoughts of the future and past aside. The body resets itself to a lower level of action preparation" (Collins 2011, 76).

> "When others don't see things as we do and don't understand our perspectives, we can become frustrated and impatient. From there, it's not a far leap to becoming unnecessarily controlling and directive, thereby abandoning the preferred neutral role" (Goerling et al., 2007, 20)

> **Understanding Emotional Intelligence allows one to develop a *Teflon Character*.**

Teflon character: "The ability to deflect insults and not allow verbal assaults to 'stick' is a necessary skill in modern law enforcement" (Goerling et al., 2007, 3). Taking a cue from the martial arts, officers with a Teflon character do not allow insults or verbally aggressive people to distract them from trying to defuse people and situations. These types of officers essentially allow verbally aggressive behavior to *deflect* from them without distracting their immediate goal of controlling people in crisis. Verbally aggressive people are attempting to provoke and thereby assume some measure of control over a situation they see as negatively impacting them.

> "Who is in control when our anger causes us to do or say something that is unprofessional or which would embarrass us, our family, our department, or our profession? Who is in control? Are we in control or being controlled?"
> (Goerling et al., 2007, 29).

➤ **Police officer *Emotional Intelligence*, developing a *Teflon Character*, and being prepared mentally as well as physically – what are the imperatives?**

- To remain focused, centered, and balanced.
- To demonstrate a neutrality of presence that even aggressors are able to recognize as a professional command presence that does not indicate bias or prejudice (thereby enhancing credibility).
- The more officers "take the 911 call personally," the greater the obstacle to achieving a Teflon character.
- Officers need to recognize that the insults a disputant hurtles at an officer are not personal – they are a way to deflect the heat from them and foist it onto the responding officers. "Many gangsters, thugs, and criminals are master manipulators and take great pleasure in 'getting inside your head.' Making you lose your composure is often a personal victory for them; it's their last grasp for control in a situation they know they ultimately can't win" (Goerling et al., 2007, 28).
- And the more the officers appear professional, the greater their credibility; the more they participate in the argument, or become aggressive themselves, the more they lose the ability to effectively communicate and control. These types of officers are assertive but do not act offensively or appear to be aggressive to those they are trying to defuse and control.
- By taking this psychological stance – which certainly does take emotional discipline - the more an aggressive person verbally attacks (again, not compromising officer safety) the more the officer allows the insults to pass without a negative or defensive response. With the officer refusing to get sucked into the antics of an aggressive person, the aggressor essentially loses any psychological advantage in the confrontation with the police... and their aggression dissipates because they are not effective with this tactic.

> **"The true master studies his or her environment, tracks challenges, and maintains a sense of internal balance. By doing so, he or she can quickly decide what to do, what level of force to use, and the best time to take actions"** (Goerling et al., 20076).

➤ **Understanding Self-Concept and Self-Disclosure: How a person sees himself or herself affects how that person communicates with others.**

(R Dan Small

- A person with a strong self-concept, such as someone who is self-assured and confident, as well as assertive in interpersonal relationships (like many police officers) may have a difficult time trying to communicate with someone who has a poor self-concept. The poor self-concept type of person has difficulty conversing with others, admitting when wrong, accepting constructive criticism and expressing feelings; this is the type of person the assertive police officer frequently comes in contact with at the 911 call. The challenge for the police officer is how to communicate without alienating someone who is already vulnerable when it comes to establishing a dialogue.

- The responding officer needs to recognize that the person at the other end of the 911-call is most likely experiencing a negative self-concept (from embarrassment related to the call or through life long negative reinforcement) and may respond by being defensive and aggressive. The responding officers are not trained psychologists, but they should be trained in how to communicate with people because it is a significant part of their job. Practicing active listening skills as well as displaying empathy can be an effective way to initiate a crisis intervention-type call.

> ***Understanding oneself through self-disclosure (the ability to talk truthfully and fully about oneself) is necessary to become an effective communicator.***

 The officer who miscommunicates through false bravado or a swaggering demeanor is not in control of a situation and most certainly lacks the credibility to encourage people to cooperate (as can be seen and verified on cop reality TV shows).

- The key point to recognize is that self-concept and self-disclosure is another dimension of officer Emotional Intelligence. Officers need to be understood to be effective as outside third party communicators. Traditional police officer training does not ask the officer to *question self* but rather to intervene as if not only people will listen, but somehow ignore that the officer's communication skills are subordinate to the uniform.

- In essence, it's all about the officer long before he or she enters the 911 scene; it's about the psychology of crisis-involved interpersonal communication and being emotionally prepared.

 Understanding how your messages are refracted: There are many factors that impact how verbal and non-verbal messages are sent and received. Understanding how messages are sent from the sender's emotional and physical perspective will help to understand if the message will be received as intended.

 Much like how the sun is projected through the atmosphere or light through a prism is distorted by refraction, the same can be said how a message (what you want to say) passes through the mental refraction of your own experiences, moods, prejudices, personal needs and biases. Examples include understanding how messages are refracted by being self-absorbed and preoccupied; mind

(Photo Dictionary)

wandering; emotionally blocking; historical and past experience hostility; being inarticulate, regional accent or limited English; and effects of the physical environment. **The following are some examples of message refraction:**

- **Being self-absorbed and preoccupied:** As the responding officer, you are sent to a call, **but most of what is on your mind may be unrelated to what you are supposed to be focusing on.** An example is someone who superficially greets you, then not only ignores what you have to say, but may even forget your name (think of the glad-hander and back-slapper at a convention). This type of person is preoccupied and self-absorbed. This type of person may only be interested in greeting people and "showing good face" without any intention to communicate on all but the most surface and superficial levels.

 - **Mind wandering:** Similar to being preoccupied; **this type of person is not only disinterested, but is usually displaying non-verbal cues that signal lack of interest.** The officer needs to *focus* and concentrate on the immediate call, not the next call or the report that still needs to be written.

> **This focusing is known as *centering* and an officer unable to *center and remain focused* on the call is not at his or her optimum for officer safety.**

- **Emotionally blocking:** These are words and concepts that trigger and surface emotions. They can be in the form of words, such as someone using racist labels or patronizing words and tones or concepts, such as politically charged topics (from the death penalty to undocumented immigrants). These words and concepts touch one's true values and can provoke a negative response, seemingly out of proportion to the context. Let's say an officer used the words *you people* to a group of people who are having a dispute with one another. Now, all of a sudden, the focus is on the police officer and what is interpreted as a bigoted phrase. The pain and hurt of racism now surfaces and the police officer is overwhelmed with the hostility that he/she naively initiated through a poor choice of words. And the same can be said of the police officer who interprets a trigger word or phrase as hostile and responds in kind. So watch what is said and deflect (i.e., *teflon character*) the trigger words or insults.

- **Historical and past experience hostility:** Much like the trigger words and phrases, one may be predisposed (both the officers and people they come in contact with) **by negative past experiences**. These negative past experiences form the emotional starting point of the contact and usually the contact slides downhill as the initial contact surfaces deeper hostile feelings.

"The biggest obstacle to accurately listening is that we tend to listen to the voices in our own heads first. Especially when we are emotional or we are dealing with emotional people, the conversation tends to follow very common scripts. At this point you are no longer listening to what was said, but planning your response to what you expected the subject to say" (Miller 2011).

> o If the officer is able to recognize how this dynamic impacts communication, he/she can make quick adjustments. At the least, the officer needs to recognize the hostility demonstrated by an aggressive person is not personal and not take it as such.
> o The more personal this is internalized, the more biased will be the response.
> o The more this is recognized as not personal, the more prepared one will be to move beyond the initial hostility and attempt to establish a communication link (and better officer safety frame of mind).

- **Being inarticulate, regional accent, or limited English:** The first is lack of education and verbal skills; the second is regional or geographic bias, and the latter is language-based. They all impact communication clarity which in turn impacts interpretation and how people are perceived.

- **The physical environment:** Both sides may want to talk, and the intervening officer may be ready to defuse, **yet the physical environment is not conducive to having a conversation**.

  ✓ Once there is some level of control (such as the disputants are arguing but not appearing to escalate to physical contact), the officer needs to find an acceptable location, away from crowds and onlookers. If in a residence, try to get the disputants to sit down. The officer may also sit, and appear *comfortable* but needs to be ready to jump up if the disputants appear to be escalating.

> **Factors that Negatively Impact Emotional Intelligence and Developing a Teflon Character – *What contributes to Peak Performance?*** (Ross 2007, Graham 2007, Force Science News #75, 2007):

Dr. Darrell Ross, Dept. of Law Enforcement and Justice Administration at Western Illinois University, analyzed 86 high-profile, police-suspect confrontations to determine which federal lawsuits were filed, alleging excessive force and civil rights violations. The study analyzed 121 male officers from 94 police agencies across the U.S.   In these confrontations, the suspects were killed 97% of the time and all of the officers survived. The question in the Ross study was: "What guided them toward peak performances their first time out?" The study identified specific essential skills that these officers possessed to enhance their decision-making and the study identified which type of training developed these skills (Force Science News #75, 2007, 1):

> **This is an example of how being Self-Absorbed and/or Preoccupied or Mind Wandering can seriously impact officer safety.**

- With reaction time at a premium, "decisions tend to be made according to the 'recognition-primed' model – you quickly 'read' what you're dealing with on the basis of certain cues and patterns that seem familiar from past training and experience and you choose a course of action based on what those indicators seem reasonably to be predicting. The decision may still be rational and logical, but it's not reached through a rational sequence." (Force Science News #75, 2007, 2).

- Using sports terminology this is called *reading the play*; officers were able to formulate flexible anticipations. "En route to the scene, these officers usually began constructing an impression of what they'd be encountering. They generally had some limited information from dispatch. Often they'd been to the location before or knew some of the history of the people they were responding to" (Force Science News #75, 2007, 2).   The key point is that the officers mentally pre-planned as they approached the 911 call; this is centering and focusing.   This preplanning (known as *the Pre Contact Phase* of a 911 call) will be discussed in Chapter 9.

> **"Under ideal circumstances, decision-making is a deliberative process that follows schematic, sequentially ordered steps, with time to conjure and evaluate options, to weigh relative risks and potential benefits, perhaps even to field-test possibilities. In academic circles, this is called the 'rational analysis' model"**
> (Force Science News #75, 2007, 1)

> **Factors that Negatively Impact Emotional Intelligence and Developing a Teflon Character – What contributes to peak performance (kayakers and Marines)?**

How can getting back into an overturned kayak be analogous to tactical communication and crisis intervention training and maintaining peak performance? It has to do with the *psychology of survival* (Brooks 2008) and scenario-based training in real time exercises is an effective method of peak performance skill building. The more one trains and practices, the more these experiences become part of a *reactive repertoire* that forms the reaction basis for responding to emotionally charged, high stress situations. ***The more realistic and situational-relevant the training, the greater the enhancement of peak performance.***

The psychology of survival deals more specifically with how people react in a life threatening emergency, such as attempting to re-enter an overturned kayak in frigid waters, but the cognitive and leaning principles are the same for crisis intervention training:

Wayne Horodowich

- "The brain usually manages to function very successfully even in a whirlwind environment. What psychologists refer to as 'human information processing' is capable of handling a lot of decisions in quick fashion. Unfortunately, however, in life-threatening situations, our brain is very limited in its ability to process information and to respond quickly and correctly" (Brooks 2008, 26).

- "From the brain's input selector, information is entered into the short-term or working memory where it is compared with other similar experiences that may already have been encoded in long-term memory or schemas or routines. The stored schemas – routines that have been learned and reinforced by practice – are available for comparison to any new information entering into the working memory. The connection with the schema provides a quick path to deciding upon an appropriate response to the emergency. If no schema is present, a plan of action has to be formulated using working memory alone" (Brooks 2008, 27). This is a very time-consuming process and there is a limit to how much information can be processed at any one time.

When a kayaker is unexpectedly dumped into a freezing body of water, the kayaker will suffer an immediate *jolt* from the cold immersion. Without the benefit of training or schema experience, the more expected reaction is to quite literally *panic* and flounder about the overturned water craft.

But those with schema training experience (meaning they have practiced water reentry) start to reflectively follow a set of precise procedures to gain reentry into the overturned kayak – seemingly *without really thinking about it*. These complex maneuvers need to be immediately performed, otherwise the kayaker will perish from exposure. (This is why Marines are trained to field strip their rifles in the dark, because if a weapon malfunction occurs, especially in the heat of combat, they can quickly disassemble their weapon and clear the malfunction without really thinking about it.)

This is where the old Marine Corps adage of "the more you sweat in peace, the less you bleed in war" becomes the guiding motto for kayakers … and police tactical communication and crisis intervention training.

The officers – recruit and veteran – need to continually practice these interpersonal communication skills and crisis intervention techniques in real-time schemas or what Dr. Darrell Ross (2007) identifies as *recognition-primed models*. "The process of decision-making in normal, non-stressful circumstances takes about a tenth of a second to happen. If no schema has been developed for such ordinary situations, then the information processing is done by the *supervisory attentional system* (SAS) in the brain. The SAS takes care of planning, decision making, troubleshooting, error correction and solving novel problems. It also helps us perform in technically difficult or dangerous environments and overcome strong habitual responses" (Brooks 2008, 27).

This *supervisory attentional system* operates best when the person experiencing an emergency or stressful event has had prior experience and training. If no experience or training reference for the brain to refer to during a stressful situation, the SAS "...is slow and takes 100 times longer to process information compared to information stored as normal schemas. In an emergency, it can be quickly saturated with information and, as a result, be disabled just when it is most needed" (Brooks 2008, 27).

- Taking a page from police use of force training: "...officers should undergo scenario training for such situations. Frankly, training scenarios that call for officers to shoot a suspect who just shot a 7-eleven clerk are easy. It's the call-to-assist (the typical crisis intervention 911 call) that proves problematic because there's so much gray area and room for a variety of responses" (Scarry 2008, 75).

(Cmdr. Joel Wilson)

➤ Negative impacts on Peak Performance: Fatigue and Lack of Sleep.

Noted police liability attorney and training specialist Gordon Graham contends that "...our cops are ticking time bombs for lack of sleep" (Graham 2007). He urges police administrators to recognize "fatigue (as) an identifiable risk; let's take responsibility and manage that risk." Graham recommends that officers take care of three basic needs while on duty: ***to eat, to nap, and to work out to stay in better physical shape***.

- "After surveying 5,296 law enforcement officers in North America, a Harvard Medical School group reports that nearly 40% of active-duty officers are suffering from sleep abnormalities. These include apnea, insomnia, shift work disorder, restless legs syndrome, and narcolepsy with temporary paralysis" (Force Science News #80 2007, 1).

Fatigue and lack of sleep may also be a function of the shift hours officers and others in public safety and emergency services are required to work. One study indicates that of those working shift work at least 20% report falling asleep while at work (Healthcommunities.com 2000). In another shift work example, a recent study of nurses working 12-hour shifts concluded "...a pattern of sleep deprivation and slower reaction times" (Bottino 2011, 26). The study of 80 full-time nurses also revealed:

- In the short term, impacts on attention failures, impaired mood and loss of sense of humor.
- In the long term, greater risks for obesity, heart disease, stroke, hypertension, glucose regulation and GI disorders.

> ## And when fatigued, officers experience a significantly lessened ability to:
> ✓ Comprehend complex situations that require processing a substantial amount of data within a short time frame;
> ✓ Manage events and improve strategies;
> ✓ Perform risk assessment and accurately predict consequences;
> ✓ Be innovative;
> ✓ Take personal interest in the outcome of action;
> ✓ Control mood and behavior;
> ✓ Recollect the timing of events;
> ✓ Monitor personal performance;
> ✓ Communicate effectively (Force Science News #80, 2007).

For responding officers to be experiencing any of the above symptoms, they will be at a serious … and potentially dangerous … disadvantage that will impact the peak performance required for 911 calls. "When an officer is deprived of sleep, actual changes occur in the brain that cannot be overcome with willpower, caffeine, or nicotine" (Lindsey in Force Science News #80, 2007:1-2). **Current studies indicate that "fatigue is four times more likely to cause workplace impairment than alcohol and other drugs."**

"Studies have shown that sleep deprivation causes our nervous systems to work improperly and our memory and concentration to become impaired, while others suggest that it affects the immune system in detrimental ways" (Scott 2008, 30).

Police management is usually very responsive to officer chemical/alcohol abuse, but seem to ignore how officer fatigue and sleep deprivation can be just as pernicious to officer performance. Those officers who do not eat properly, get enough sleep before going on duty, and have no time to periodically rest while on duty, are at greater risk of being irritable, angry and tired. And the more fatigue, the less one can maintain "peak performance" and the psychological discipline to recognize Emotional Intelligence and maintain a Teflon Character when confronting aggressive people (Louie 2007c).

In reviewing citizen complaints, it comes as no surprise that a large portion is related to "officer attitude." And the more irritable and tired, the greater the probability this will influence how the officer communicates…or miscommunicates with the public.

 Clearly there is a critical need to minimize fatigue and lack of sleep, otherwise peak performance during critical incidents will be compromised.

➢ **How we cope with stress directly impacts how we communicate; therefore, our stress management directly impacts how the public perceives us.**

(Col. Charoen-Rajapark, Royal Thailand Police, 2009)

Stress reduction Eastern Style: Photo of meditation session taught by a Royal Thailand Police official.

Effectively coping with chronic stress, which accumulates over the years, is an officer survival imperative. (Thompson 2007). To effectively cope requires organizational support, support from immediate supervisors, personal recognition and adaptation – known as internal coping skills. **The public safety agencies that recognize the impacts and costs of employee stress are the ones that acknowledge the value of responding to these needs through the budget as well as leadership training and awareness** (Louie 2007a).

➢ **Coping with stress by having a positive and *winning attitude* at the workplace and in the field ... *qualities of the ideal crisis intervention practitioner*.**

What are the qualities that consistently emerge as one attempts to define and identify strong Emotional Intelligence? Those that recognize and emulate the list of qualities below need only to continue with confidence. For those in need of improving their interpersonal skills, this list (Oregon Employment Department 2004, Louie 2010a) can serve as a behavioral guide:

- **Respect: Showing respect in the workplace and with co-workers.** In the field, recognizing the necessity to demonstrate respect with people, especially those experiencing stress and emotional upset.

- **Confidence: This is "getting the job done" and being a good partner and co-worker.** In the field, this is more a demonstration of "command presence" and delivered in a professional and personable manner.

- **Patience:** In the workplace, **recognizing that co-workers need your patience.** In the field, recognizing that practicing patience with people in need of defusing can actually be a way to eventually control a situation. Part of this patience is understanding that when dealing with people in stress, it is important to "slow things down" to enable people to cope with internal and external stressors.

- **Helpfulness: Going the extra mile with co-workers and being a supportive team member.** In the field, being seen not only as a police officer but as one who is actually there to help! This quality may be demonstrated by providing community resources to assist people in need, such as counseling and support programs for people needing help to maintain their daily lives.

- **Empathy: Empathy in the workplace means you are practicing good listening skills and reinforcing being a team member.** In the field, this means demonstrating that you are practicing effective communication skills. You are understanding, but you are not necessarily agreeing.

➤ New study: Anger sets the stage for seeing threats where none exist

Recognizing one's emotional intelligence goes beyond merely how well an officer communicates under stress. A recent Northeastern University study that looks at how anger impacts perception suggests that this could possibly be the difference between "seeing" a cell phone or a gun. **"If you are angry when you confront a suspect, are you more likely to mistake a cell phone or other nonthreatening object in his hand for a gun? Recent findings from university-based research suggest that indeed is the case"** (Force Science News 2010, 1).

This study has discovered that "angry participants were significantly more likely to misidentify an object as a gun than were test subjects experiencing 'happy' emotions or even other 'negative' emotions, such as sadness or disgust" (Force Science News 2010, 1).

The study suggests that anger may change peoples' perceptions and expectations such that when they are angry, they may have a "higher anticipation" to encounter more guns than neutral objects compared to those who were not angry. The interpretation is that angry subjects may "set a much lower threshold for saying that a target is holding a gun" meaning they needed less information to determine a threat, such as a person holding a gun versus a cell phone.

Although the study does not specifically state, it maybe that a hypervigilant officer who happens to be angry sees more threats than are present; at the least, more threats than an officer who is not angry and possess a more balance emotional intelligence.

 Speaking of the Northeastern University study, Dr. Bill Lewinski of the University of Minnesota and the Force Science Institute suggests that *"this appears to be well done, empirically solid work that supports the psychoanalytic concept that angry people project their anger onto others and see a more threatening world around them than actually exists"* (Force Science News 2010, 1).

- **Some of the points highlighted in the Northeastern University study indicate:**

  ✓ Threat assessment "can frequently occur in the presence of heightened emotional states." The researchers sought to determine "whether strong emotions might 'constitute a primary influence on threat detection,' and, in fact, might 'push individuals' judgments toward [mistakenly] favoring the existence of a threat, thereby leading them to actively aggress against others who may not have posed an actual danger'" (Force Science News 2010, 2).

✓ "Anger is an emotional state that signals the presence of potentially violent or aggressive threats." To innately "favor one's own safety and survival" in that situation, it is more useful "to mistakenly harm a nonthreatening (unarmed) person than to risk being harmed or even killed by a threatening person; survival-wise, it is better to be safe than sorry when one's emotions are signaling the presence of potential dangers" (Force Science News 2010, 2).

✓ **"In other words, an angry person, feeling an exaggerated emotional need for self-protection, is biased toward finding threats where none exist, and for good reason from a preservation standpoint"** (Force Science News 2010, 2). Clearly more research needs to be conducted, especially with in-field police officers, however the implications appear evident that a balanced emotional intelligence may be the best preparation an officer can make when preparing to confront a potentially dangerous situation.

"Training people to be aware of their emotions as well as the potential influence of those emotions on assessments of threat may represent one possibility for enhancing accuracy"
(Force Science News 2010, 6)

The training implications for police officers are significant: "Even 'brief amounts of additional processing time' can drastically reduce errors … but in the police and military worlds 'allowing such additional time is not always an option, as some decisions must be made very rapidly.'" (Force Science News 2010,2).

It appears that people who "typically attend to their feelings are less likely to allow their emotions to influence judgment of risk than those who do not typically attend to their feelings" (FSN 2010, 2). Awareness of one's emotions at a particular point in time, and awareness overall of the impacts of balanced emotional intelligence may impact the perceptions that anger may bias. The researchers conclude that "programs designed to improve the accuracy of individuals who must make rapid decisions (e.g., police officers) might find the most success in eliminating emotion-based biases by training individuals to be aware of their emotions and the sources of those emotions" (Force Science News 2010, 2).

Speaking on the *hypervigilance* of both the military and police, former San Diego police officer Steve Albrecht (2001, 34) describes the hyper-vigilant officer as not wanting to "get too comfortable, too complacent" otherwise one will "lose their edge." But this constant hypervigilance can lead to: anger issues, anxieties, sleep problems, diet and sexual disorders, an inability to relax or think about pleasant things, and even when exhausted, there is a need to approach every situation in polite society as a tactical problem to be solved. Albrecht comments on the need to balance one's professional life and "don't let your emotions blind you to the realities of your job."

"It's Ok to feel angry toward people who press your hot buttons in the field – just don't let them know it. And don't take them home in your head with you"

Angry police officer on a call: In a recent Oregon case, an officer responded to a call at a restaurant of two patrons "sleeping at the counter," but according to witnesses, the officer was already "angry"when he arrived: The officer arrived at 1:57 a.m. "Although this was a low-priority call, (the officer) arrived angry, according to (two) witnesses." The jury awarded the plaintiff $35,000 for the officer's misconduct. "Why is the police officer escalating a situation?" asked Circuit Judge Kathleen Dailey, who presided over the case. "The officer should be trained to manage the situation without escalating it." (Duin Feb. 5, 2011)

Police excessive force case: A jury awarded $175,000 to three plaintiffs who alleged two police officers used excessive force, and as verified by two independent witnesses, the officers **appeared to be angry** when they first contacted the three men (Duin, Feb. 9, 2011).

"...a small percentage of officers may deal with their anger by losing sight of their professionalism, ethics and training." (Albrecht 2011, 33)

Road Rage incident - "He appeared angry": And in a rare sustained citizen complaint against an Oregon police sergeant, a Police Review Board found the sergeant "escalated the situation," and "acted inappropriately, used profane language and shouldn't have drawn his weapon during an off-duty traffic confrontation in April with another motorist who (the sergeant) says flipped him off at a traffic light and later unholstered his gun." (Bernstein, Feb. 9, 2011).

Wikipedia

> ## Reinforcing Emotional Intelligence; Don't Let Anger Hurt Your Health

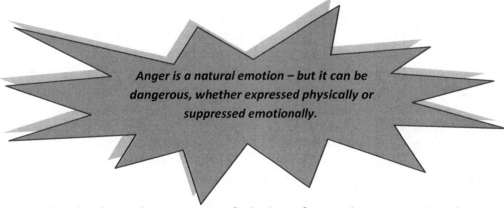

Anger is a natural emotion – but it can be dangerous, whether expressed physically or suppressed emotionally.

People who tend to *bottle-up their anger* may feel a loss of control over situations, brewing a boiling potion of pent-up anger, resentment and unhappiness. Suppressing these emotions may lead to "coping mechanisms" such as self-destructive as substance abuse and suicide.

Officers do not check-in their emotions at the door, but they can evaluate their emotions to determine if they are experiencing greater levels of anger. **One such check lists the following questions** (CIS 2008, 3):

> ### *Is Anger a Problem for You?*
>
> ✓ Do you often feel angry or hostile?
> ✓ Does your anger stay with you?
> ✓ Do you regularly hide negative feelings?
> ✓ Do you turn to alcohol or drugs to calm your anger?
> ✓ Does your heart race or do your muscles tense up when angry?
> ✓ What can you do when something angers you?
> ✓ What's really bothering you?
> ✓ Are you reacting because you are tired or depressed?
> ✓ Can you express your feelings in a way that will help rather than hurt?

Find a Healthy Release:

- **"Reach out to a caring friend; everybody needs a good listener."** For police officers, peer support is important and should be solicited. Many police agencies now have effective peer counseling programs, chaplains' programs and employee assistance programs (EAP) to support officers in time of emotional need.
- **"Consider writing about your anger; you might learn to control your mouth with your brain."** You can self-analyze to at least focus on where you need to do more work on your emotions. This list may be helpful when discussing with others (such as a loved one, close friend, counselor or peer support).
- **"Anger may take time and practice to control."** This may be seen as the *Zen* part of the discussion…but it is critical to acknowledge one's emotions and decide how to control them. This is where *mindfulness based training* can be invaluable.
- **"If your negative feelings continue, don't delay getting help before they hurt you and those around you."** This is the stage where many people continue to bottle-up their feelings and are reluctant to seek help…and this is when help is the most critical.
- **"Talk to a counselor, clergy or staff from your employee assistance program."** All police agencies need to make sure they are addressing emotional intelligence issues.
- **Practice Self-reflection:**   Debrief yourself from the stress of an emotional event to help lessen the deleterious impacts on the mind and body.   One technique is to keep a journal to write about a specific event. Although sounding too much like homework, writing about what has happened may actually aid in relaxation.   "People who have experienced trauma often use journaling. Writing about traumatic experiences reduces stress reactions and improves the response of T-lymphocytes, making a person less susceptible to illness" (Collins 2011, 78).

Mindfulness Based Training: "Studies suggest the practice of meditation can ease pain, improve concentration and immune function, lower blood pressure, curb anxiety and insomnia, and possibly even help prevent depression. Newer research tools, such as high-tech brain scans, show how meditation might have diverse effects" (Elias 2009).

Brain-scan studies of long-time meditators indicate they have increased thickness in parts of the brain associated with attention. Evidently, experienced meditators recognize when their muscles tense as a result of feeling angry. Sensing this reaction to anger prompts the meditators to "practice" their mindfulness based training.

And in a UCLA study, "meditators' brains have larger volume in areas important for attention, focus and regulating emotion. They also have more gray matter, which could sharpen mental function" (Elias 2009).

Emptying the Mind and becoming Centered: "Mindfulness has beneficial effects on vital signs, lowering pulse rate and blood pressure, and has been helpful in managing chronic pain. Controlling breathing and emptying the mind by being in the present is the essence of mindfulness" (Collins 2011, 77).

This type of self-awareness allows the practitioner of mindfulness training to become *centered* as a means to focus on the job at hand. For the police officer, this becomes an officer safety skill building exercise, allowing one to set "aside extraneous thoughts and focus on being present" meaning that the present is the *situational awareness* of the 911 scene. As an example, as the officer approaches the door of a disturbance call, he or she may merely stop short of knocking on the door and just take a few deep breaths, trying to concentrate on the information that had been relayed regarding the 911 call. To help concentrate, the officer may listen for any noises or voices coming from the other side of the door (*stop, look and listen* really does work!).

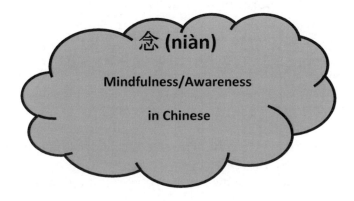

念 (niàn)

Mindfulness/Awareness

in Chinese

Chapter VIII: Use of Force

> For active duty public safety professionals, use of force is dependent upon departmental policy, guidelines and training, which may or may not include these concepts.

All crisis intervention calls have the potential for violence and although this tactical communication in crisis situations training focuses on non-physical contact with people, officers must always be prepared to use defensive tactics to control and subdue aggressive and potentially violent people. This section will explore two contemporary perspectives on use of force: the **Confrontational Continuum** and **Dynamic Resistance Response (DRRM)** models.

➤ The Confrontational Continuum Model:

There are situations confronted by police where no amount of questioning or interviewing, listening, empathy, rapport, persuasion, mediation or negotiation will affect the outcome of the contact. The police officer must *play the hand the officer is dealt* and sometimes must do so without the option of time or opportunity to retreat. Yet, the officer is not asked to *play the hand* and *be a gambler* (Blitz 2008).

> *In confronting a situation, the police officer is expected to seize control as necessary to protect himself and others – and to be assured that the measures taken will be effective 100% of the time in controlling the situation and/or stopping the threat*
> (Blitz 2008).

- In making choices, the officer must control effectively in order to guarantee that he or she is successful in protecting self and others from the threat that is the officer's duty to confront and stop. It is not and cannot be acceptable that the officer's choice is effective 50% or 75% of the time – because the consequences to society and to the police of such a result (death and injury to the police and innocents) simply are unacceptable (Blitz 2008).

- "Gordon Graham, noted lecturer and expert on emergency services risk management, remarks that 'contemporary policing is the most difficult job in America today.' Not only must the officer be prepared to 'get it right the first time' in a myriad of difficult, unpredictable and fast moving situations, but the officer must react sometimes in the split of a second and do so in compliance with statutes and law as handed down by the appellate courts. The officer does not have the luxury of the surgeon who is able to read the patient's charts, x-rays and scans and plan his every move days in advance; nor the reflective and consultative opportunities of the judge who can ponder over a record until satisfied that the decision is as correct as the judge is capable of making it. And, when the judges second guess an officer's actions after the fact, they sometimes cut little slack" (Blitz 2008).

> "The responsibility for keeping abreast of constitutional developments in criminal law is squarely on the shoulders of law enforcement officials. Police must be cognizant of how far their authority extends, and the point where it ends. Given the power of the police over our liberty and sometimes our lives, this responsibility is entirely proper"
> *(Ward v. County of San Diego, 1986)*

➢ The Confrontational Continuum Model; Legal Precedents

In matters concerning the use of force, police officers are governed by state laws related to justification for the use of physical and deadly force. In addition, police decisions in America must be consistent with the Fourth Amendment of the federal Constitution which, among other things, guarantees that citizens shall not be arrested without probable cause and reasonable grounds supporting the belief that they are committing or have committed a crime.

In addition, all situations concerning justification for the use of force are governed by the standard of objective reasonableness as stated by the Supreme Court in <u>Tennessee vs. Garner</u> (1985). In that case the Supreme Court held that an officer's use of deadly force against fleeing felons violated the Fourth Amendment, thereby establishing the Fourth Amendment as a basis for resolving claims of excessive force by the police. Then, following that decision, the Supreme Court held that all claims of excessive force in the course of an arrest, investigatory stop, or other "seizure" are governed by the Fourth Amendment objective reasonableness standard, rather than by a substantive process "shocks the conscience" approach.

- **Under Garner, the officer may use deadly force when:**
  - ✓ There is an immediate danger to the officer or others;
  - ✓ The suspect demonstrates dangerousness by the previous use of or threatened use of force;
  - ✓ The officer reasonably believes the suspect has committed a crime involving the use or threatened use of serious physical harm;
  - ✓ Whenever reasonable the officer first must issue a verbal warning or challenge before using deadly force.

> **Note the complexity of this determination and the latitude given by the Court to the officer on the street under this legal standard.**

➢ The Confrontational Continuum Model; Among the factors to be considered to determine reasonableness"

In <u>Graham v. Connor</u> (1989), the Supreme Court stated that reasonableness must be evaluated in light of the particular circumstances "from the perspective of a reasonable officer at the scene, rather than with the 20-20 vision of hindsight." Thus, in order to justify use of force choices, the officer must be able to demonstrate that the person posing the threat presents a danger to the officer or the community, with the following factors considered to determine "reasonableness":

- ✓ The severity of the crime at issue;

✓ Whether the suspect poses an immediate threat to the safety of the officer or others;
✓ Whether the suspect is actively resisting arrest or;
✓ Whether the suspect is attempting to evade arrest by flight.

Reasonableness of the officer's action is determined by balancing the nature of the intrusion on the individual's Fourth Amendment interest against the importance of the governmental interest alleged to justify the intrusion (Terry v. Ohio, 1968, in Blitz 2008).

> **"Street encounters between citizens and police officers are incredibly rich in diversity. They range from wholly friendly exchanges of pleasantries or mutually useful information to hostile confrontations of armed men involving arrest, or injuries, or loss of life. Moreover, hostile confrontations are not all of a piece. Some of them begin in a friendly enough manner, only to take a different turn upon the injection of some unexpected element into the conversation"**
> (Terry v. Ohio, 392 U.S. 1, 13, 1968).

Other decisions have expanded on the manner in which "reasonableness" should be evaluated. The Fifth Circuit admonished lawyers and judges in Grandstaff v. City of Borger (1985) stating that "Judges must never forget that peace officers stand at the front of law and the ordering process of society."

Nevertheless, the point is that the legal factors to determine what is and is not lawful and justified are complicated. An officer who must contemplate these legal complexities before reacting appropriately is likely to freeze in indecision, the result of which could be injury or death to the officer or another person.

> **In applying Use of Force options, several concepts are important to understand – the goal is to control the situation; the odds of achieving control must be 100% because the police cannot lose 50% or even 90% of the time. Thus, the officer must employ such force as is necessary to maintain an advantage for control (Blitz 2008).**

> ## The Confrontational Continuum Model: Dialogue; Escort Compliance; Compression or Pain Compliance; Mechanical Compliance; Impact Weapons/Batons to Impede; Weapon to Stop

The material presented in this text emphasizes nonverbal and verbal persuasion, typically described as *dialogue* in use of force training. However, dialogue is not always effective. If dialogue is inappropriate or deemed ineffective to control the situation and control the threat to self or others, the officer may have to use other levels of force such as escort techniques which requires physically taking hold of a resisting or combative person (Blitz 2008). The following summarizes this Confrontational Continuum:

- **Dialogue.** Reduced to the simplest of terms, dialogue can be characterized as directive or calming. The nature and elements of dialogue need not be addressed here, for this is the subject of this entire work on interpersonal communications in stressful situations. The key is to gain control through calming and voluntary compliance with officer requests and directions communicated artfully. The officer's presence, uniformed appearance, body language, and his capacity to use force coupled with persuasive dialogue are employed (Blitz 2008).

  There is no downside to effective verbalization and communication. This will have a positive effect on the individual and the individual's personal life at home and at work. It's not always easy, but will take practice and the anticipation of situations. Each officer is responsible for his or her own interpersonal communication (Thompson 2007).

  > *Presence and body language, emphasized with verbalization, are the building blocks for a use of force situation (Thompson 2007).*

  However, dialogue is not always effective… If dialogue is inappropriate or deemed ineffective to control the situation and control the threat to self or others, the officer may have to use other levels of force such as escort techniques, which require physically taking hold of resisting or combative people (Blitz 2008).

- **Escort Compliance:** Although this text recommends avoidance of touching someone who is experiencing an emotional event, there are times when police officers need to react quickly to aggression. Escort compliance is the physical taking hold of the person by the arm, or using a come-along technique in directional contact. It may include placing the person under arrest and leading him or her away. However, the escort is sometimes inappropriate or deemed ineffective to control the situation. The officer may need to select the next appropriate higher level intervention on the continuum (Blitz 2008).

  > *At any stage in the unfolding of a scenario it is the officer's responsibility to observe the circumstance and determine the corresponding response that the officer is confident will enable him to control the situation. The next higher option above escort is pain compliance.*

- **Compression or Pain Compliance:** Here the officer manipulates a joint to create pain and cause surrender, such as a come-along or a wrist lock technique, and digital control.   However, pain compliance techniques may be inappropriate or deemed ineffective to control the situation (Blitz 2008).

  > *As pointed out elsewhere in this text, the mentally disturbed or the person impaired by substance abuse may not perceive or respond to pain. The next level of force option is mechanical compliance.*

- **Mechanical Compliance:** Here the officer repositions the body to gain compliance by one or more techniques such as a punch, kick, blow or throw. Techniques may include hair or joint take downs, pressure points and joint *come-alongs* (Blitz 2008).

> *However, these techniques sometimes will be inappropriate or deemed ineffective to control the situation. The next level of option is to resort to impact weapons.*

- **Impact Weapons/Baton to Impede:** At this level a baton, ASP (collapsible baton), flashlight, Billy, sap or sap glove, bean bag, or TASER is used to impede a threatening person who presents the potential to inflict harm. Other less than lethal techniques including canine deployment and bite, CS/CN gas or Mace and the carotid-neck hold may be used. The officer responds to a higher degree of threat based on his perception of jeopardy and need to control in light of the assailant's/threat's actions (Blitz 2008).

> **Impact weapons sometimes will be inappropriate or deemed ineffective to control the situation. At this juncture, the threat is very high and the officer perceives the immediate need to stop and control to avert death or serious injury to him or others. The remaining alternative to stop will be either a Taser or other impact weapon, or a firearm** (Blitz 2008).

- **Weapon to Stop:** Lethal force is used to stop.

> **In the context of this model that discusses levels of force in *a Confrontational Continuum of Officer Responses*, officers are taught to take into account officer-subject factors such as age, sex, size, strength, combat skill level, the presence of multiple subject threats, and the threat's mental state.**

➢ The Confrontational Continuum Graph

The "Confrontational Continuum" (relied upon in Blitz 2008) as portrayed in the following graph initially was developed by police use of force consultant Kevin Parson Ph.D. and also has been referred to since its use in the 1980's as the "Force Response Continuum" and the "Use of Force Continuum," a version of which was later adapted and published by Armament Systems and Procedures, Inc. It is an illustration, a graphic portrayal, which allows an officer to understand easily the complexities of the law of justification for the use of force. This illustration lends itself to easy explanation by the officer in reports and in court testimony. It provides a model the officer may apply in any context with assurance that the choices made based on the model will be objectively reasonable, legally defensible and justified.

It is a training aid intended to enable the officer to appropriately respond to every emergency situation involving the potential use of force, without pause or concentration.

The graph depicts "Assailant Action" on the vertical axis, "Levels of Force" on the horizontal axis and the appropriate level of "Officer Reaction" in order to control along the 45 degree diagonal line. The key point to understanding the continuum is this: The proper point along the diagonal line is never precise and the officer's appropriate reaction is not susceptible to being characterized as within the one and only one correct "box" or single control technique. The continuum was designed to match the officer's reality in police responses to confrontational behavior.

The Continuum emphasizes the core concept to its correct application — that the officer must maintain control, and do so only with such force that is a reasonable response to the threat as the officer perceives it. The diagonal line conveys the concept that the degree of force employed is escalated and deescalated in response to the actions taken by the threat. The image of the continuum conveys vividly and powerfully at a glance the concept that reasonableness is defined by the officer's perceptions of the assailant's threat actions and that the threat actions dictate the response, starting at the lowest appropriate level (Blitz 2008).

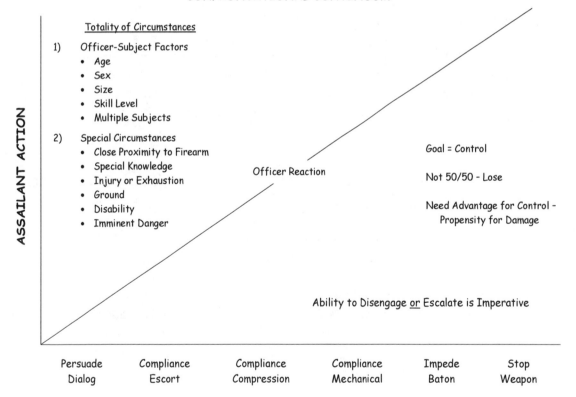

CONFRONTATIONAL CONTINUUM

Totality of Circumstances

1) Officer-Subject Factors
- Age
- Sex
- Size
- Skill Level
- Multiple Subjects

2) Special Circumstances
- Close Proximity to Firearm
- Special Knowledge
- Injury or Exhaustion
- Ground
- Disability
- Imminent Danger

Officer Reaction

Goal = Control

Not 50/50 - Lose

Need Advantage for Control – Propensity for Damage

Ability to Disengage or Escalate is Imperative

ASSAILANT ACTION

| Persuade | Compliance | Compliance | Compliance | Impede | Stop |
| Dialog | Escort | Compression | Mechanical | Baton | Weapon |

PASSIVE CONTROL -------------- EXPLOSIVE POWER

Also emphasized in the depiction is that the ultimate goal is to control the situation, and to be successful in doing so 100% of the time!

Controversy regarding Use of Force Continuums: *Have Force Continuums Outlived Their Usefulness?* ⬅➡

Within the law enforcement community, some contend that the "original need for force continuums (guidance) has been reduced because the judicial system has now provided adequate guidance in force standards. The U.S. Supreme Court defined the Fourth Amendment's objective reasonableness force standard in <u>Tennessee v. Garner</u> and in <u>Graham v. Connor</u>. Garner gutted the common-law fleeing-felon rule, while Graham held that an officer's use of force, when seizing a free person, will be analyzed under the Fourth Amendment's objective reasonableness standard" (Peters et al, 2006, 1).

Some use of force continuum graphs appear to indicate (or at least are frequently interpreted by the Defense Bar) that officers need to start at a lower level of force and work their way up the graph until they are able to overcome the resistance. "Force continuums often give the perception that officers must use minimum force, but that is not the constitutional standard" (Peters et al, 2006, 1).

Under this more simplified analysis (meaning, no need for complex graphs), the Fourth Amendment "objective reasonableness standard" does not require that an officer use the least intrusive means to overcome resisting force. This reasonableness standard is based on the appropriateness of an officer's decision to use force and will be analyzed on the totality of the circumstances that the officer "reasonably perceived" at the time of the incident.

> ### How to Visualize Use of Force Concepts: The Dynamic Resistance Response Model (DRRM); An alternative model to the Use of Force Continuum.

> "Officers faced with potentially life-threatening situations need simple, clear, unambiguous, and consistent guidelines in the use of force. To this end, the dynamic resistance response model (DRRM) combines a use-of-force continuum with an application of four broad categories of suspects" (Joyner and Basile 2007, 23)

Terms:

- **Dynamic:** "Dynamic indicates that the model is fluid. Suspects can move rapidly from one level of resistance to the next. The public must realize that situations can quickly and dangerously transition from one category to another. Officers never should assume a suspect currently complying will continue to do so. Also, they always should be prepared for an attack no matter how compliant an individual initially appears" (Joyner and Basile 2007, 23).

120

- **Resistance:** "Resistance demonstrates that the suspect controls the interaction. A major failing among current use-of-force models is the emphasis on the officer and the amount of force used. This places officers in a weak position during accusations of excessive force as the *focus is on the officer's actions, rather than on the suspect's. The DRRM emphasizes that the* suspect's level of resistance determines the officer's response and delineates suspects into one of four categories: not resistant (compliant), passively resistant, aggressively resistant, and deadly resistant" (Joyner and Basile 2007, 23-24).

➢ The Four Categories of Suspects:

1. Not Resistant: "Suspects who do not resist but follow all commands are compliant. Only a law enforcement officer's presence and verbal commands are required when dealing with these individuals; no coercive physical contact is necessary" (Joyner and Basile 2007, 25).   The skillful use of defusing techniques is able to control the situation and prevent any escalation of violence or aggression (Louie 2007c).

2. Passively Resistant: "A passively resistant suspect fails to follow commands and may be verbally abusive. He may attempt to move away from the officer, escape from the officer's grip, or flee. The suspect's actions are neutral or defensive, and the officer does not feel threatened by his actions" (Joyner and Basile 2007, 26).

3. Aggressively Resistant: "An aggressively resistant suspect takes offensive action by attempting to push, throw, strike, tackle, or physically harm the officer or another person. To defend himself, the officer must respond with appropriate force to stop the attack. The officer feels threatened by the suspect's actions. Justified responses include the use of personal weapons (hands, fists, feet), batons, pepper spray, and a stun gun" (Joyner and Basile 2007, 26).

4. Deadly Resistant: "A deadly resistant suspect will seriously injure or kill the officer or another person if immediate action is not taken to stop the threat. The officer is justified in using force, including deadly force, reasonably necessary to overcome the offender and effect custody. For each of the four suspect categories, officers have all of the tools in the preceding categories available. In each instance, officers constantly should give commands to the suspect when doing so does not jeopardize safety. Further, the DRRM is flexible. Departments can apply the four categories of suspects to their current use-of force continuum and insert the tools available to officers in that particular agency" (Joyner and Basile 2007, 26).

> **If not a criminal matter, many times people are released after physical resistance because they have been defused by the officers and there is no longer a need to keep them in custody or restraints such as handcuffs** (Louie 2007c).

➤ Application of the DRRM Diagram

As can be seen in the DRRM triangle diagram, compliance or "no resistance" is in the center of the triangle, emphasizing that is the goal of every encounter with people.

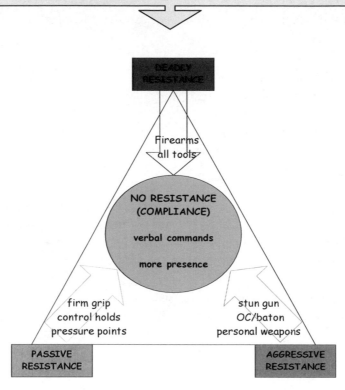

If a suspect's resistance level places him on one of the three corners of the triangle, the officer's response (appropriate use of force) is intended to move the suspect's behavior to the center of the triangle and compliance. If force is used by the officer in response to the suspect's resistance level, the sole purpose of the application of force is to gain compliance (Joyner and Basile 2007, 27).

"Law enforcement officers are tasked with a difficult responsibility and must make life-or-death decisions at a moment's notice. The intense public scrutiny resulting from alleged misuse of force sometimes results in unnecessary restrictions placed on the use of viable, effective tools in restraining combative suspects. Departments would better serve their officers and citizens by establishing a single use-of-force policy directly related to suspects' behavior and easier to comprehend and apply. Law enforcement agencies will significantly benefit from instituting a legally defensible use-of-force model that protects the rights of the public without decreasing the safety of officers" (Joyner and Basile 2007, 27).

Agencies that adopt the dynamic resistance response model can gain several advantages. First, the structure of the model brings every confrontation to a compliant resolution. The DRRM is based upon the obvious presumption that law enforcement officers seek no resistance (compliance) in all cases. Traditional use-of-force models guide officers into a pattern of escalation of force. Second, a resistor's behavior is placed in one of four easily recognized categories, providing more guidance to officers in the selection of the appropriate use of force. Third, the DRRM accurately focuses the initial use-of-force analysis on the resistor and better reflects the actual events that cause a police-citizen confrontation. Most other use-of-force models first direct attention to the acts of the officer and then belatedly explore what initiated the action.

Finally, the DRRM simplifies training on use-of-force options as officers can explain any encounter in a resistance –response or action- reaction equation. With appropriate training, officers have a clearer understanding of their force options, enhancing their safety and the effectiveness of the department" (Joyner and Basile 2007, 27-28).

> ## According to FBI agents Charles Joyner and Chad Basile (2007), agencies that adopt the dynamic resistance response model can gain several advantages:

First, the structure of the model brings every confrontation to a compliant resolution. The DRRM is based upon the obvious presumption that law enforcement officers seek no resistance (compliance) in all cases. Traditional use-of-force models guide officers into a pattern of escalation of force.

Second, a resistor's behavior is placed in one of four easily recognized categories, providing more guidance to officers in the selection of the appropriate use of force.

Third, the DRRM accurately focuses the initial use-of-force analysis on the resistor and better reflects the actual events that cause a police-citizen confrontation. Most other use-of-force models first direct attention to the acts of the officer and then belatedly explore what initiated the action.

Finally, the DRRM simplifies training on use-of-force options as officers can explain any encounter in a resistance—response or action—reaction equation. With appropriate training, officers have a clearer understanding of their force options, enhancing their safety and the effectiveness of the department" (Joyner and Basile 2007, 27-28).

> ## A brief additional word about "objectively reasonable force" in "response" to someone who is aggressive (Louie 2008):

Although this training material has focused on non-physical control of people, public safety professionals frequently have to go *hands-on* when attempting to defuse and control aggressive and violent people. It is the physical restraint that must be objectively reasonable. This reasonable standard can be defined as "would another officer with the same or similar training and experience, given the same or similar circumstances as presented to the officer being evaluated, do the same thing or use similar judgment?" (Graham v. Conner, 1989). In the aftermath of a serious or fatal police use of force, the question that will surely surface (most likely as a banner new headline) is "was the force the officer(s) used reasonable given the circumstances?" Once control is achieved, the officer can decide if the person will remain in restraints or be released after calming down to a level where the officer is able to communicate effectively with the threat and with other disputants without risk.

A more contemporary approach to police use of force, such as the above DRRM model, realigns terminology to more accurately reflect the true nature of the police-to-disputant contact: "response to resistance and aggression" (Faulkner 2007, 3).

As reported in *Force Science News* (#88, 2007, 3): "The word 'response' denotes that the subject must be engaging in an action either resisting or aggressing toward the officer or others. These are external factors the courts want to hear in judging the efficacy of an officer's conduct." Stated differently, the assailant's action determines the officer's reaction; the degree of force or resistance to control determines the extent of force employed by the officer to overcome that resistance and be able to control with 100% assurance of maintaining control.

> **Whenever a person is not exhibiting or indicating any increase in or elevating aggression, then officers should be mindful of their respective Emotional Intelligence and not become the provocateur. If there is no increase in aggression, and if time is on your side, then it is best to stabilize the situation and attempt to communicate with the aggressor** (Louie 2007c).

➤ Words of Caution: How responding to a disturbance call can become a Fourth Amendment use of force issue (Louie 2008; Scarry 2008).

What can happen if a suicide threat or disturbance call, with no initial and overt criminal violation, suddenly escalates into a police use of force? This is a common 911 call where the responding officers attempt to "control" someone who has threatened suicide or another violent act, and in the process of controlling, the police use of force escalates, sometimes with tragic and deadly results.

In reviewing an actual case, officers responded to a "threats of suicide call," relayed to 911 from a social service agency that was in telephone contact with the threatening 32-year old male. Four officers responded and one knocked on the man's door which was opened halfway. The man was only wearing shorts and therefore was not holding or concealing any weapons. When asked if he was threatening suicide, the man replied "yes."

Appearing "nervous and agitated," the man said he wanted to get his shoes. As the man tried to slam the door shut, one of the officers placed his foot in the door, and the officers pushed their way into the home. The officers then say the man "grabbed a Samurai sword" and held it in a threatening manner. The man then lowered the sword, grabbed a telephone, and said "help me" and "they are coming to get me."

While the man was talking on the phone, one of the officers pepper- sprayed him in an attempt to get him to drop the sword. The man then "turned the sword toward the officers and began to move in their direction." The officers were in and near a doorway but were unable to retreat because "it was too crowded." As the man was moving in their direction, two of the officers fired their guns; the man died at the scene. The entire incident is reported to have lasted less than four minutes (Scarry 2008).

In a civil rights lawsuit filed by the deceased man's brother against the two officers who fired their guns, it was alleged that the officers violated the deceased's Fourth Amendment right to be "free from unreasonable searches and seizures." The officers responded by filing for qualified immunity, stating they were acting in self-defense. The officers contended they acted reasonably under the circumstances (i.e., they were being threatened by a man wielding a deadly sword, in a confined area). The lawsuit contended that the "officers' actions were unreasonable" and constituted excessive force. Further, "...the officers weren't responding to a crime or attempting to arrest," instead, "they were responding to a call for help from a suicidal subject" (Scarry 2008, 73).

Although the reasonableness of any police use of force must be judged from the perspective of "a reasonable officer on the scene, rather than with the 20/20 vision of hindsight," this particular case surfaces significant issues relative to how the officers handled the call before the need for deadly force.

> **"As such, the officers knew they were dealing with a potentially mentally ill or emotionally disturbed individual. Therefore, according to the Plaintiff, the officers' training required them to de-escalate the situation. Instead, the officers escalated the events by entering the home, confronting Hastings in the bedroom and pepper spraying him, which forced them to use deadly force"** (Scarry 2008, 73).

In this case, the deceased's brother did not dispute the fact that the officers were acting in self-defense; the issue was what did the officers do, and not do, that resulted in a self-defense response. This case, now at the appellate court level, focuses on whether the officers' "actions unreasonably led to the need to use deadly force."

- ✓ The deceased had not committed a crime;
- ✓ Was a potentially mentally ill or emotionally disturbed person;
- ✓ Was reported to be attempting suicide;
- ✓ Had called for help.

In following the subsequent sequence of events when the officers arrived, the court noted: "...instead of helping ...the officers squeezed themselves into a bedroom doorway, leaving no room to retreat." Further, the officers "used loud commands; and sprayed him with OC, which caused him more distress" (Scarry 2008, 74).

And in a more ominous analysis, former police officer and now attorney Laura Scarry states: "...the court concluded a jury could find the officers' actions unreasonably escalated the situation, calling for the need to use deadly force" (Scarry 2008, 74).

> **The relevance of this case is obvious for all first responders: when called to assist someone asking for help, and absent any apparent criminal behavior or activity, the officers need to constantly assess each use of force escalation when attempting to control someone.**

If the escalation approaches serious physical injury or need for deadly force, the issue of how to continue will be scrutinized. If the officers have an opportunity to retreat and secure the scene by containing the person in question, say within a residence, and call for additional resources (such as trained negotiators) then the officers will most likely be judged as "responding to contemporary tactical communication and crisis intervention training." If, on the other hand, officers find themselves "squeezed into a predicament" such as in this case, they will most likely be judged (both internally within their respective agency and externally by the media, public and survivors) by the standard of "what should they have done when it appeared the situation was escalating" (Scarry 2008, 74-75).

"Frequently, police officers are called to 'assist.' Those who want assistance are typically complaining about an individual who has not committed a crime but is in some sort of physical and/or mental distress. Often something goes wrong through no fault of the officers, particularly when officers are called to deal with distressed individuals. And sometimes, the mere fact that police are called to the scene escalates a situation" (Scarry 2008, 75). The point to note is that police actions preceding a serious and/or deadly use of force may very well be called into question.

(Cmdr. Joel Wilson)

This chapter focuses on how public safety officers should respond to *disturbance calls* using a Crisis Intervention Model. From start to finish, one can visualize identifiable phases in a *typical* (but never routine) disturbance call. Understanding these phases will better equip responding officers with a strategic schema on how to handle these calls (Louie 1986).

1. Pre Contact

The Pre Contact Phase is the critical time for responding public safety officers to learn as much as they can about the call, and to prepare themselves mentally and emotionally.

- **How the call is relayed to the officer:**

  ✓ Radio; dispatch information – dispatchers play a vital role in conveying information to the responding officers;
  ✓ Officer observes the incident or is contacted by a witness or reporting party;
  ✓ Prior experience of responding officers; prior history at address;
  ✓ Type of call;
  ✓ Type of location.

- **While enroute to the scene:**

  Make a plan in your mind and talk it over with your partner - be prepared!
  "Anticipation is a forerunner of perception" and "...it can be helpful in 'interpreting environmental cues and patterns' and can assist in 'processing the situation and selecting options. It tends to bring your body and mind into unison" (Ross 2007, 1).

 The time spent responding to a 911 call is the time to start preparing mentally. And although it is unknown what will happen, the officers can still prepare. "En route to the scene...officers usually (begin) constructing an impression of what they'd be encountering. They generally had some limited information from dispatch. Often they'd been to the location before or knew some of the history of the people they were responding to. A number of the officers said they had mentally rehearsed being in the kind of situation they ended up in" and "this mentally prepared them to recognize danger cues" (Ross 2007, 1).

- **Approaching the scene – Situational Awareness mindset:**
  - ✓ Officer safety precautions!
  - ✓ Stay *centered and focused* on the call.
  - ✓ Parking of vehicle (and the noise you make)
  - ✓ Approaching the scene; day and night
  - ✓ Stop, look and listen...and listen again! What can (and cannot) be heard from the people inside?
  - ✓ This pre-contact phase is where many police officers make officer safety mistakes!

CAUTION	**"The only thing that is predictable about the calls that police respond to is that they are unpredictable!"** (Sergeant Debra Case, Police Crisis Intervention Instructor)

2. Contact

This initial Contact Phase is where the officers need to *read the play* and be alert – the initial *situational awareness* time – as the officers are making contact with the disputants.

- **Making contact: *Walking through the door...***
  - ✓ Visually frisk; look for visual cues and behaviors (drunk vs. mentally ill or maybe … diabetic?);
  - ✓ The entry; vulnerable time since the location may be unfamiliar and those inside may still feel they have an advantage;
  - ✓ Search area for disputants, witnesses, victims, etc.;
  - ✓ Take note of potential weapons (from ashtrays to trophies – to grandpa's sword on the wall);
  - ✓ Clues to the dispute;
  - ✓ Bring disputants together (avoid kitchen and bedroom);
  - ✓ Determine who belongs at the scene before you get any further in the process.

DANGER	*Situational Awareness - making contact; the critical time to visually scan and quickly draw inferences from people and the environment*

This initial contact phase is the critical time when the officers need to not only anticipate the unexpected, but also to visually scan the environment at the 911 scene.   This is known as *situational awareness* whereby officers are "...keenly attuned to potential danger signals from the surrounding environment" and "were particularly aware visually" (Ross 2007).   And those officers unable to develop this "situational awareness" usually are selected out of the profession, either during the field training program or as a result of subsequent injuries and poor performance evaluations as a post recruit (Louie 2007c).

- **Bring disputants together:**

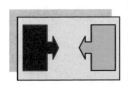
Look for nonverbal cues; read body language, facial expressions; hand movements and body positioning as officers approach. During this critical initial contact, the officers should only be focusing on situational awareness to enhance officer and disputant safety. Once officer safety can be established or assured, then the officers can attempt to determine what has happened and hopefully, develop enough information that will lead to resolution.

   ✓ Officers need to "draw reasonable inferences quickly" and be prepared to quickly make multiple decisions (Ross 2007). *This is Situational Awareness!*
   ✓ Screen out distractions and try to minimize noise (loud TV, radio or machinery).
   ✓ As the officers attempt to make contact, part of minimizing the distractions may be to ask one or more of the disputants to take off their earphones or stop playing with their electronics (a common nervous ploy as one or more of the disputants pretends to ignore the officers).
   ✓ Determine who belongs at the scene before you get any further in the process. Many times police start the defusing process with people who should not be at the scene – bystanders or neighbors or other people who don't need to be there. If you let these uninvolved people remain, they become cheerleaders and spectators, creating an even greater defusing challenge.
   ✓ If disputants are too angry to face each other, then re-position them *B-to-B* (Back-to-Back) such that the officers maintain eye contact but the disputants are unable to see one another.

- **Determine if this is an arrest situation:** If yes, establish the elements by interview and evidence. If appropriate, and not a compromise to officer safety, you may still want to calm the disputants (remember, you may still need their cooperation for your investigation, even if they are in handcuffs). Always take disputant(s) into custody when officer safety is at issue.

Tactical Communication Techniques: Pointed questions to ask to assess lethality at beginning of domestic violence call (Campbell 2007)

Since a large portion of police disturbance calls are related to domestic violence, there is a need to address violence-preventing protocols that police officers are incorporating into their domestic violence investigation procedures. As the officers are attempting to communicate with people at a domestic violence call, they should incorporate the following script. Developed for Maryland police agencies, the following set of questions are designed as an assessment check list for violence and suicide potential in domestic violence calls. "These inquires are intended to surface common precursors of deadly violence" (Campbell 2007, 1).

The first three questions are designed to "reveal direct deadly violence." In the participating Maryland police agencies, if the answer to any of the questions is yes, officers call a domestic abuse counselor to confer with the domestic violence victim.

1. *Has your partner (or whoever the aggressor is) ever used a weapon against you or threatened you with a weapon?*
    2. *Has he or she ever threatened to kill you or your children"*
        3. *Do you think he or she might try to kill you?*

If the answers are no, then officers are instructed to ask the following questions:
4. *Does he or she have a gun or can he or she get one easily?*
5. *Has he or she ever tried to choke you?*
6. *Is he or she violently or constantly jealous or does he or she control most of your daily activities?*
7. *Have you left him or her or separated after living together or being married?*
8. *Is he or she unemployed?*
9. *Has he or she ever tried to kill himself or herself?*
10. *Do you have a child he/she knows is not his/hers?*
11. *Does he/she follow or spy on you or leave threatening messages?*

For jurisdictions other than those participating in Maryland, the above questions are optional. However, post analysis of domestic violence calls does indicate that responses to these questions may lead to earlier intervention and perhaps prevent further violence.

Many officers begin the initial contact too aggressively!

Such demeanor may actually *spike* the emotion index. Keep in mind the scene: you may be in someone's home. Think of what you would do if a stranger - even a police officer - came in to your home and started shouting commands. Officer ego will determine how this is done. This is where the Emotional Intelligence of the officer is critical. Will the officer recognize he/she needs to manage the moment (his or her stress) as well as that of the disputants?

- **Difficult balance to strike; not too soft, not too hard.** If you recognize you may *have come on too strong*, then maybe good tactic is to apologize; people are normally not expecting this from police officers and your apology may actually help defuse. Although it may seem awkward for the officer to apologize, this can be an opportunity to start on the track to establish rapport and perhaps some trust with the disputants.

An apology from the officer can actually be a defusing tactic. An apology has three basic parts: **1.** What I did was inappropriate or wrong; **2.** I regret that what I did or said may have hurt or angered; and **3.** What can I do to make this better?

By and large, people are rather forgiving when there is an acknowledgement that they have been wronged. Contemporary patient care research suggests the healing power of an apology: "Hospitals that allow doctors to say 'I'm sorry' for mistakes are less likely to be sued, which can lower malpractice insurance rates and free up money for better patient care" (Nielsen 2011, B8).

Many police contend that to apologize is a sign of weakness or loss of authority, but that is not correct. As an example, if the officer "came on too strong" during the Contact Phase, and quickly apologizes ("Hey folks, sorry I yelled…I shouldn't have…but I was trying to get your attention") for that, people will tend to appreciate hearing that from the officer and may even be taken off balance when a police officer actually apologizes…that's the defusing aspect of making an apology. And once the apology is made, quickly move the conversation to "OK, tell me what happened here today?"

- **Do not *Unreasonably Escalate*.** Having the police authority to intervene in a disturbance does not give one the license to be a jerk. One of the most frequent police officer complaints from the public is that "the officer was a jerk; was rude; was overbearing; was way out of line," etc., (Louie 2007c).

    ✓ Create an atmosphere for discussion; treat the disputants as partners in a conversation (albeit
    probably heated for the moment);
    ✓ Difficult balance; not too soft, not too hard;
    ✓ Do not escalate;
    ✓ Be aware of your body language, tone of voice, mannerisms, etc., (remember, tone of voice and non-verbal cues are most important in communication);
    ✓ Create an atmosphere for discussion.

➢ **Tactical Communication Techniques: Creating first impression of non-hostile authority with a smile** (Conniff 2004; Forman 2003)

   Recall that nonverbal cues are the most effective means of communication.

> **For humans, as for monkeys, smiling is a way to disarm and reassure those around us.** And apparently, the quicker the better. Once officer safety has been established, a cordial smile (not humorous or sarcastic) sends a reassuring non-verbal message and may help to defuse people who are angry. Just don't try to force the smile … try to be as natural (or normal) as you can.

(Photobucket)

> **The impact of a smile:** POWs of the Korean War were taken off balance when their "Chinese captors greeted them with a cigarette, a smile and a friendly 'hello'" (Keckeisen 2002). Even the dreaded religious police of Saudia Arabia are now trained to smile to enable them to "deal effectively and pleasantly with the public" (Whitaker 2003). Knowing when to smile can be very powerful and is part of effective non-verbal tactical communication.

Mee-sho
(Smile in Korean)

الإب تـسامة
(Smile in Arabic)

> **But be cautious when smiling:** "Most people cannot consciously do the eye movement that makes a smile look genuine. A fake smile can look fake, which will shatter your rapport or it can even look like a primate threat display" (Miller 2001).

> **A smile can demonstrate non-aggression, friendliness or, it can disguise true feelings, so don't force the smile … be natural.**

- The *Medium of the Face* came before words and we humans still send tremendously powerful messages (and receive those messages) with our facial expressions. Remember - Non-verbal cues are 55% effective in communication – the most effective way to communicate a message or feeling!

There are seven clear facial signals: anger, sadness, fear, surprise, disgust, contempt and happiness. Police officers have to master which facial signal is appropriate for attempting to communicate with someone who is experiencing emotional stress (Forman 2003). Research suggests these facial expressions may be universal so even when there is a language barrier, *there is not a facial and emotional barrier*. This works in the police officers' favor because nonverbal expressions may convey a positive or helpful message.

> **"Putting on a poker face is a way to avoid contact, preserve privacy and anonymity."** Many police officers also "put on the poker face" in the mistaken belief that it signals authority, but what this type of face signals is impersonality and insincerity. When you combine this poker face with a harsh tone of voice (and poor choice of commanding words) the intervening officer may actually escalate the negative emotions. It then takes a lot of work to defuse and bring people back to a position where you can have a conversation. It is easier to commence the contact with a smile and pleasant tone of voice; if this is not effective, you can change your facial expression and body language, along with your tone of voice and words used.

- ➢ **Tactical Communication Techniques; Defusing and calming the disputants**

  - • **On the initial contact, be aware of:**
    - ✓ **Body language;**
    - ✓ **Voice and words used**. *It's all in the voice...the officer's #1 tool! The way something is said (tone, inflection, rate of speech) can be five times more important than what is said.* Tone of voice, demeanour, and projected sincerity are more important than any single phrase that you may use (Vance 2006). Recognize Alpha vs. Beta commands;
    - ✓ **Give Reassurance;**
    - ✓ **Display Empathy;**
    - ✓ **Defuse** – as an example, you may use distraction techniques;
    - ✓ **If you "come on too strong," say you are sorry you yelled and ask "tell me what happened**?"
    - ✓ **Do not threaten** – this is a poor strategy;
    - ✓ **Don't forget the seven clear facial signals** (anger, sadness, fear, surprise, disgust, contempt and happiness).

  > *That all will have an opportunity to give their side, but only one person speaks at a time*

  - • **Defusing and calming the disputants:**
    - ✓ **Separate and *announce ground rules*** – a critical time at the beginning of the contact;
    - ✓ **Use of humor** - when appropriate, so be careful;
    - ✓ **Use others present to help** - but be careful whom you choose;
    - ✓ **Be prepared to ignore some statements** - remember your *Teflon Character* and *Emotional Intelligence*;
    - ✓ **Firm response when necessary** - but be seen as fair and impartial;
    - ✓ **Exclude outsiders** – they become distractions;
    - ✓ **If practical, make disputants comfortable** - when they are seated, they are most comfortable, etc.;
    - ✓ **Physical restraint** - if officer safety demands it.

- ➢ **Distractions can be identified as either Physical or Psychological and they have to be employed as part of an overall strategy to defuse and gain control. The officers need to decide which of these *Pattern Interrupts* are best for the situation.**

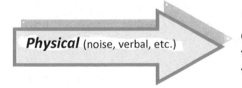

Physical (noise, verbal, etc.)

What can readily be seen or heard? Distractions that tend to divert briefly - such as a loud noise - or other type of defusing technique that breaks the momentum of anger and violence of the moment can be very effective.

For an example, as the responding officers enter a bar scene with people fighting, one of the officers blows a police whistle then announces in a loud voice "OK, everybody out of the pool." If successful, people will be stunned momentarily, maybe even laugh. "But it's at this moment when the officers have to quickly separate and continue to defuse. It only takes a split second to distract, and another split second to lose the distraction advantage" (Louie 2006). Or, flicking on and off lights, maybe even rapping a baton on the floor to get attention. Whatever the technique, timing is important immediately after attention has been momentarily diverted – this is where the skilled officer starts to defuse the situation by quickly separating disputants and gaining control through selected "conversation" (i.e., "you can help me...tell me what happened here") and prevent continuing violence or disruption (Louie 2006).

Once the disputants have been separated, it is very important to minimize other distractions occurring at the scene – such as patrons in a bar continuing to encourage the subjects to fight, or annoying bystanders, or, in the case of a domestic call, a loud TV or radio, barking dog, or crying children. All these ancillary distractions need to be dealt with if genuine communication between the disputants and the officers is to occur (Louie 2006).

> **This "lost keys" distraction technique:** While two people were arguing in their apartment front room (not violently, with no officer safety issues), they continue to ignore the two polite officers who have been called to their apartment regarding a family disturbance call. In a rehearsed role play, the officers try a new technique: One officer looks at the other, ignoring the disputants, and asks "Do you have the patrol car keys?" The partner responds, "No, I thought you had them!" The other officer, now raising his voice slightly, "It's your job to keep the keys; you are the rookie!" At this moment in time, the couple now stops arguing, staring almost incredulously at the two arguing officers. Once the officers see this break in the emotional momentum, they immediately separate the two, walking them to opposite corners of the living room, breaking eye contact between the disputants. The key is the distraction, followed by quickly separating the disputants, then initiating a conversation by stating : "I am Officer Smith … please tell me what happened here today?"

Psychological distractions probe more to surface emotions and inner feelings from within.   This may be in the form of a question that provokes the subject to think and   eventually touch on feelings.   The strategy is to provoke a response that hopefully will initiate a dialogue with the officers.

The key here is to skillfully surface an emotional response from the subject; something that's enough to influence them (Lewinski 2007).   For example, a domestic dispute situation at a residence where officers notice militaria items, sports trophies or a family portrait may provide the officers an opportunity to distract psychologically. Taking note of a football trophy, the officer says: "Hey, I see you played football …me too," or "Hey, isn't that a civil war sword on the wall…I am a civil war history buff" (of course with the latter, you take note of a potential weapon as well!).

The high risk/high gain with this technique is that, although the subject may seem to get even more emotional, may even cry, you have touched on some other emotion for the moment. Use this as a distraction strategy and quickly defuse this new emotion being expressed – hopefully this will open the door for dialogue (Louie 2006). By provoking acknowledgment of something that may be near-and-dear to the subject, you have steered the communication in another direction, away from the disturbance-provoking issue of the moment.

Once you have people talking is when you start to practice genuine "listening with understanding," taking mental notes of what is being said, processing this information, then feeding back into the conversation. Although perhaps the disputant is still emotional, at least you have him/her talking **with you** and **not at you.**

Taking the previous example of the military medals on the wall: "I can see you are a veteran and an honorable person. Let's talk about what happened here today and see what we can do to help. We can work this out..." The "we" comments are also helpful in establishing rapport and building trust.

Try to minimize **ordering** people to do an action or follow directions. Many times officers do not effectively diffuse those "self-agitating" and rather than apply tactical communication tactics, merely yell and command others to stop their aggressive or angry behavior thereby inadvertently escalating an already tense situation. "Good officers, by contrast, start reading the level of a subject's emotional intensity from the beginning of the encounter and are always looking for clues to psychological strategies that might help control the situation. For example, if you're dealing with a drunk who's starting to get worked up but is still at a relatively low level of agitation, you might tell him that you need to know all the addresses where he's lived for the last 5 years. This can be a challenging intellectual task for someone in an altered state, and may fully consume his diminished mental capacity" (Lewinski 2007, 3).

"On the other hand, subjects displaying a high emotional intensity – a couple bent on tearing each other apart in a domestic dispute, for instance – 'may require a distraction that's much more visceral. You might say, 'just a minute. I know you have children. Before we get into your situation, can you tell me if your kids are safe and where they are?' This distraction is likely to be important to them and offers an opportunity to calm them a bit while they respond" (Lewinski 2007, 3). As the subjects are responding to the officers' diffusing tactics is the time the officers need to be ready to not only continually defuse, but also to move the discussion towards an analysis of how each side sees the argument. "Remember, distractions don't always work and officers need to be able to quickly move away from one topic – if it appears to be too emotional or agitating – to do something else that may still distract, if even for a moment" (Louie 2006).

Timing is everything in challenging situations such as these. Officers need to be always thinking of where they are going next in the conversation and what the risks and gains are. Their primary objective is to distract and defuse so that the people involved can at least have a conversation - albeit lively and probably emotionally charged. None the less, at least there is a dialogue starting to develop, which may lead to building temporary rapport and trust with the officers (Louie 2006).

> **Pattern interrupts**: Distraction techniques are sometimes called 'pattern interrupts,' and their effectiveness in circumventing undesirable subject behavior is well researched (Butler 2007, 3). "Police communications must be designed around the psychology of persuasion. Powerful verbal and non-verbal communication can work to modify a subject's behavior in such subtle ways that they are not detectable by the individual being influenced. However, officers who are not properly trained in these strategies may unwittingly use words and body language that undermine their attempt to positively influence behavior" (Butler 2007, 3).

- **Have You Tried These Distractions? Some tips from officers in the field.** (Force Science News #81, 2007; Louie 2006)

    ✓ **Sometimes humor;** but be careful because humor can be high risk/high gain. One officer would ask those clearly inebriated (and not violent) to name the 7 dwarfs. In the process of recalling, all present would start to laugh and once attention redirected and the subject defused, the officers would try to communicate (Force Science News #81, 2007).

       Actually, genuine humor that elicits laughter "… releases neurochemicals that promote relaxation" (Collins 2011, 77).   And the use of humor, under tense circumstances, can "lighten the mood" and even surface the absurdity of stressful situations, but needs to be judiciously applied and one must remain keen to recognize if humor is not working.

    ✓ When approaching a subject that may have been drinking, or is appearing to be upset, rather than start directly with questioning, ask if the subject has seen something, such as a speeding car, or perhaps a small child walking in the area. As the subject is attempting to recall – and be distracted – feign hearing from the radio that the car or child has been located, then start your investigative conversation, again in a conversational and not accusatory tone. (Force Science News #81, 2007).

    ✓ Feign being casual and nonchalant; if not a compromise to officer safety, walk up to the subject and maybe offer the person a candy bar or even a cigarette. For someone who can be seen sitting on a curb, grab a bottle of water and offer to the person as you casually ask him if he has seen anything unusual. If not a compromise to officer safety, sit on the curb with the person as you engage in conversation (Louie 2006).

> **The dropped change technique:** While two people are arguing, ignoring the officers who are attempting to intercede, a preplanned distraction is used. One officer pulls out a handful of coins, then drops the change onto the floor, causing the disputants to momentarily stop arguing and look down at the change (*people will always look down at the coins!*).   At that strategic moment, the officer quickly introduces himself, then asks one of the disputants to walk to the opposite side of the room while the officer's partner remains with the other disputant and asks what happened, making sure to position the disputants so that eye contact is broken.

➤ Contact Phase; Deflecting rage and creating a void where it's aimed
(McRedmond 2007)

Use the common judo principle of *pull when pushed*, such as an obviously drunk person *squaring off* against the officer. Rather than accommodate by being aggressive (and raising the voice to command), ask a silly or humorous question…"did ya hear the one about an old lady they called Gummy Bear because she has no teeth," or something else humorous – but not insulting to the person   (McRedmond 2007).

Officers are trained to quickly control situations and when someone assumes a fighting stance, most officers oblige by preparing for defensive tactics. But, if not a compromise to officer safety, and if time is on your side...then use time to your advantage! Don't be in a rush to take the person into custody if you don't have to! Stand back, show your hands in an open gesture, lower your voice (Louie 2006).

Throw the person off balance psychologically by asking if they needed anything or if there is anything you can do for them. Don't forget, the subject is preparing to fight you and you are diverting and defusing by *not going to blows*. Since the person is obviously drunk, then he/she is most likely dehydrated, so offer a bottle of water – that should really throw the person off mental balance since the person is expecting to fight (Louie 2006). People who have had previous contacts with the police are not expecting this type of compassionate or caring attention.

Many times people are in a panic when confronted by police, so if you are shouting commands at them – say from a distance – they may not be paying attention to you; they may be fumbling around for their driver's license, or trying to hide contraband. If you are not going to approach any closer, why keep on shouting? Take a few moments to see if they are going to refocus on you – you cannot control what's going on inside the vehicle anyway – at least, not yet. Think: is time on your side? If not a compromise to officer safety, take the time to see if waiting for them to acknowledge you will work. If you are covered and concealed – such as behind your squad car door - all the better. If people are not complying, it's not necessarily because they are belligerent, it's most likely because they are in a panic (Louie 2006).

> **Distraction tips from a former mental health worker:** Distractions can be a quick ice breaker when attempting to defuse an emotionally distraught person. One former mental health worker, now working as a police officer, reported that: "I used such simple things as 'I really like that pair of boots you have there' and 'it sure is hot here today. Let's move over to the shade and talk.' These worked very well in conveying that I was interested in the person I was dealing with and his immediate well being. There were times when this approach did not work, and I just responded in a quiet and respectful voice, addressing the person as Sir or Miss" (Schumpert 2007, 3).

➢ Contact Phase - Tactical Communication Techniques; Which Command Voice and Style to Use: Alpha or Beta?

> **Current research is suggesting that officers who shout more vague commands to offenders may not be as effective as those officers who are more precise and measured with their commands.** "The quality of commands officers issue tends to deteriorate drastically in potentially life-threatening confrontations, possibly leaving suspects confused about what they're expected to do to comply" (Houlihan 2006,1).

Alpha Commands α "In nonviolent situations ... officers overwhelmingly issued so-called 'Alpha' commands. **Alpha Commands... are simple, direct and explicit**, so that even someone in a chemically or emotionally induced fog is likely to understand. Examples are: 'Take your hands out of your pocket,' 'stop talking,' 'Quit resisting,' and "don't leave your vehicle'" (Force Science News #43, 2006, 2).

Research indicates that in nonviolent encounters, "84 percent of the commands given were alpha commands. But in violent situations, only 16 percent were alpha," suggesting that many times the responding officers resorted to the less effective and more imprecise beta commands (Houlihan 2006). Further, officers not only changed their tone and volume, but also changed the "emotional context" of the words they used: "Instead of non-inflammatory, specific commands there was a more intense emotional tone, much more swearing. The 'f' word was flying all over the place" (Houlihan 2006).

For some reason, many officers would resort to a "Dirty Harry" style of communication; sarcastic and abrupt, laced with vulgarities and Hollywood phrases such as: "bite the curb, barf bag," "make my day, punk," "don't continue to be an idiot or you die," etc. It's as if the officers were on camera for a cop reality show - and many of these same types of phrases can be seen in daily TV reruns (Louie 2007c).

Beta Commands β **These commands are more vague:** "'Don't make me shoot you'. An officer uttering that kind of order...may really be stating what he doesn't want to do or what he doesn't want to happen, having gotten sidetracked from expressing exactly what is needed for the subject to comply" (Houlihan 2007, 3).

Theatrics aside, these Beta Commands can become potentially deadly barriers to communicating with someone who is already under extreme stress – irrespective if under the influence or not. "The closer a given situation came to the flash point of violence, the more frequent both beta commands and profanity became" (Houlihan 2007).

Dr. Bill Lewinski of the Force Science Research Center, Minnesota State University-Mankato, suggests this transition from the more communicative Alpha to the more barrier-producing Beta may be a reaction to the officer feeling less in control of the situation. And as those officers become more "beta-vague" they also tend to shout and yell, further exacerbating the situation, not to mention confusing and at the same time angering the person. A better command would be to utter in a clear tone and precise word of direction: "put down the knife," "stop walking," (but don't follow with "don't make me shoot you," or "keep it up and you will get hurt," etc.)

> "When you're dealing with subjects who may be mentally impaired or under the influence of drugs or alcohol or even just emotionally keyed up, ambiguous commands throw all kinds of possible confusion into the situation" (Houlihan 2006, 2).

Research on "beta" and "alpha" commands needs to continue, however it is clear that the more times officers resort to an aggressive tone of voice, plus vulgar choice of words, the more others (including the officers' partners) will become angry and uncooperative. And the more vague the command, the greater the burden on the person you are trying to control to interpret what you mean.

Although it may seem obvious to the officer shouting "don't make me kill you" implies that the suspect is expected to either drop a weapon or stop, *it is still a vague command and not specific enough* for someone who may be mentally ill or emotionally upset.

> ## Distraction Supplies – never leave the briefing room without them! (Louie 2006):

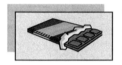

Water/Juice: Many times, those drinking alcohol, taking drugs, or even mentally ill or emotionally distraught, are dehydrated. So, bring a couple of water bottles with you in the patrol car. Offering the water not only distracts, but starts to build trust and demonstrates caring – and, is usually much unexpected for a police officer (which are what distractions are supposed to be).

Cigarettes: Not a value statement about smoking, just good business. Bring regular and menthol. If it does not compromise officer safety, offer one – not to "calm" but to distract and demonstrate caring. This also is unexpected and may have a dramatic effect on the person you are trying to calm and communicate with. Oh yes, don't forget the matches!

Wrapped food/fruit juice: Such as candy bars and fruit juice (for the diabetic or just plain hungry or thirsty) or energy bars: Again, the action is unexpected and a great distraction technique. Offer it to the subject – the very act of unwrapping distracts and is an opportune time for the officer to start a dialogue.

Small stuffed animals: Keep these in the trunk and once officer safety has been assessed, give them to young children related to the 911 call. Ask the parent(s) first and if OK, give to the kids. Nothing warms a parent's heart more than to see their child comforted –and it doesn't hurt for the officer to be seen as human and caring.

As with all of these distraction tools and *tricks-of-the-trade*, make sure you keep timing on your side: As they are drinking, or lighting up the cigarette, or unwrapping the energy bar, they are engaged in your dialogue.   The subject may still be agitated, but at least you now have the person "refocused," albeit momentarily, and you need to be skillful about timing.

3. Interview

Once order has been established through defusing (and remember, you may need to defuse throughout the contact) you move to the Interview Phase.
It is during this phase that you initially establish the basic ground rule, and that is only one person speaks at a time. As one disputant is reciting his or her version of what happened, the other may interrupt. That is when the second officer needs to use perhaps body language (a quick nod of the head) or *soft words* ("OK, you will have a chance to talk but let's first hear what is being said").

➤ **Tactical Communication; Establish the ground rules:**

- Let disputants know each will have a chance to talk but only one may speak at a time;
- Let them know what will happen next – explain the process. Don't forget, when people are arguing and being separated, they need to be told they will have an opportunity to tell their side of the story. **Many times police fail to announce these ground rules, causing angst and frustration among the disputants.** They may even need to be constantly reminded they will have their opportunity as the other side is reciting their version of what happened;
- Bring disputants together;
- Allow for ventilation (but control; defuse and paraphrase if they continue to repeat issues);
- Allow for feedback (it should be specific, not general);
- Be prepared to constantly calm and diffuse disputants;
- Remember, reduce their anxiety about the situation as much as possible (it is not knowing what to do next or how to resolve that keeps disputants stressed).

➤ **Tactical Communication; Skills in directing** (Schwartz 1977):

- Help the disputants face the crisis;
- Assist those involved to face the crisis in manageable doses;
- Assist fact finding;
- Avoid false reassurance;
- Discourage blaming of others;
- Encourage the individuals to accept help;
- Assist with everyday tasks if they needed.

Chapter 3

➤ **Tactical Communication; Use empathy** (Parker and Meier 1975; Louie 1981; 2006):

- Show understanding;
- Do not patronize;
- Use statements plus body language to communicate concern;
- It is all about how you treat people and how they feel you are treating them.

➤ **Interview Phase; how do police normally gain information?** (Louie & Vance 2007)
Police usually use an *official voice* in the mistaken belief that it demonstrates authority, but it is usually interpreted as impersonal and offensive. And if the official voice comes out of a *poker face*, it will be more difficult for the officer to establish rapport. Questions are usually in the form of police-trained formal interviewing and *interrogation style*. Accusations and confrontational tone are usually employed. Police need to eliminate the "Investigatory" style of communication when they are interviewing people who are experiencing stress and emotional trauma.

Physical presence plus using an official voice many times becomes a barrier to effective communication. How police are traditionally trained to gather information – the interrogation mode – is not always the most effective means to communicate with someone who is upset.

- ➢ **Characteristics of traditional law enforcement questioning** (Louie and Vance 2007):
  - **Rapid fact finding:** Usually too quick and impersonal for people in crisis to effectively comprehend.
  - **Quick problem solving:** Police tend to *jump to a solution* or a quick way to end the 911 call.
  - **Intrusive:** Police seem to forget they are foisting themselves into the middle of an argument or incident, not recognizing how disruptive they may be seen by others.
  - **Focus on the questioner's agenda:** *Just the facts* – which is related to the quick problem solving mode of the street cop who is looking for an expedient justification to end the contact (but not necessarily resolving the issue(s) that provoked the 911 call).
  - **Seeking to control more than actually *listening*:** Again related to the *police norm* of controlling vs. communicating.

- ➢ **Phrases that damage rapport** (Louie and Vance 2007):
  - **"Calm Down":** This may be perceived as an order which may provoke intense anger. Don't tell people "to calm down"; they realize they are upset, and most likely are not ready to calm down! Work on defusing at this point without giving impotent and inciting orders.

  - **"Hey, I told you to shut up!"** The latter is heard daily on *COP reality shows*. When an officer says this, he or she merely makes the situation worse by creating even greater tension (and remember, the officers are supposed to reduce the tension by appropriately defusing!).

  - **"I am not going to tell you again."** Aside from the threatening tone, this phrase may cause the disputants to actually provoke the officer to either "tell them again," or to do something even more drastic, such as retaliate against the disputants. Many times disputants encourage the officers to act this way because it exposes the officers to criticism and demonstrates their inability to control a situation. In essence, this may be a way for those being controlled to attempt to control the situation through the proxy of the officer's negative response to being challenged. Those officers with poor Emotional Intelligence fall easy prey to this intellectual mind game.

  - **"I understand."** This is often the phrase that officers use to interrupt people in order to jump into problem solving. This is well intentioned, but could be counterproductive. You may in fact understand, however, understanding must be demonstrated by the speaker to maintain rapport. Better to say: "I hear what you are saying." It is not fatal to say "I understand," however, if the phrase is used, the speaker needs to be demonstrating both verbal and non-verbal cues that he/she is truly understanding, otherwise, the statement will be interpreted as patronizing and insincere.

  - **"Why?"** This may be interpreted as accusatory and may create defensiveness. Rather than ask a direct question, pose this as an interview response. For example, rather than ask someone why they did something…seeking a motive that may also be inciting or provoking, ask this type of question: "So, tell me what happened after that?" As the person is responding, ask further

questions, in a conversational and non-accusatory tone, such as: "So as I hear what you are telling me, you did this...because you felt..." This latter question not only answers the "why" but also seeks to clarify a feeling and is a perception checking strategy to avoid the "why did you do that" tone.

- **"You Should"** or **"You Shouldn't!"** A judgmental (advice giving) statement. Implies a superiority of the advice giver and may cause the receiver to feel inadequate or at the least, on the defensive.

➢ **Better phrases to use**:
  - **Use of "I" messages to confront.** "I feel... when you... because..." Use this phrase to confront the subject about behavior that is counterproductive, without being accusatory. "I feel frustrated when you yell at me because it stops me from listening to you." "I can see this is upsetting...what can I do to help?"

  - **No Zingers** - watch the impulse to be sarcastic or abrupt! *Maintain your Emotional Intelligence!* If you really want to say something, and you can just taste how good those words will feel ... they're probably wrong, so don't say them!

  - **We/Let's** – keep the "we" and "let's" in the conversation. The more the officers can include themselves as a partner with the speaker, such as "let's do this," or "we need to help," or "what can we do," the more the disputants may see the officers as actually trying to help. This implies "we are here to help," or "I am here as long as you need me."

➢ **Tactical Communication - Gather relevant information** (Goldstein, et al., 1977):
  - **Explain what you want**: This is part of establishing ground rules for the conversation;
  - **Ask what happened:** Do not be accusatory; watch your demeanour and/or body language/tone of voice;
  - **Practice interview and active listening skills, in a conversational tone;**
  - **Ask open ended questions**: Try to avoid close-ended questions; remember, you want them to talk about the dispute/issue/problem;
  - **Listening responses:** Show that you are actively listening;
  - **Perception Check:** Ask them to repeat and confirm what they feel; also demonstrates you are listening;
  - **Confirming what you interpret the person may feel:**
    - ✓ "It sounds like you are angry that..."
    - ✓ "Am I hearing that you are angry?" "Does this make you sad?"

> Police tend to ask too many closed-ended questions, requiring only a yes or no response. Ask open-ended questions to encourage dialogue and don't talk too much! Don't forget the *20/80 Rule* when seeking to get people to open up and talk.

- ➤ **Mirroring / Reflecting** (Louie and Vance 2007).
  - **Brief follow-alongs (also known as "echoing"):** Repeating the last few words. This is a good initial technique – it helps the officer get oriented to the subject and appears more conversational than investigative:
    - ✓ **Subject:** "She doesn't pay attention to what I say to her and it makes me angry."
    - ✓ **Officer responds:** "It makes you angry...?" Here the officer is using what are known as *brief follow alongs*: Voice inflection at the end of statement (upward or downward) can be used to either demonstrate understanding, or encourage them to go on. This is subtle but very important and signals you are listening without having to appear as "interrogating."

- ➤ **Summarize frequently - periodically covering main points.**
  - Summarize by combining what you are told with the feelings and emotions interpreted and observed by you: "OK, what you've told me so far is this...and as a result, you feel... and seems like ... do I understand correctly?

> **Summary Statement: Statements made, feelings and emotions, and interpretations by the officer.**

- ➤ **Active listening skills.**

  - Active listening, *with a conversational tone*, helps to establish rapport and empathy, all the components of effective communication. Once a give-and-take dialogue has been established, though it may take many hours, negotiation for peaceful resolution can begin.

  - Active listening is "...a way of paying attention to what the other person doesn't say, not just what is said. It's a way of listening in which you do not let yourself get tangled up in your own emotions" (McHattie 2010, 1).

  - Active listening skills are specific communication techniques designed to demonstrate understanding, encourage the subject to talk, verbally vent emotions, and build rapport between the individual and the officer. A variety of different active listening skills exists, all of which involve reflecting back to the subject the facts or content of what the person is saying and the emotions surrounding the content (Regini 2004, 4).

 What active listening is not:
(Louie 2008;105)

It is important to recognize from perspective of the person experiencing the crisis. You cannot be effective if you don't understand and acknowledge this.

  - ✓ **Not giving advice**, judgment or persuasion;
  - ✓ **Not offering your ideas** or what you have done in a similar situation;
  - ✓ **Not an opportunity to inject your values**;
  - ✓ **Not asking "why?"** because "directly asking a question beginning with the word why can make the person you're talking with (be) defensive. When a person is already angry adding defensiveness to the conversation will only slow down the progress you are trying to make" (McHattie 2010, 1);
  - ✓ **No discussion of topics not expressed by the subject**;
  - ✓ **Statements and opinions from people are what count.**

What is important are the subject's feelings, values, and what he or she is saying.

Tone and sincerity of voice can be critical to establishing rapport with a person experiencing emotional upset. When attempting to establish rapport, recall that there is a *continuum* of how sincere a person is interpreted and received. And remember that "words are usually 7% effective in communication, tone of voice is usually 38% effective, and non-verbal cues are usually 55% effective" (Mehrabian 1971).

> **Common Barriers to Effective Listening** (Mayer 1990, in Zinkin 2000, 10):
> When an officer is able to engage disputants in a conversation is also the point in time when active and effective listening discipline needs to occur. Any one of the following will negatively impact that effectiveness:

- ✓ Discounting the entire message if you find even one flaw;
- ✓ Deciding from the sender's appearance and/or delivery style whether or not the message is worthwhile;
- ✓ Allowing your own biases on the subject to interfere with hearing the message;
- ✓ Listening selectively for what you want to hear or believe the other person will say;
- ✓ Responding before hearing the other's viewpoint;
- ✓ Allowing the status of the person to color the content of what your hear;
- ✓ Mentally rehearsing your response rather than paying full attention to what the sender is saying;
- ✓ Listening for agreement rather than understanding;
- ✓ Allowing your mind to wander;
- ✓ Having to be right, to win, or to have the last word;
- ✓ Filtering the other's message through your own judgments, *shoulds* and *shouldn'ts*;
- ✓ Being out of touch with your own feelings (so that you are unaware of the messages behind them);
- ✓ Failing to use your eyes, as well as your ears, effectively;
- ✓ Getting a button pushed and seeking revenge or turning off;
- ✓ Not exercising sufficient empathy for the other person;
- ✓ Rejecting the other in any way;
- ✓ Responding in an unbalanced manner by suppressing or discounting your gut responses and intuition in favor of a demand for *logic* or *rationality*.

> **Tactical Communication: Steps in Active Listening** (Zinkin 2000, 11).

- • **Give the speaker a verbal door-opening**, showing your readiness to listen ("you sound down today"). Stay with the content of the communication first, then listen for and identify the basic general feeling – anger, fear, joy, etc.
- • **Feed that general feeling back to the speaker.** "Am I hearing that you are angry?" (known as Perception Checking – checking out how you think the person "feels").
- • **If and when you identify a more specific feeling, feed that back to the speaker**, both to clarify and to show your acceptance of it. "This is what I am hearing..." (known as "Paraphrasing" – checking out what you think you have heard)
- • **Stay an inch ahead of the speaker, not a mile.** Don't jump to conclusions and solutions – you won't be listening, or you'll be thinking about a response. There is a "...tendency to start preparing a response before the other person has finished speaking. We want to jump ahead to the important things that we have to say" (Miller 2011, 1).
- • **Remember that you are a facilitator**, and an enabler – not an oracle to provide the answers.

- **Also, recognize your emotional intelligence;** how are you able to handle the emotions of others as well as your own (Saville 2006).

➢ Instrumental and Expressive behavior

In 1997 FBI agent Gary Noesner and RCMP officer Dr. Mike Webster researched how active listening skills were fundamental to critical incident negotiations, such as hostage and barricaded subject calls. Their research continues to be valid today as public safety agencies throughout the nation reassess how they train their officers to tactically communicate with the emotionally distraught, the mentally ill, as well as barricaded subjects and those holding hostages.

Although intended for the intensely trained police hostage negotiator, these skills are just as fundamental to the more common 911 police call when dealing with those who are emotionally distraught and experiencing non-life threatening crises in their lives. What this means is that all first responding police officers should be trained in these communication fundamentals.

Usually the media covers the more notorious hostage or barricaded call where the suspect is demanding specifics, such as money and an escape route. The more common type of police call deals with people who are "motivated primarily by emotional needs and exhibit expressive behaviors such as outrage, passion, despair, anger or other emotionally laden type of behavior" (Noesner and Webster 1997, 1).

These types of critical incidents break down even further, distinguishing hostage from non-hostage or barricaded subject types of calls. "Hostage incidents involve a subject who has taken hostages and has a substantive demand, something that the individual cannot attain without extorting authorities through the act of hostage-taking. In non-hostage incidents, on the other hand, the subject does not have any demands, or the demands are non-substantive" (Regini 2004, 2).

With the non-hostage type of call, the subject may demand that the police leave. Usually in this type of call, no one has been injured, although there may have some type of violent demonstration such as a shot fired from the residence or vocal threat over the phone or face-to-face threat to a neighbor. This non hostage call may also be the prelude to a suicide attempt or more provocative "suicide-by-cop" incident.

> **Demanding specifics, such as money or concessions from the police negotiator is known as Instrumental Behavior, whereas the more emotional response is known as Expressive Behavior (Noesner and Webster 1997, 1). And it is with the more common *Expressive Behavior* type of call that the responding officer needs to practice active listening skills.**

In this scenario (such as someone who is barricaded inside his home after learning that his wife has left him...and he just got fired from his job) the subject may be shouting demands (such as "bring my wife here") but is in reality ventilating and expressing himself through more or less self-destructive behavior. This person has "lost equilibrium" of life, may have lost his or her usual support system (known as the sphere of influence: loved ones, family and friends) and may now express despair, anger and fear.

> **These types of people are angry, appear irrational, and usually have difficulty articulating their true needs because of their emotional state of mind.**

It is at this point that the best strategy is to practice active listening, in the hopes of developing some type of rapport that may eventually lead to a true give-and-take conversation (as opposed to the traditional police mode of ordering and demanding). It is important for the first officer on the scene who makes contact with the subjects to understand that he/she need to *switch* from a normal, police verbal demeanor of asserting control through *commanding and demanding* to the more *conversational tone* of someone attempting to establish a dialogue. **Both first responding officers and specially trained police negotiators need to be able to use their *communicative voice* and muster all their active listening skills so as not to be interpreted as officious and disconnected** (Louie 2008).

The officer (again, this may be the first responding officer to make contact or a specially trained crisis intervention negotiator) needs to recognize that the subject is in a heightened, emotional state – with behaviors very visible such as shouting or intense, threatening body language. Not as visible in the situation is an individual who has an impacted self-esteem which may motivate him/her to act even more recklessly. During this time of confusion and imbalance, the officer needs to concentrate on how to communicate, not as a friend, but rather as someone who is listening (that's the key). **By listening during this time of crisis, the officer becomes, however briefly, someone of support … support that the subject does not have for the moment.** And by being supportive (as an active listener, then as a give-and-take conversationalist), the officer may be able to reestablish some of the balance that the subject needs to be able to start making rational decisions.

➤ **Active listening techniques that encourage communication**

There are a few established techniques as core elements to active listening skill building (Noesner and Webster 1997, Regini 2004 and Louie 2008). These active listening techniques are just as fundamental in a non-threatening 911 call (such as a neighborhood dispute) as they are in the hours-long hostage or barricaded subject call. It is imperative to practice these skills at all first responder levels.

- **Minimal encouragers:**

  "OK" One effective method of signaling that you are listening to someone is by the use of verbal and non-verbal minimal encouragers. Verbal minimal encouragers may be a simple "uh huh" or "OK" or "I see" "go on," etc. This is truly "acknowledging without interrupting" but one needs to be cautious "…because many of us have practiced this as a skill to not listen without insulting someone we care about. It can trigger the same non-listening mode" (Miller 2011).

  Although police hostage negotiators are rarely face-to-face, first responding police officers are. The non- verbal minimal encouragement to motivate someone to continue to talk may be a simple and silent nod of the head, or raising the eyebrows with the head ever so slightly tilted upwards and the eyes focused on the subject (but not staring). "These responses will encourage the subject to continue talking and gradually relinquish more control of the situation to the negotiator" (Noesner and Webster 1997, 4)

> Minimal encouragers are brief responses (or sounds) that indicate you are present and listening. Minimal encouragers are best used when the person is talking for an extended period of time: *"Uh-huh…really….yeah…OK, etc."*

People want to know you are there and listening to them. If you are asked if you are still listening, the speaker may perceive that you are patronizing and not listening (Louie 2008, 104). Use silence wisely since it may invite an opportunity for our minds to wander or be distracted. This is also what the subject is used to hearing when the listener is simply waiting for a chance to speak.

Minimal encouragers are also effective in combination with other communication techniques such as paraphrasing (repeating what has been said), or mirroring and reflecting (using key statements to motivate the speaker to acknowledge what has been said and to continue to encourage the conversation). This indicates that you are listening and at the same time, provokes more conversation with the speaker (Louie 2008, 104).

Minimal encouragers are best used when the person is talking for an extended period of time. People want to know you are there and listening to them. Too much silence from you will cause the speaker to break concentration and ask if you are still listening. And if you are asked this, the speaker may perceive you are patronizing, not listening.

- **Paraphrasing:**
  Paraphrasing is merely repeating, in your own words, what you believe to be the meaning and intent of what the subject has stated. *This is not verbatim repeating as much as restating the general theme.*

  This is effective whether the subject agrees or not. If you paraphrase a statement that the subject disagrees with and corrects you, well, you now know what the subject intended to say. If you paraphrase a statement and the subject agrees with your interpretation, you now know you are on track. Either way, you not only have a clearer understanding of your interpretation of the subject's message, but also you have demonstrated you are listening which will help build empathy and trust.

  You may say something like: "So as I understand it, your wife left you today and you were also fired from your job." The subject may respond: "Ya, that's what happened and now you can see why my life is over now." Or, the subject may respond: "Ya, my wife left me but I wasn't fired…I am not a loser…I was laid off because of the economy and it wasn't my fault." Again, either way you have demonstrated that you are trying to truly listen.

  - ✓ **Paraphrasing:** Repeat what they said or meant; this is used to clarify and also to demonstrate you are listening. Put the meaning in your own words – Summarizing: "…restatement…giving the meaning in another form." (Webster's Collegiate Dictionary). Used for brief confirmations of meaning and to display attentiveness/active listening (Louie and Vance 2007):

    - ❑ **Subject:** "She is always talking and doesn't pay attention to what I say."
    - ❑ **Officer:** "She doesn't listen to you?"

Cmdr. Joel Wilson

- **Emotion labeling and perception checking:**

  Emotion labeling (also known as perception checking) goes beyond understanding what was said to the deeper understanding of what was felt.
  "Emotion labeling allows negotiators (referring to those intervening in a crisis) to attach a tentative label to the feelings expressed or implied by the subject's words and actions. Such labeling shows that negotiators are paying attention to the emotional aspects of what the subject is conveying. When used effectively, emotion labeling becomes one of the most powerful skills available to negotiators because it helps them identify the issues and feelings that drive the subject's behavior" (Noesner and Webster 1997, 4).

I was really excited...

A person intervening in a crisis and attempting to diffuse it may say: "You sound as if you are angry that your wife left you and you are now lonely." The subject may respond: "Well, wouldn't you be angry if that happened to you!" Or, the subject may say: "It's not the anger as much as being betrayed by my wife and best friend that I am feeling distraught. There just isn't anything left for me...we were together for 20 years."

In this latter response, the crisis intervener now learns this may be a love triangle, provoking a possible sense of revenge or need to punish. The active listening has developed into a conversation that is now getting closer to a "give-and-take" conversational mode, which is where the negotiator wants to go. **It is very important to understand that emotions don't die and they must be acknowledged through emotion labeling and perception checking.**

Almost everyone has encountered depression, anger, and frustration in their lives. Emotional labeling and perception checking essentially attempts to confirm what the subject is feeling and demonstrates that you are listening as well. *Emotions are the great human common denominator; people can identify with those of another person without having had the same experiences.*

"One of the first principles in crisis intervention is to listen for the emotions exhibited by the subject and how they relate to the facts of the situation"
(Regini 2004, 4)

- **Establishing empathy:**
  By demonstrating that you are listening and acknowledging the subject's emotions, you initiate the essential steps in establishing empathy. "Empathy involves demonstrating the act of listening to the subject and acknowledging the individual's situation and the emotional reaction to it with the purpose of establishing a basic trust relationship. This trust is necessary to achieve a behavioral change in the subject. No peaceful resolution can occur without some degree of trust between the individual and the negotiator" (Regini 2004,3).

Empathy is not pity; feeling sorry for the person – or being perceived as such - does not promote a true communication link with the subject. Empathy is understanding the content and emotions that the individual is communicating, and then reflecting it back to demonstrate you are listening and that you understand what the subject is saying. Simply stating "I understand what you're saying" is not an empathic communication approach and may be perceived as patronizing. "The demonstration of empathy most effectively is accomplished through the use of active listening skills" (Regini 2004, 4).

Another aspect of empathy involves listening for the subject's values or what he/she feels is important. Officers then can demonstrate that they have heard and understood this critical information. These actions denote a significant step in rapport development because this often requires an officer to read between the lines (also known as listening with the third ear) of what the individual states. For example, if a subject becomes violently angry over his wife leaving him for another man and, subsequently, takes her hostage to prevent her from moving out of their house, a hostage negotiator could say to the subject, "It sounds like your relationship with your wife is very important to you." Though the statement sounds trite, it will establish that you are listening without passing judgment or agreeing with the subject.

Values are typically associated with another person or allegiance to a concept. Values also can be the source for potential theme development, or "hooks." For instance, a subject who identifies himself as having old-fashioned values may have a potential hook in his allegiance to his family or certain relatives (Regini 2004;4).

Rapid establishment of rapport through a demonstration of empathy combined with a nonjudgmental approach indicates negotiation progress in an emotionally charged hostage-barricade situation. A nonjudgmental approach requires conveying acceptance and neutrality. The officer must ensure that personal opinions and values are not apparent or stated.

> *Crisis interveners do not have to agree with the subject's actions; they simply can validate his or her emotions as understandable and treat him or her with respect and dignity.*

- **Mirroring:**

Mirroring is another demonstration of active listening that not only shows you are listening, but may also encourage the subject to continue talking without having to sound like you are interrogating.

For an example, a subject may say: "I just can't live with it anymore" and the officer responds with an *echoing* "live with it anymore?" The response tone rises up with "anymore" giving emphasis to the word which usually provokes a response such as "well, ya know, it's happened to me so much...being fired ... that I am just a loser who is tired of sponging off my mom and dad...and they see me as a loser also." The simple mirror of a few words (or "echo" of a word or two) provoked a deeper response from the subject, providing valuable information and an indication now of some of the low self-esteem roots.

"Mirroring can be especially helpful in the early stages of a crisis, as negotiators attempt to establish a non-confrontational presence, gain initial intelligence, and begin to build rapport. This technique allows negotiators to follow verbally wherever the subject leads the conversation. Consequently, negotiators learn valuable information about the circumstances surrounding the incident, while they provide the subject an opportunity to vent" (Noesner and Webster 1997; 4).

The officer is "directing" the conversation but in such a subtle way that the subject does not realize he or she is providing necessary information. This type of directing requires an officer's finesse because the officer does not want to be portrayed as manipulative or patronizing.

 Nurses practicing mirroring techniques to help calm patients: Since breathing techniques can reduce the effects of stress, Nurses are trained to practice slow and deep breaths to help "stabilize" the nurse/patient environment. " Another breathing technique is for the nurse to mirror the patient's respirations and then slow down gradually. The patient's breathing will slow down, as well, and when the breathing slows, the patient is calmer" (Collins 2011, 77).

➢ Asking open-ended questions to encourage a dialogue

It is very important not to ask questions requiring a simple yes or no (closed-ended), because if you do, the subject may very well only answer "yes," or "no." People experiencing emotional trauma may simply not want to talk. Questions that require more than a yes or a no are better to use such as: "What...?" "How...?" "When..." "What happened here today?" "How would you like this to work out...?" "When would you ......" The benefit of open-ended questions is that it conveys an interest in gaining understanding as well as encourages people to talk.

Open-ended questions are designed to seek elaboration. Open-ended questions give freedom of response while framing the parameters of what the officer is seeking, and limits the feeling of interrogation. The more a person elaborates, the more you are able to generate a conversation (which is where the negotiator initially wants to go). "Effective negotiations focus on learning what the subject thinks and feels. If negotiators do most of the talking, they decrease the opportunities to learn about the subject" (Noesner and Webster 1997, 5).

A simple "tell me what happened here today," or, "tell me what I can do to help you" can start the conversation rolling. Skillful negotiators don't have the gift of gab; they are very strategic in which words to use and when to use them. And they are very strategic in how much not to say!

- **"I" and "We" messages** *(i + i = We)*
"I" messages are a means for a negotiator to express how he or she feels and still continue the give-and-take of a conversation. The negotiator may say: "when you yell, I cannot hear you. I don't want to make you angry but you have to know that I can't help you if I can't understand what you want to tell me."

  This type of conversation may take some time to develop because "I" messages can signal an argument or disagreement with the subject. The negotiator needs to make sure that the "I" messages are more in the realm of stating the feelings of the negotiator without being too judgmental (don't forget, the subject most likely has been judged by many and most likely is sick and tired of hearing it!).

  "While employing this skill--and all active listening techniques--negotiators must avoid being pulled into an argument or trading personal attacks with a subject. An argumentative, sarcastic, or hostile tone could reinforce the subject's already negative view of law enforcement and cause the subject to rationalize increased resistance due to a lack of perceived concern on the part of the police. Use of 'I' messages serves to personalize the negotiator. This helps to move the negotiator beyond the role of a police officer trying to manipulate the subject into surrendering" (Noesner and Webster 1997, 5).

  In conjunction with the "I" messages, it is important for the negotiator to frequently use *we messages* as well. Statements such as "let's see what we can do," or "we can work through this together; I am here with you as long as you need me" frame the situation now as one with the subject and negotiator working together. These "we" statements can be both subtle and powerful; but they have to be reinforced as the conversation continues. In a very subtle way, the "we" messages provides a balance against the feeling of isolation.

> *Trained Hostage Negotiators are very adept at "I" and "we" messages and are very strategic about when to use them.*

➢ Effective pauses and silence

Pausing and using silence are **strategic moments in time** during the communication. The use of a pause may give the subject time to reflect on what was just said, or, may also give both sides time to breathe and get some oxygen in their respective brains.

One way to use a pause and silence may be the not so obvious technique of saying "wow, I am tired also, let's take a breath and let me drink some of my water." After stating the latter, do take a deep breath (hopefully the subject will model your behavior) and be heard drinking the water. Then say nothing to see if that provokes a continuation of the conversation from the subject's perspective. This also may be a great opportunity for the negotiator to offer water, coffee or juice to the subject (who no doubt, is very dehydrated!).

Silence may also slow down the tempo of the conversation or emotional level of the subject. "Silence also is an effective response when subjects engage in highly charged emotional outbursts. When they fail to elicit a verbal response, subjects often calm down to verify that negotiators are still listening" (Noesner and Webster 1997, 5).

> ***Statements and opinions from people are what count. What is important are:***
> ***The subject's feelings, values, and what the person is saying.***

- **Are you a good or bad listener?**
  In his book *Are You Communicating*, Donald Walton (1989) lists common reasons for having a "turned-off attitude." The more often you see yourself on the below list, the greater the barrier to being an active listener and effective communicator. Walton recommends that you **"try to stop yourself when you realize you are 'tuning out' from others"** (Walton 1989;27).

- **Common Reasons for Not Listening:**
  - ✓ I want to talk first;
  - ✓ I'm thinking about what I'm going to say;
  - ✓ I'm not interested in the subject;
  - ✓ That's too hard to understand;
  - ✓ I don't like you;
  - ✓ I don't like the way you talk;
  - ✓ I'm too upset, or worried, about other things;
  - ✓ I don't want to believe what you're about to tell me;
  - ✓ I'd rather give my attention to people or activities around me;
  - ✓ I'd rather daydream or doodle.

Cmdr. Joel Wilson

Active listening may involve the eyes as well as the ears...
"Active listening may involve the eyes as well as the ears, strange as that may seem. If you watch the speaker's face closely, you may sense that he or she doesn't really mean what is being said. Tone of voice may also indicate certain feelings that will alter your perception of the message" (Walton 1989, 33).

The more someone experiencing stress talks, the more they may make disjointed and rambling statements. They may talk about unrelated topics, even complex themes that don't seem to be connected. **But the negotiator needs to focus on the "core of the message" (Walton 1989, 33) and connect this core and key themes that are woven throughout the fabric of responses.**

Active listening requires concentration with your eyes and ears. "Talk rambles, repeats, and backtracks. It often contradicts itself and can confuse you. It may be loaded with important details that hide just a nugget or two of worthwhile information. So you have to sift and sort – bounce the raw input around until you can identify the gold from the mass of gravel" (Walton 1989, 34).

To aid in concentration, Walton (1989, 34) suggests an exercise that lists words and phrases heard, then identifies the key ideas and important concepts as well as words (like "connecting the dots").

"Look for...ideas, not details" because people cannot remember everything (don't forget: the police negotiator is experiencing stress as well!).

Interview Phase; Listening with the Third Ear

Psychologists and counselors practice listening from the perspective of what is not being said as much as what is being said. Reik (1948) identified this form of active listening as "listening with the third ear." In his book *Deep Listening: Hidden Meanings in Everyday Conversations*, Robert Haskell (2001) discusses techniques for identifying and understanding deeper, hidden messages that people leave along the wayside of even casual conversation. Haskell contends that an astute listener (such as someone practicing active listening skills) can pick up and identify "sub literal nuances" which translates into how the speaker feels.

And when agitated, these feelings, even if unconscious and not readily identifiable by the speaker, can be revealed by the words spoken. For the objective third party, such as an intervening police officer, actively listening (and processing the words at a quicker rate than the spoken rate) is an effective technique to enhance understanding of not only what the speaker is saying, but also "meaning." Frequent use of paraphrasing and perception checking as well as periodic summarizing promotes feedback and validation from the speaker.

Although these concepts have been developed for longer term contacts, such as a patient or client in counseling, a police officer can also practice deep listening with the third ear. Listening in this context requires that one not only tries to "read between the lines" but to also identify the non-verbal communication cues that the speaker is displaying. Just as in physics when two objects come in contact, there is some transference, if only at the particle level. The same is true with human beings.

When people come in contact, both are affected (Fromm's, 1989, "law in human relations"). Some police officers see their role as more clinical yet ignore that they are impacted and affected by contact with others, especially in stressful situations.

Establishing a communication bond, if even for a brief time such as the 911-call, can provoke genuine connection between people. Establishing this connection as an eventual positive experience, for both the disputants and the officers, can have a long lasting impact on how people relate. And the more positive the contact, the greater the enhancement of the self-concept will be. Assertive police officers, may not readily acknowledge this self-concept growth, but for the people they come in contact with, this can be a significant experience. The experience may very well influence how they react to police officers in the future.

(Jo Taylor, RN)

An effective communicator will ALWAYS keep the third ear open.

> **Interview Phase: Active listening coupled with recognition of one's Emotional Intelligence sets the intervention environment.**

The crisis intervener needs to recognize personal biases and prejudices and suspend judgment while intervening. The interview location needs to be as comfortable as practical and distractions need to be minimized to enable concentration on the observable and hidden messages (such as from loud music to removing people who should not be present).

- Practice active listening verbally (minimal encouragers) and non-verbally (body language)!
- Paraphrase what the speaker is saying to not only signal you are listening but also to seek clarification.
- Perception Check what you interpret to be the speaker's feelings about what is being said. Skillful use of the Paraphrase and Perception Check will provoke the speaker to respond and may encourage a dialogue.
- Recognize what the important points and themes of the speaker are this will help to recognize what the "insurmountable obstacles and barriers" (Caplan 1961 in Parker and Meier 1975, 185) the speaker is facing. Recognizing what the speaker is facing will help to understand what needs to be done to allay fears and concerns.
- Active listening is listening with your eyes as well as your ears (all three of them!). The meaning of spoken words and messages comes from what is seen – how the speaker appears. Active listening requires clarification as well. Whether people are arguing or casually talking, they still need to clarify what they mean for effective communication. **Many times, people are upset because they fail to recognize how imprecise language can be.** ⬇

How far is Yonder?   Like a San Franciscan trying to understand how far is *yonder* to someone from Arkansas...it's just not going to be clear unless the Arkansan identifies some distance that can be mutually seen and understood by both people. The San Franciscan is not dumb (although he may dress funny and talk fast) he just does not understand the concept or meaning of how far yonder can be.   Now if both sides are locked in a verbal dispute, it

(desiwalls.com/lonely-road)

may take a third party intervener to seek clarification on the distance implied by the Arkansan and misunderstood, albeit innocently, by the San Franciscan. The third party needs to always be alert to identify and clarify the *yonder terms* (metaphorically speaking) and phrases that only the speaker may understand. The consequent confusion merely contributes to the already heated tension about how far is yonder.

- Once there is an understanding – and clarity - of the overall issues and concerns, try to lead the disputants toward a discussion that focuses on resolutions.
- **The way words are spoken:** Anthropologists will tell you that these are fundamental communication cues for primates...we humans merely are higher primates, but none the less, evolutionarily determined to communicate in the same way. (*This is why the words used are not as effective in communication as the way the words are spoken – the tones and accompanying non-verbal cues.*) Again, as with all primates, we are very facially expressive, utilizing the many variations of facial expressions to convey what we are saying and meaning (Conniff 2004). This is where Reik's (1948) third ear concept comes into play...***we are listening with more than our two ears!***

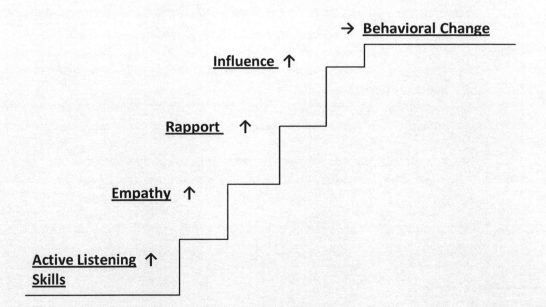

<u>*Influencing Behavioral Change - The Change Stairway*</u> (Vance 2006)

→ <u>**Behavioral Change**</u>

Influence ↑

Rapport ↑

Empathy ↑

<u>**Active Listening**</u> ↑
<u>**Skills**</u>

Active Listening becomes the foundation that supports each step in the *Change Stairway*. As **Active Listening Skills** are employed, this establishes the development of Empathy. As **Empathy** is perceived, then genuine **Rapport** develops, leading to **Influencing** people to effect **Behavioral Change**. This Behavioral Change may be what motivates a disputant to accept help, or agree to a suggestion that leads to resolving a dispute - and the initial reason why the police were called (Louie 2007c).

➤ **Active listening is the only skill set designed to work toward all these goals at the same time** (Louie and Vance 2007):

  ✓ To lower emotions and return the subject to *normal*;
  ✓ To establish rapport and influence;
  ✓ To gather information;
  ✓ This is not long term or even lasting behavioral change; it is behavioral change for the moment, usually long enough to establish communication by defusing, establishing rapport, basic interviewing (trying to find out what happened), then seeking a resolution through mediation and problem solving.

> *For the police officer, active listening is used to encourage behavioral change.   Like the Hostage Negotiator, the officer's role is essentially the same...to influence behavioral change.*

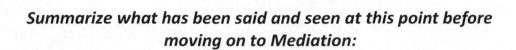

> **Summarize what has been said and seen at this point before moving on to Mediation:**
>
> - When you feel each side has had a chance to talk, then summarize what they said and check it out with the other side.
> - Your role is to constantly check out with each side; you are making sure that the issues and feelings are clear to each other.
>
> *Once both sides acknowledge your summary (although they may not agree on responsibility or guilt), it is time to move them towards resolution by way of mediation techniques.*

4. Mediation

 **Once the disputants have had an opportunity to relate their respective stories, and the officers have accurately paraphrased and summarized, it is now time to mediate the dispute and seek a mutually agreeable solution.**

> ➤ **As discussed above in other chapters, if practical, use mediation as your first approach.** Inform the disputants that you cannot resolve their problems, and that they must do so themselves – you are there to help and facilitate.

- **Avoid suggesting solutions** at the beginning of the phase; you may have to be more suggestive later on if there is an apparent impasse.
- **Elicit suggestions** on how to resolve the problem.
- **Check out each proposal** with the other side, until there is acceptance or compromise. Summarize and paraphrase the resolution to reaffirm clarity.
- **Avoid criticizing the solutions** (unless absolutely unworkable), even if you don't agree; do not impose your values or suggest the way you would handle the situation.
- **Offer encouragement** for follow through with any agreements.
- **Summarize** - most important at this point: summarize all the agreements; put it all together for both sides.

> *Review Chapter III for discussion of Mediation principles*

> ## Summarize Again – most important at this point:

- Summarize all the agreements; put it all together for both sides.
- May be very brief and only takes seconds, but it is important to continually bring all the issues together (Goldstein, et al., 1977; Zacker and Bard 1973).

5. Negotiation

Elledge Mediation Group

> ## In negotiation, unlike Mediation, you are more *directive* and you do suggest solutions, although you need to encourage buy-in from disputants.

The crisis intervener is now negotiating and being more active in seeking solutions because being an objective mediator has not worked with the disputants. This may be because the disputants are either so distraught or angry that they cannot visualize solutions. You need to take a more active role by:

- Summarizing to the disputants your perception of the problem;
- Checking out this summary with them;
- Listening openly to their response; this is a critical moment in time because you will get clues to what they may accept (and not accept);
- Proposing a compromise and measure their response (Goldstein et al., 1977; Zacker and Bard 1973).

6. Arbitration

> ## If unable to compromise through Mediation or Negotiation, then you may need to "arbitrate," which means to "directly impose" upon the disputants what they will have to do.

This is the least desirable of options since you are *ordering* the disputants to do something. However, this may be your only option, short of arrest for police officers, or ending the contact for non- police negotiators.

If the dispute continues, you may have to resort to arrest and only as a last resort. Police officers are required to fall back on the basic safety and peace keeping role. Also, the officer may have to arrest because of not only a criminal complaint but also state statute or liability issues.

7. Referral

Columbia County Social Services

➤ **This phase is optional, depending on complexity of the issues identified, and need to refer the disputants to a more specialized alternative, such as counselling services, substance abuse services, veterans' services, etc.**

- Determine if appropriate or necessary;
- If problem is too complex or requires long-term solution, you may have to call another agency or specialists (i.e., professional counsellors, neighborhood mediation program, etc.)
- Be specific with your referral (and be familiar and up to date with the services);
- Assist the disputants in planning out how/when they will contact the referral and follow through ("Help the individual accept help; Assist with everyday tasks")
- Have Community Resources and Referral Guide available
- When agreements are made, summarize, reassure and...leave!
- If appropriate, maintain record keeping for future contacts or referrals
- Do a personal quality control on yourself and spot check with previous calls to determine what worked and did not work.

Overview of Crisis Intervention Process

1. **Pre-Contact** *(Receiving the 911 call; emotionally and physically preparing for the Contact)*

2. **Contact** *(Officer safety first – Situational Awareness; establishing if arrest or non-arrest situation; recognizing your Emotional Intelligence; defusing, separating and preparing to interview the disputants)*

3. **Interviewing** *(Finding out what happened through active listening and communication techniques; establishing the ground rules; may need to constantly defuse as well as summarize what disputants are saying – or not saying)*

4. **Mediation** *(The give-and-take process of active listening, then paraphrasing and perception checking feelings and emotions; continuing to defuse and summarize solutions for final phase)*

5./6. **Negotiation/Arbitration** *(may need to refer to others for help in resolving; if not, then seek final agreement resolution, making sure to artfully summarize the agreement)*

7. **Referral** *(if appropriate, refer to more specialized services such as counseling, substance abuse intervention, veterans' assistance, etc.)*

Police Leave

When the officers are satisfied order has been restored and people are willing to agree, it is time to leave (it is OK to periodically check back to make sure people are following through with agreements and/or referral)

Chapter X: Summary

Crisis intervention as a procedural strategy of dispute settlement has gained acceptance in many police training programs. Unfortunately, many TV reality cop shows continue to portray officers as abrasive and uncaring while handling disturbance calls (a successful call would probably be boring since people would be seated and trying to communicate with the help of the mediating officers.)

Police officers have been employing many of the procedural steps as outlined by Bard (1970) without even recognizing that they are following a systematic model. To a police officer, his or her defined procedures and behaviors have survival value; they change their methods of approach when they perceive an enhancement of this survival value.

The sections addressing the issues of Emotional Intelligence, how to deal with the mentally ill, those under the influence of drugs and/or alcohol, and the suicidal, are designed to enhance the responding officers' survivability as well as reinforce the skills it takes to resolve disputes.

It is a fallacy to assume that just because an officer is a veteran, he/she will be resistant to change. The veteran officer changes his or her procedures and behaviors when the credibility of a new concept, such as crisis intervention and mediation (Cooper 2000), has proven to work in the field and has gained greater acceptance as standard police training throughout the law enforcement community.

The concept of crisis intervention training appears to be more difficult when applying the training program to recruit officers. The recruit has little or no frame of reference to base a judgment on *what works* when handling a disturbance call. Many of these recruits have been attracted to law enforcement by strongly identifying with the more commercial (i.e., TV and the action media) stereotype of *what is a cop*. Many people join the military for the same reasons - the influence of the media and the "action" image projected on the screen.

In some cases, the recruit is actually disillusioned when he or she is told that they must perform a service in response to the needs of the community. This type of officer feels that the reverse is true and his or her response to the community is based upon personal perceptions and not the needs of the community.

> *In summary, crisis intervention is a communication strategy and approach to be used by police officers because of its survival value for the officers and its more community policing and problem solving effectiveness when serving people in need.*

Training Strategies and Teaching Aids

The following sections will focus on the actual training strategies and aids used when teaching crisis intervention and tactical communication.

Note for field training officers: By diagramming how trainees respond to these types of disturbance calls, a visual record can be produced that will highlight the pluses and minuses of the trainee's performance.

The training officer needs to identify which tactical communication techniques worked and which did not work – and why they worked and did not work. By isolating a particular phase, and conversely showing which phase was handled well, the trainee may not feel that he or she *blew the entire call* but rather needs improvement in one or more of the phases. The latter reduces the overwhelming nature of handling disturbance calls that recruits commonly complain about (unfortunately, sometimes their complaints are heard in exit interviews after they have been unsuccessful in a field training program).

One approach to teaching police crisis intervention is to focus on the above phases of a particular conflict. By diagramming each phase (Louie 1981; 2006), the officers can visualize their roles, identify tactics and techniques, and concentrate on skill building. The procedure is to graph the contact and identify the phases of the contact (example of graphs on following pages):

- The ***vertical axis is a subjective measure of the stress or anger level*** of the disputants; as the graph line "climbs," the disputants become increasingly agitated and in greater need to be calmed and defused by the officers.

- The ***horizontal axis is the objective representation of time***. Combining the two axes, you have a fluctuating anger level of the argument, with each phase of the process identified and diagrammed. In the diagram, the argument was still developing when the officers arrived (**"C"** in the graph, which represents the initial *Contact Phase*) on the scene; as an example, a husband and wife argument in their home.

- The officers may allow the disputants to continue their argument; this is a defusing technique whereby the officers are allowing people to vent, and at the same time, exhaust some of that volatile energy so they won't use it against the officers (but it doesn't always go this way!)

- Another reason for the technique *is to listen* – you may get some idea of what they are arguing about. But don't let them go too long, otherwise they may get so angry that they start a physical fight (**F**)!

- After defusing and calming the disputants (individual preference on which techniques to use), the officers announce the ground rules and begin the *Interview Phase* (**I**), and from here on, the disputants are telling their respective side of what happened and why the police were called.

- During this *Interview Phase* (**I**), there may be continuing outbursts of anger as the argument is reignited as each side presents their version (albeit biased) of what happened and there is a continuing need to constantly be vigilant lest the anger erupt once more. Utilizing defusing techniques is always an on-going process.

- If the officer is unsuccessful in controlling the anger, the situation may lead to a true physical conflict (**F** for Fighting). One must remember that this calming strategy, by utilizing defusing techniques, is not a specific phase of the process, but rather, it permeates the entire contact.

- Once the disputants have an opportunity to explain, the officers now *put it all together* by restating through Paraphrasing or Perception Checking, then Summarizing what has been said. This is known as the *Mediation Phase* (**M**). This phase also serves as a calming strategy because the officers are soliciting solutions and eliciting agreements as to how the disputants view ending the argument (although the disputants may still disagree on the facts and the role each other is playing). As people start to recognize that they may be able to overcome the "obstacles" that provoked the argument, they start to think in terms of which solution will best meet their needs.

- The next phase (**A**) is to maneuver the disputants into a workable Agreement whereby they agree to follow a course of action that will reduce the danger and bring about a solution.

- Finally, Summarize (**S**) the Agreements made, then Leave (**L**).

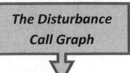

The Disturbance Call Graph

Disturbance Call Graph

One approach to teaching police tactical communication and crisis intervention is to focus on the above phases of a particular conflict, such as a *911 disturbance call*. By diagramming each phase, the officers can visualize their roles, identify tactics and techniques used, and concentrate on skill building. The procedure is to graph the contact and identify the phases of the contact.

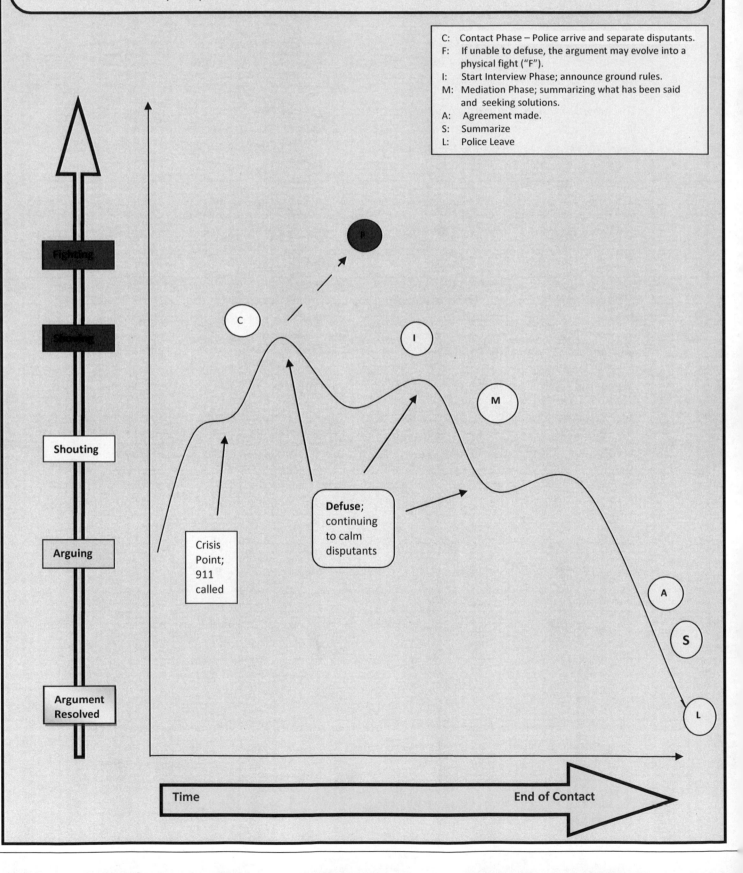

C: Contact Phase – Police arrive and separate disputants.
F: If unable to defuse, the argument may evolve into a physical fight ("F").
I: Start Interview Phase; announce ground rules.
M: Mediation Phase; summarizing what has been said and seeking solutions.
A: Agreement made.
S: Summarize
L: Police Leave

Fighting

Shouting

Shouting

Arguing

Argument Resolved

Crisis Point; 911 called

Defuse; continuing to calm disputants

Time

End of Contact

- The following graph illustrates the flexibility of the Disturbance Call Graph and how *each call is different and can be diagrammed and labeled differently*, although the overall phases of the crisis intervention model (Pre Contact, Contact, Interview, Mediation/Negotiation, Referral) remains similar from call to call.

- In this hypothetical example, disputants are shoving each other as officers arrive (**X**). Once the officers arrive, they need to continually defuse (**D**) the disputants; since they were shoving, the officers need to separate beyond "combat distance" (meaning far enough apart such that they cannot lunge or strike one another). This is the critical time when each officer has to attempt to communicate with each respective disputant, redirecting the focus on to the officers and away from each other.

- Although the disputants are farther apart, they are still angry. There are three distinct defusing events (**D**) which take a few minutes. The graph indicates that the continuing Defusing has been successful because the anger level has been reduced. The utility of the Disturbance Call Graph is that it allows each defusing technique to be identified. In this hypothetical call, perhaps the first defusing technique was to quickly separate the two and break eye contact. The second defusing technique, a few minutes later, may be a verbal acknowledgement of what each disputant is saying and a reassurance they each will have an opportunity to tell their side of the story. This is reinforced with empathic responses, non-verbal assurances and body language (nodding of the head, non-aggressive body posture, etc.). The third defusing technique may be a restatement of the ground rules and verbal as well as non-verbal reassurance of the disputants as they are brought back together in eye contact that they will each have an opportunity to talk about what has happened.

- The disputants are now at the Interview Phase (**I**) and the officers are encouraging each to talk more about what happened. As each side has an opportunity to talk, they start to calm down. The graph now shows a more horizontal pattern, indicating no need for further defusing.

- Over a period of minutes (the exact time left blank on the graph but in a real situation, the time would be identified) the disputants eventually reach a Mediation Phase (**M**) and agreement (**A**), assisted by the skillful use of paraphrasing and perception checking from the officers (there is no need for a Referral). Finally, the agreements are summarized (**S**), the argument resolved and the officers leave.

- As indicated by the steadily falling curve, the following disturbance was quickly defused and resolved.

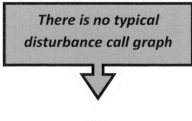

There is no typical disturbance call graph

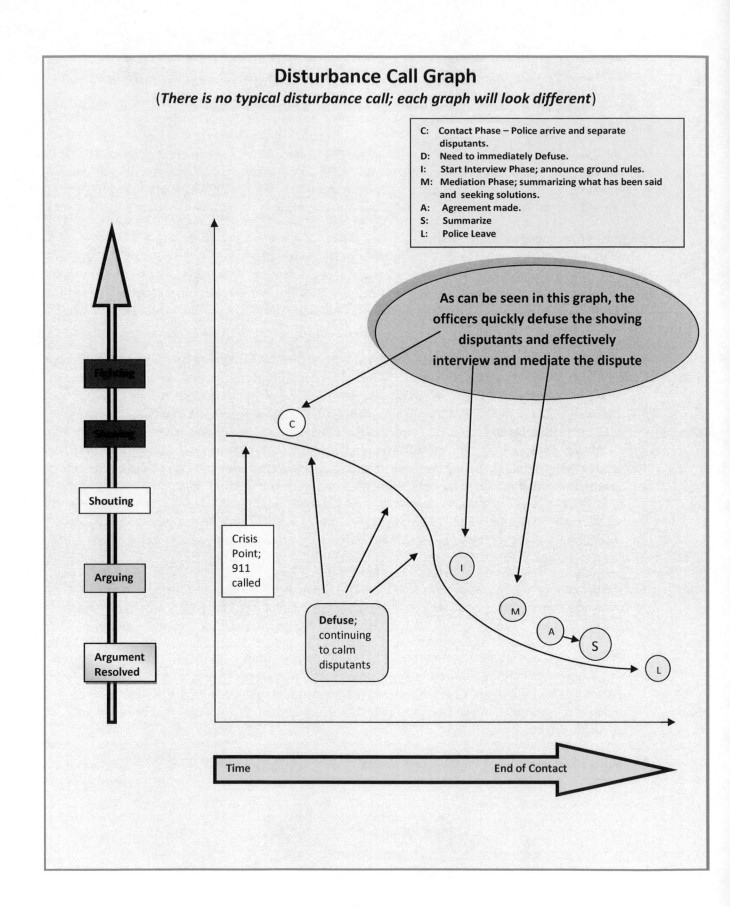

Disturbance Call Graph
(There is no typical disturbance call; each graph will look different)

C: Contact Phase – Police arrive and separate disputants.
D: Need to immediately Defuse.
I: Start Interview Phase; announce ground rules.
M: Mediation Phase; summarizing what has been said and seeking solutions.
A: Agreement made.
S: Summarize
L: Police Leave

As can be seen in this graph, the officers quickly defuse the shoving disputants and effectively interview and mediate the dispute

Fighting

Shoving

Shouting

Arguing

Argument Resolved

Crisis Point; 911 called

Defuse; continuing to calm disputants

Time   End of Contact

What is the best training model for teaching tactical communication and crisis intervention?

San Jose PD FTO Program

Many times those in law enforcement training have the correct information, but present the material incorrectly. The following, modified from Robert M. Gagne's (1988, 1974, 1965) *Events of Instruction*, is an effective adult learning model for public safety professionals.

❖ **Gain Attention of students**. Start with the daily headlines, emphasizing the critical nature of crisis intervention calls and events. Let the students know that their safety will be paramount and the crisis intervention and tactical communication protocols are designed to enhance safety for not only the first responders, but all of those involved in the call.

❖ **Share Objectives of training with students.** List objectives and seek expectations from students; review these at end of class.

❖ **Connect to Prior Knowledge.** What do the students know about how to defuse and calm people; how to approach angry or emotionally distraught people? Use "Identifying Out of Control Situations and Responses" and "Defusing Techniques" forms (below) to initiate class discussion on which defusing techniques worked and did not work. *Do not rush through this instruction event because it is important for the students to recognize their pre-class skill level.* This step is very important to cover for in-service students who already possess a demonstrated skill level.

❖ **Present Information.** *Most teachers/trainers erroneously contend that this is where most learning occurs, but this is not the case!* Present the information, incorporated within the principles and concepts of adult learning.

❖ **Guide the Learner**. Coach them in class, using role-playing scenarios (below). Use the emotional intelligence exercises (below) to guide the student towards self-awareness. For post-class, use the above *Disturbance Call Graphs* to identify how well the student handled the call (this is where it is important to make sure the Field Training Officers are trained also in crisis intervention and tactical communication skills).

❖ **Practice Purposefully.** *Students learn best from peers*; have peers provide feedback (using the below *Role Playing Evaluation* forms). *Significant adult learning occurs when the students practice role-playing scenarios and the class participates by grading how well the role players performed their roles.* For the role playing scenarios, start with short scenarios that focus primarily on defusing techniques. Basic interviewing and mediation can come later, once the students are more experienced with the role playing scenarios.

❖ **Give Feedback**. This is where adult learning is reinforced for both the role players and the student assessors.

❖ **Assess Performance.** Assess the above objectives and expectations. How did the students demonstrate their knowledge and practice of crisis intervention and tactical communication techniques?

Role playing is acting, and like actors, students need *rehearsals where the stimuli is limited and organized*, such as a stage or classroom with props. Attempting new tactical communication and crisis intervention techniques, in the real world of a police 911 call, is not the time to practice! High stress situations bombard the brain with stimuli. The more students have practiced and are comfortable with new skills, the more competency they will perform in the real world. Experience in the classroom has demonstrated that by asking students to identify those times when they may have experienced or witnessed out-of-control or tense situations (see page 172), and then used these examples as role-playing scenarios, adult learning and retention has been shown to be effective. Below are actual student-supplied role playing scenarios that have been used in the classroom.

Scene: Two cars have collided on a residential street. One driver is arguing with the other about the collision. There are no injuries and only minor damage to the vehicles.

Driver #1: Another car has struck your car from behind, at a slow speed and there are no injuries. But as you get out of your car, the other driver confronts you and is angry at you "for causing the accident."

Driver #2: You are angry that the car in front of you suddenly stopped, for no reason, causing your car to rear-end the car. You get out of your car and approach the other driver, accusing the driver of causing the accident.

Police Officers: You receive a call of two drivers arguing at the scene of a non-injury auto collision.

Scene: Apartment complex. It is late at night and roommates are overheard arguing. When a window is broken, neighbors call 911.

Roommate #1: You have been drinking with your roommates and start to argue with Roommate #2. You feel the roommate has not been keeping up with the assigned chores (taking out the garbage, cleaning, etc.). You are not "fighting" as much as loudly arguing.

Roommate #2: You have been drinking with Roommate #1 and start to argue about who should be cleaning up the apartment. You are angry with Roommate #1 because the roommate is consistently late with the rent. You throw a large ashtray that breaks a small window.

Roommate#3: You were sleeping when you hear loud arguing from two roommates. You get up and are in the front room when the police arrive. You have no idea why your roommates are arguing and you are not involved with the incident.

Roommate #4: You are returning to your apartment one late evening when you see your roommates arguing with the police. You enter the apartment (the door has been left open) to see if you can help.

Police: You are dispatched to an apartment complex on a report of "breaking glass with people fighting in one of the apartments."

Each student is assigned a role. The key role players are the police officers since they are expected to practice their tactical communication and crisis intervention skills by utilizing effective communication techniques: words used, tone of voice and body language. As they utilize these communication skills, they are also required to use as a performance template the Phases of the Crisis Intervention Process.

Tactical Communication and Crisis Intervention Training, and the Changing Police Culture

One of the problems encountered when trying to teach crisis intervention to police officers is that there are differing role perceptions of how they should perform their law enforcement duties.   A second problem involving crisis intervention training revolves around the matter of officer safety and security. If the goals of crisis intervention training are not clearly stated, the trainees may feel that they are being told what to do, even in potentially dangerous situations.

Culturally speaking, police officers do not emphasize communication skills in training and need to recognize their *Emotional Intelligence* (Saville 2006). Once it is clearly stated that safety and security is paramount and must always be maintained, the officers are then more receptive to the training. The point to emphasize is that crisis intervention training is a strategy to control people and reduce violence.

The area currently most lacking is skill building for dealing with emotionally distraught or mentally ill people and the critical 9-11 call such as suicide-by-cop, alcohol/drug induced trauma, and an irrational person facing a significant emotional event.

➢ *Who's your partner and how well do you get along with each other?*

Aside from regional pockets, the police ranks are still overwhelmingly white male dominated, but the police culture is changing.   Your partner may be a women, someone from a different ethnicity, even sexual orientation which are all healthy inclusions of police officer ranks. These differences may be disruptive to those police agencies that are still using older and more traditional models of handling the emotionally distraught.

How well police officers work as team members is based on how well they communicate with each other before the 911 call.   During the call, subjects can also detect subtle cues if it appears officers are not working as a team which can influence how subjects respond to the officers. If the officers are trained differently, they may seem out-of-sync as they attempt to communicate with people, at a 911 disturbance call (Louie 2007c).

Feedback such as "the officers did not seem to be on the same page or it seemed that only one officer was trying to help us as the other looked bored and even angry" are comments that police officers rarely hear because these criticisms are usually in the form of citizen complaints to the police chief.

The same comments also apply to officers who disagree about how to handle a call. The most common response is for one of the officers to remain disengaged and not show disapproval or disagreement in front of disputing people.   However, most of the time the subjects perceive that those who responded to the call are not in agreement about how to handle their situation which does impact issues of control and credibility.

The best solution is for the officers to be trained alike, using the same models and practicing the same methods of dispute resolution. The Hillsboro, Oregon, Police Department's previously mentioned 32-hour mediation training model, with an additional 32-hour advanced course is an example of an effective program (Oregonian 2006). The officers must be *on the same script*! The more you train for consistent tactical communication skills, the more successful will be your results in real life situations.

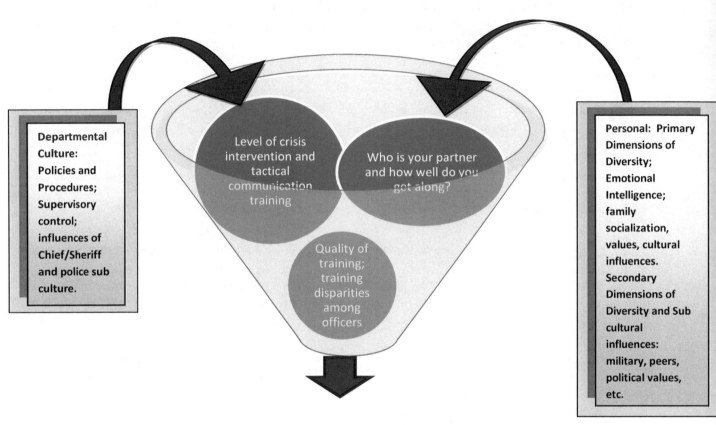

Departmental Culture: Policies and Procedures; Supervisory control; influences of Chief/Sheriff and police sub culture.

Level of crisis intervention and tactical communication training

Who is your partner and how well do you get along?

Quality of training; training disparities among officers

Personal: Primary Dimensions of Diversity; Emotional Intelligence; family socialization, values, cultural influences. Secondary Dimensions of Diversity and Sub cultural influences: military, peers, political values, etc.

What influences how officers work together and how well they communicate with people

Palo Alto Police sponsored Domestic Crisis Intervention class, April 1975, Menlo Park, California (Officer Ron Louie)

168

Alexandria, Virginia, Police Dept. Crisis Intervention Academy class graduates (Sharon McLoone, *Old Town Alexandria Patch*, March 2011)

Training Exercises

❑ *Blank Disturbance Call Graph:*
- Use this graph to practice identifying the Phases of the Crisis Intervention Process.
- As time progresses, identify defusing techniques that either reduce or spike the anger level as disputants are arguing.

❑ *Role Playing Evaluation*:
- As students practice role playing scenarios, use this form to critique and evaluate, then provide feedback to the role player. Remember, feedback is a powerful adult learning technique.

❑ *Identifying Out of Control Situations and Responses*:
- The purpose of this exercise is to identify a particular situation where the student felt "out of control" and how did the student gain control. The student is asked to identify defusing techniques by describing how he/she was able to regain control a situation.

❑ *Defusing Techniques:*
- This exercise asks the student to list which defusing techniques he or she is most comfortable using. Many times people "just do it" without thinking much about what they do that is successful.

❑ *Emotional Intelligence: Identifying What Really Angers You:*
- This exercise asks the student to look inward and explore what really angers them (domestic abusers, undocumented immigrants, drug users, etc.). The student is asked to identify how confronting these types of people and situations impacts his or her ability to be an objective third part. Police officers frequently intervene in disturbances between two people or confront groups of people that may be on this list. Building this self-exploration list is a way of recognizing his or her Emotional Intelligence.

❑ *Recognizing Your Emotional Intelligence: Managing Your Baggage:*
- By listing how the student describes himself or herself, he/she starts to recognize "who they are."
- By identifying a stereotype of how they see themselves, the student will recognize how that may influence behavior when he/she interacts with someone who is opposite them in values and preferences.

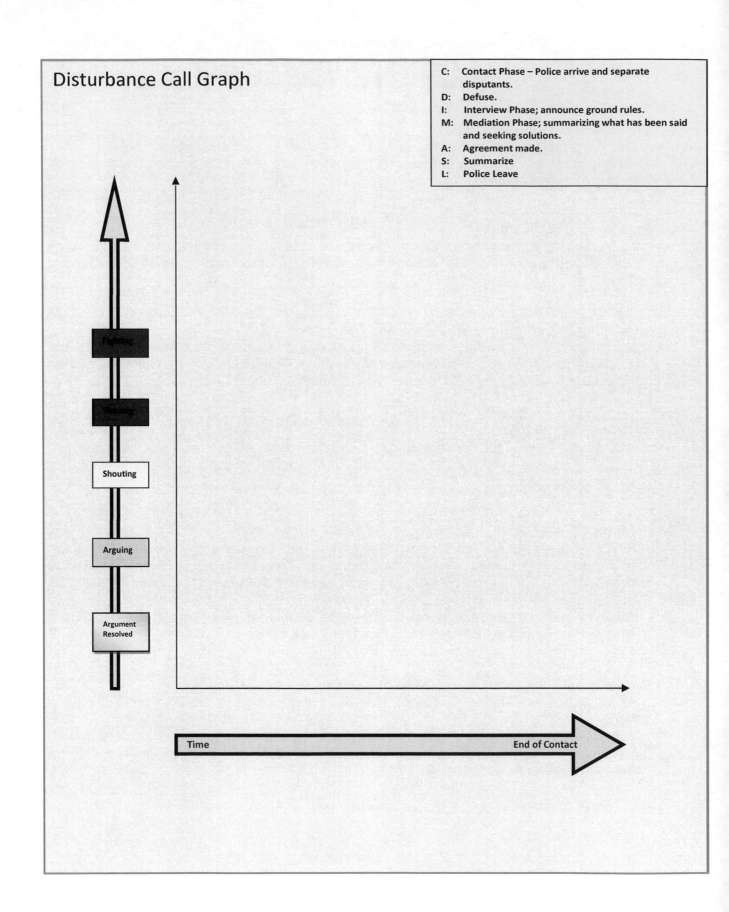

Disturbance Call Graph

C: Contact Phase – Police arrive and separate disputants.
D: Defuse.
I: Interview Phase; announce ground rules.
M: Mediation Phase; summarizing what has been said and seeking solutions.
A: Agreement made.
S: Summarize
L: Police Leave

Fighting

Shoving

Shouting

Arguing

Argument Resolved

Time   End of Contact

Tactical Communication/Crisis Intervention Evaluation for Role Playing Scenarios

Person being evaluated: _____ Date: _____

1 = Very Poor   2 = Poor   3 = Fair   4 = Good   5 = Very Good   NA = Not Applicable

	1	2	3	4	5	NA
Voice Projection/ Tone of Voice						
Speech Clear/ Slow/Understandable						
Eye Contact						
Overall Body Language						
Mannerisms (gestures, etc.)						
Defusing Ability/ Techniques Used						
Personal Safety						
Interview Skills						
Mediation Skills						
Use of Time						
Overall Poise/Bearing and Command Presence						
Other Behaviors Observed: _____ _____ _____ _____						

Additional Comments:

_____

_____

_____

_____

Identifying Out-of-Control Situations and Responses

For Public Safety Professionals: From your experiences in the field, write down a situation where you felt you were not in control, if only for a short time, and even if you eventually gained control. What made you feel out of control? How were you able to gain control?

For those not in public safety: Think about a similar circumstance but perhaps a different setting. For example, you were a retail clerk being confronted by an angry customer, or you found yourself in the company of someone yelling and/or acting unruly.

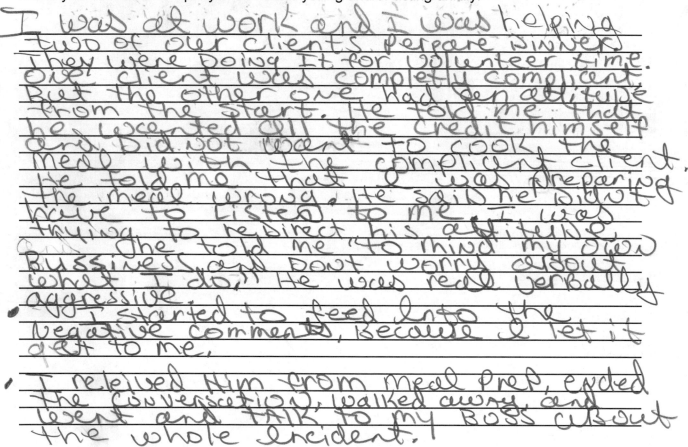

- I was at work and I was helping two of our clients prepare dinner. They were doing it for volunteer time. One client was completly compliant. But the other one had been attitude from the start. He told me that he wanted all the credit himself and did not want to cook the meal with the compliant client. He told me that I was preparing the meal wrong. He said he didn't have to listen to me. I was trying to redirect his attitude. She told me "to mind my own bussiness, and Dont worry about what I do." He was real verbally aggressive.

- I started to feed into the negative comments, Because I let it get to me.

- I relieved Him from meal prep, ended the conversation, walked away, and went and TALK to my BOSS about the whole incident.

The purpose of this exercise is to explore those instances when there was a loss of control over another person. What defusing techniques were utilized to eventually bring the situation under control? For class participation, summarize these scenarios as scripts for classroom role playing.

Tactical Communication; Defusing Techniques*

List 5 defusing techniques you commonly utilize when trying to calm and control someone who is upset/emotionally distraught:

1. Try to use a sincere tone of voice.

2. I show empathy.

3. I actively Listen.

4. I use non-threatining eye-contact.

5. I try to help the person face the crisis, assist in helping the person figure out the facts, and then help go into problem solving mode,

*Listing these defusing techniques helps identify which techniques individuals are comfortable with when attempting to calm and control others experiencing a crisis.

Emotional Intelligence: Identifying what really angers you*

List 5 things that tend to upset you. Do not list day-to-day irritants, but the more subtle, deeply felt issues/concerns that really annoy you or conflict with deeply held values or beliefs:

when you try to Be friendly with
someone and they respond in

1. a snotty or Disrespectful manor.

2. Not cleaning up after Yourself.

3. Infidelity

4. lying

5. Sexual and Physical abuse.

Many times, these are the people you will be contacting at the 911 call!

*This list represents a person's core values. Emotional intelligence is recognizing that these *core values will be challenged* as one responds to people in crisis. This exercise should follow the "five words that describe who you are" exercise. This understanding of self-knowledge and self-awareness reinforces Emotional Intelligence and how that impacts dealing with people in crisis.

Recognizing your Emotional Intelligence: Managing Your Baggage*

List 5 words that describe who you are (i.e., happy, conservative, punctual, etc.):

1. Responsible
2. honest
3. motivated
4. Loving
5. Determined

Now write a word that is critical of these descriptors (negative stereotypes):

1. Loser
2. Liar
3. Lazy
4. Cold Hearted
5. weak

*This exercise helps establish an understanding of individual officer Emotional Intelligence by asking the officer to list words that describe "who they are." The actual terms are not as significant as the second part of this exercise. Next to each word, write a negative sterotype. This exercise assists the student to realize that no matter how proud one is about how he/she sees themselves or how innocent term, there may be a negative connotation attached to that descriptor. He or she cannot leave personal baggage at the door of the 911 call but there can be an awareness of self and recognition of how that impacts personal and professional interactions.

References Cited

Acosta, J. and J. S. Prager. "What To Say When Every Moment Counts," *Police and Security News*, Vol. 18, #3, May/June 2002.

AELE Law Journal. "Police interaction with Autistic persons: The need for training," #101-1935-0007, July 2009.

Albrecht, Steve. "Vigilant … or hyper-vigilant?" *Law Officer Magazine*, June 2011, pp. 32-34.

Ambrose, Stephen E. *Band of Brothers*. New York: Pocket Books, 1992.

American Heritage Dictionary, 4th Ed. Boston: Houghton Mifflin Co., 2000.

Associated Press. "ACLU report criticizes police use of stun gun." *Oregonian*, September 14, 2007.

Bard, M. *Training Police as Specialists in Family Crisis Intervention*. Washington, D.C.: U.S. Government Printing Office, 1970.

Bard, M. *The Function of the Police in Crisis Intervention and Conflict Management*. Washington, D.C.: U.S. Government Printing Office, 1975.

Baum, David and Jim Hassinger. *The Randori Principles*. Chicago: Dearborn Books, 2002.

BBC News. "Body language and autism," August 4, 2009 (accessed April 18, 2011).

Bella, Rick. "Clackamas County deputies get new partner: crisis expert," *The Oregonian*, July 16, 2010.

Bernstein, Maxine. "Starting Monday, a business card will come with that traffic stop." *The Oregonian*, September 20, 2009, p. A7.

Bernstein, Maxine. "Portland Police Chief Mike Reese fires Officer Ron Frashour in Aaron Campbell's fatal shooting," *The Oregonian*, November 16, 2010, A1.

Bernstein, Maxine. "Portland police chief to discuss role of the bureau's mobile crisis unit today," *The Oregonian*, January 18, 2011a.

Bernstein, Maxine. "Portland Sgt. Kyle Nice acted 'inappropriately' in off-duty driving confrontation," *The Oregonian,* February 09, 2011b.

Blitz, C. Akin. "The Confrontational Continuum." *Hillsboro Police Department Training Bulletin #1-2008*, Hillsboro, Oregon, 2008.

Block, Jerald, MD. *"Unpublished Review of Empathy and Mental Illness"*; Electronic Communication," Portland, Oregon, November 29, 2006.

Borg, John. *Body Language: 7 Easy Lessons to Master the Silent Language*, Prentice Hall life, 2008).

Bottino, Barry. "12-hour shifts," *Nurse Week*, April 4, 2011, pp.26-27.

Brooks, Chris. "Cold Shock and Swimming Failure," *Sea Kayaker*, February 2008, pp. 24-28.

Butler, Chris. "The Sorry State of Police Communications Training." *Force Science News* #81, September 2007, pp.1-3.   www.ForceScienceNews.com (accessed September 21, 2007).

California Peace Officers Association. "Survivors of Suicide." Training Bulletin Vol. IV, #21, June 1983.

Campbell, Jacquelyn. "Lethality Assessment helps gauge danger from domestic disputes." *Force Science News #86*, pp. 1-4, December 2, 2007 www.ForceScienceNews.com (accessed December 2, 2007).

Caplan, G. *Principles of Preventive Psychiatry*. New York: Basic Books, 1964.

Caplan, G. *An Approach to Community Mental Health*. New York: Grue and Stratton, 1969.

Carkhuff, R.R. *Helping and Human Relations*. New York: Holt, Rinehart and Winston, 1969.

Carkhuff, R.R. and B. G. Berenson. *Beyond Counseling and Therapy*. New York: Holt, Rinehart and Winston, 1967.

Case, Deborah, "Overview of Mental Illness," *Hillsboro Police Department Training Bulletin #7-2007*, Hillsboro Police Department, Oregon, February 2007.

CIS Benefits Newsletter. "Don't let anger hurt your health," July 2008, pg. 3.

Coffey, Alan R. *Police Crisis Intervention into Family Crisis*. Santa Cruz, California: Davis Publishing, 1974.

Collins, Susan B. "From 'Distress' to 'De-stress' with Stress Management," *Nurse Week*, May 2, 2011, pp. 74-79

Conniff, Richard. "Reading Faces," pp. 44-50, *Smithsonian*, January 2004.

Cooper, Christopher. "Training Patrol Officers to Mediate Disputes," *FBI Law Enforcement Bulletin*, pp. 7-10, February 2000.

Corum, James S. "We have ways of making you talk" pp. 42-49. *World War II*, March 2008.

Danto, B. L. "Project S.O.S.: Volunteers in Action," *Suicide and Bereavement*. Virginia, U.S. Government Printing Office, September, 1999.

Domrose, Cathryn. "Calming a Storm; Psych Nurses Form Alliances with Patients to Forestall Violence," *Nurse Week*, pg. 18, September 24, 2007.

Duin, Steve. "Portland's Officer Kevin Tully perfects the use of force," *The Oregonian*, Feb. 5, 2011a.

Duin, Steve. "Portland's Officer Kevin Tully perfects the use of force ," *The Oregonian*, Feb. 5, 2011b.

Duin, Steve. "The truth about police who lie? There are no consequences," *The Oregonian*, February 9,. 2011c.

Dworkin, Andy. "Autism affects how people see faces," *The Oregonian*, June 25, 2008, p.C-4..

Dworkin, Andy. "Multnomah County awarded grant to study police encounters with mentally ill,"   *The Oregonian*, July 8, 2010.

Elias, Marilyn. "Suicide in America; suicide on the increase for middle-aged whites," *USA Today*, Oct. 21, 2008.

Elias, Marilyn. "Mindfulness meditation being used in hospitals and schools," *USA Today*, June 8, 2009.

Engleberg, Isa N. *Working in Groups: Communication Principles and Strategies. My Communication Kit Series,* 2006.

Everly, Jr., G. S. and J. T. Mitchell. *Critical Incident Stress Management (CISM): A new era and standard of care in crisis intervention* (2nd. Ed.). Ellicott City, MD: Cheveron, 1999.

Faulkner, Sam. "Ongoing survey seeks consensus on what's 'reasonable' use of force." *Force Science News*, #88, December 29, 2007, pp.1-4. www.ForceScienceNews (accessed January 2, 2008).

Fidanque, David. "How does it feel to be shocked by a Taser?" *ACLU of Oregon Newsletter*, November 19, 2007.

Fiedler, Chrystle. "Defusing Conflict: Stop health-eroding effects of fighting and improve your relationships," *The Costco Connection – For Your Health,* December 2010, pp. 57-58.

Flannery, Jr. Raymond B. and George S. Everly, Jr. "Crisis Intervention: A Review," *International Journal of Emergency Mental Health*, 2000**,** pp. 119-125.

Foreman, Judy. "The Look/Face Reading," pp. L7, L10, *Oregonian*, August 24, 2003.

Force Science News. "What Promotes Peak Performance in Lethal-Force Conflicts?" #75, June 2007a. www.ForceScienceNews (accessed September 24, 2007).

Force Science News. "Police and Sleep Problems: Are You a 40% er?" #80, September 2007b. www.ForceScienceNews (accessed October 26, 2007).

Force Science News. "Have You Tried These Distractions?" #81, September 2007c. www.ForceScienceNews (accessed September 24, 2007).

Force Science News. "Lethality Assessment helps gauge danger from domestic disputes." #86, December 2, 2007d. www.ForceScienceNews (accessed January 1, 2008).

Force Science News. "Ongoing survey seeks consensus on what's 'reasonable' use of force." #88, December 29, 2007e. www.ForceScienceNews (accessed January 2, 2008).

Force Science News. "Suicide by Inches," #101, Oct. 6, 2008.

Force Science News. "New study yields best profile yet of suicide-by-cop offenders and their threat," #126, July 3, 2009a, www.ForceScienceNews (accessed March 28, 2011).

Force Science News. "Emergency doctors confirm excited delirium does exist," #136, November 6, 2009b.

Force Science News. "Cops use wrong tactics in questioning witnesses," #149, May 7, 2010a (accessed April 3, 2011).

Force Science News. "Anger sets the stage for seeing threats where none exist," #163, November 19, 2010b, www.ForceScienceNews. (accessed November 19, 2010).

Frier, Scottie. "Verbal Containment; Negotiation skills for the first responding officer." *Law Officer*, September 2007, pp. 44-47.

Fromm, Erich. *The Art of Being.* New York: Continuum Publishing, 1989.

Gabel, Jakie T. "Mentally ill are not criminals." *Oregonian*, pg. A6, December 18, 2007.

Gagne, Robert M. *The conditions of learning.* New York: Holt, Rinehart & Winston, 1965.

Gagne, Robert M. *Essentials of learning for instruction.* New York: Holt, Rinehart & Winston, 1974.

Gagne, Robert M. *Instructional technology: Foundations.* Hillsdale, NJ: Erlbaum ,1988

Garner, Gerald W. "Handling people Under the Influence," *Police Magazine*, pp. 48-50, December 2006.

Giancola, Peter. "Distractions and Aggressive Subjects," *Force Science News*, #79, pp. 1-4, August 29, 2007a. www.ForceScienceNews (accessed September 24, 2007).

Giancola, Peter. "Have You Tried These Distractions," *Force Science News*, #81, pp. 1-3, September 21, 2007b. www.ForceScienceNews (accessed September 24, 2007).

Goldstein, Arnold P., Phillip J. Monti, Thomas J. Sardino and Donald J. Green. *Police Crisis Intervention.* Michigan: Behaviordelia Press, 1977.

Goerling, Rich, Scott Hewetson and Mike Rouches. "Minimizing Volume of Citizen Complaints." *Hillsboro Police Department Training Bulletin #2007-6*, Hillsboro Police Department, Hillsboro, Oregon, January 2007.

Goerling, Rich, Scott Hewetson and Mike Rouches. "Teflon Character; Dealing with Criticism." *Hillsboro Police Department Training Bulletin #2007-7*, Hillsboro Police Department, Hillsboro, Oregon, January 2007.

Graham, Gordon. "Our Cops are Ticking Time Bombs for Lack of Sleep." *Force Science News*, #71, 2007. www.ForceScienceNews (accessed October 26, 2007).

Graham v. Connor, 490 U.S. 386 (1989).

Graham, John L. and N. Mark Lam. "The Chinese Negotiation" pp. 82-91. *Harvard Business Review*, October 2003.

Grandstaff v. City of Borger, 767 F, 2nd (5th Cir. 1985).

Green, Aimee. "Jury awards $82,000 after woman is arrested when asking police for a business card," *The Oregonian*, April 15, 2011.

Harper and Row, "Officer Survival: An Approach to Conflict Management." Hagerstown, Maryland: Harper and Row Media Film Series, 1976.

Harvard Business Review. "Negative Stress." July 2003.

Haskell, Robert E. *Deep Listening: Hidden Meanings in Everyday Conversations.* Cambridge, MA: Perseus Publishing, 2001.

Hatton, C. L. and S. M. Valente. "Bereavement Group for Parents Who Suffered a Suicidal Loss of a Child," *Suicide and Life Threatening Behavior,* Fall, 1981.

Healthcommunities.com. "Shift work overview, causes for shift work disorder," Dec. 1, 2000 (downloaded April 28, 2011)

Hendrickson, Robert (ed). *QPB Encyclopedia of Word and Phrase Origins.* New York: Facts on File, 2004.

Herald International Tribune. "From afar, Americans are asked to pay up; Debt collection gets a polite Indian touch," Malaysia Edition, April 25, 2008, pp. 2,12.

Honig, A.L. "Police Assisted Suicide: Identification, Intervention, and Investigation." *The Police Chief,* October 2001.

Houlihan, Dan. "Cops Give Weaker Commands in Violent Encounters." *Force Science News* #43, pp. 1-5, April 2006. www.ForceScienceNews (accessed October 26, 2007).

Hutson, H.H., D. Anglin, D., J. Yarbough, K. Hardaway, M. Hussell, J. Strote, M. Gantur and B. Blum. "Suicide by Cop," *Annuals of Emergency Medicine*, December 1998.

Jourard, Sidney. *The Transparent Self.* New York: Van Nostrand Reinhold, 1971.

Joyner, Charles and Chad Basile, J.D.. "The Dynamic Resistance Response Model A Modern Approach to the Use of Force," pp.21-30. *FBI Bulletin*, Vol. 76, #9, September 2007.

Keckeisen, George L. "The Korean War 'brainwashing' myth led to U.S. counter techniques against Communist indoctrination," *Military History*, August 2002, pp.70-77.

Klugiewicz, Gary. "Combat Verbalization," *Law Officer*, pp. 38-41, July/August 2005.

Korn, Peter. "Portland Crisis Intervention training takes some cues from Memphis," *The Portland Tribune*, September 11, 2008.

Korn, Peter. "Experts say police training flawed. Recent shootings involving mentally ill raise questions about program," *The Portland Tribune*, Jan 13, 2011.

Korn, Peter. "Program guides lives out of danger; Agency efforts save money, avoid conflict with police," *The Portland Tribune*, Feb 3, 2011.

Las Vegas Metropolitan Police Department. "Excited Delirium Video Training Series." 2005.

Law, Steve. "New mental health center fills a gap for police, patients," *The Portland Tribune*, June 17, 2010

Lawrence, Chris. "Is Excited Delirium a Fake Condition Invented to Whitewash Abusive Force; A Critical Look at NPR's Recent Reports." *Force Science News*, #67, March 2007. www.ForceScienceNews (accessed October 26, 2007).

Lawrence, Chris. "Excited Delirium Gets More Complicated; What To Do About It." *Force Science News*, #55, October 2006. www.ForceScienceNews (accessed October 26, 2007).

Legislative Report. *Oregon Association of Chiefs of Police*, pg. 29, August 2007.

Levine, Deena R. and Mara B. Adelman. *Beyond Language*, New York: Prentice Hall, 1993.

Lewinski, Bill. "New Excited Delirium Protocol Issued by San Jose PD." *Force Science News* #73, June 2007a. www.ForceScienceNews (accessed October 26, 2007).

Lewinski, Bill. "Distractions and Aggressive Subjects," *Force Science News* #79, August 2007b. www.ForceScienceNews (accessed September 24, 2007).

Lindsay, M.S. "Identifying the Dynamics of Suicide by Cop," in D.C. Sheehan & J.I. Warren, eds. "*A Compilation of papers submitted to the Suicide and Law Enforcement Conference*," FBI Academy, Quantico, Virginia, 1999.

Lindsey, Dennis. "Police Fatigue." In *Force Science News* #80, pp.1-4, 2007. www.ForceScienceNews (accessed October 26, 2007).

Loden, Marilyn. *Implementing Diversity*, New York: Harper and Row, 1996.

Louie, Ronald J., Sergeant. "Crisis Intervention: A Police Model for Dispute Settlement." *Journal of California Law Enforcement*, pp. 70-77, Vol. 15, No. 2, Spring, 1981.

Louie, Ronald J., Chief. "Crisis Intervention Training for the 1990s," *Oregon DPST Reports*, pp. 8-10, Vol. II, No. 2, Summer, 1990.

Louie, Ronald J., Chief. "Crisis Intervention: Handling the Difficult Person." Management and Supervisory Development Course, *Portland Community College*, Portland, Oregon, Spring, 2006.

Louie, Ronald J. "Crisis Intervention and Tactical Communication: Models for Dispute Settlement when Dealing with People in Stressful Situations." *Hillsboro Police Department Training Bulletin #1-2007*, Hillsboro, Oregon, January 2007a.

Louie, Ronald J., Chief (Ret.). "Cultural Diversity in Law Enforcement Professions," *Justice Administration 101 Course, Portland Community College*, Portland, Oregon, Fall, 2007b.

Louie, Ronald J., Chief (Ret.). "Tactical Communication in Critical Incidents," *Justice Administration 244 Course, Portland Community College*, Portland, Oregon, Fall, 2007c.

Louie, Ronald J., Chief (Ret.). "Tactical Communication in Critical Incidents,' *Justice Administration 244 Course, Portland Community College,* Portland, Oregon, Winter 2008.

Louie, Ronald J., (Ret.). "Tactical Communication in Crisis Incidents," *Criminal Justice Course 410, Portland State University,* Portland, Oregon, July 2010a.

Louie, Ronald J., Chief (Ret.), ed. "The Nature of Conflict." *Unpublished Training Seminar, Hillsboro Police Department,* Hillsboro, Oregon, December, 13, 2010b.

Louie, Ronald J., Chief, and Ed Vance, Detective, Eds. "Active Listening Skills; Tools for Crisis Negotiation," *FBI National Crisis Intervention Course*, FBI Academy, Quantico, Virginia, June 2006.

Louie, Ronald J., Chief, and Ed Vance, Detective, eds. "Responding to Suicide," *Hillsboro Police Department Training Bulletin #2-2007*, Hillsboro Police Department, Oregon, January 2007.

Mayer, Richard J. *Conflict Management: The Courage to Confront.* Battelle Press, 1995.

Mayo Clinic. "Schizophrenia," *MayoClinic.com*,(accessed December 13, 2010).

Mayo Clinic. "Post Traumatic Stress Disorder," *MayoClinic.com* (accessed March 4, 2011).

McElvain, James. "Drunk, Drugged, Violence-Prone suspects Most Likely to be Shot by Police," in *Force Science News*, #65, February 9, 2007. www.ForceScienceNews (accessed October 26, 2007).

McHattie, Sarah. "The art of conversation: How active listening and empathy can help calm an angry person," *Associated Content*, 2010.

McRedmond, Paul. "Deflecting Rage by Creating a Void Where it's Aimed" pp. 1-4, in *Force Science News*, #81, September 2007. www.ForceScienceNews (accessed September 24, 2007).

Mehrabian, Albert. *Silent Messages.* Belmont: Wadsworth Publishing, 1971.

City of Memphis, Tennessee. "Memphis Police Crisis Intervention Team," City Web, (accessed March 28, 2011).

Miller, Rory. "Tactical Listening; Conflict Communications," *conflict communications web,* (accessed April 12, 2011).

Miller, Rory. *Meditations on Violence.* Wolfeboro, N.H.: YMAA Publications, 2008.

Monahan, J., "Mental Disorder and Violent Behavior: Perceptions and Evidence," *American Psychologist,* 47, 511-521, 1992.

Newsweek. "How police can better handle emotionally disturbed citizens," July 31, 2008.

Nielsen, Susan. "Not part of a hospital horror story? Think again," *The Oregonian,* April 10, 2011, p. B8.

Noesner, Gary and Mike Webster. "Crisis intervention: using active listening skills in negotiations," *FBI Law Enforcement Bulletin,* Aug. 1, 1997, pp. 1-7.

Oregon Employment Department. "Defusing Difficult Situations: Discovering the keys to a positive workplace," 2004.

Oregonian. "Hillsboro police require all officers to train as mediators," August 24, 2006.

Oregonian Editorial Board. "Inviting Portlanders in from the cold," January 22, 2011.

Owen, Wendy. "Fashion doesn't make the teacher, but it gets respect from students." *The Oregonian,* October 12, 2009.

Page, Jonathan. "Cops Give Weaker Commands in Violent Encounters." *Force Science News,* #43, April 2006. www.ForceScienceNews (accessed September 26, 2007).

Parad, H.J. and G. Caplan. "A Framework for Studying Families in Crisis," *Social Work,* July 1960.

Parker, L. and R. Meier. *Interpersonal Psychology for Law Enforcement and Corrections.* St. Paul, Minn.: West Publications, 1975.

Parsons, Kevin, Ph.D. "Trial record testimony explaining justification for the use of deadly force." Stomps v. City of Gresham, U.S. Dist. Ct. for Oregon, May 15, 1985.

Perrou, Barry. Crisis Intervention: Suicide in Progress - A Working Document. *Public Safety Research Institute,* 1999.

John G. Peters Jr., Ph.D., John G. Peters Jr. & Associates, "Force Continuums: Three Questions," *Police Chief,* Jan 2006 (accessed April 14, 2011).

Puhn, Laurie. *"Fight Less, Love More: 5-Minute Conversations to Change Your Relationship Without Blowing Up or Giving In"* Rodale, 2010.

Pyers, Louise. "Suicide by Cop –The Ultimate Trap," *FBI National Academy Associates*, July/August, Volume 3, No. 4, 2001.

Regini, Chuck. "Crisis Intervention for Law Enforcement Negotiators," *FBI Law Enforcement Bulletin*, Vol. 73, October 2004.

Reik, Theodor. *Listening With the Third Ear*. New York: Pyramid, 1948.

Reiter, Lou. "Are You Providing Reasonable Training and Policy Direction on the Handling of the Mentally Ill and Emotionally Disturbed Persons?" pp.1-6. *Public Agency Training Council*, January 2007.

Rogers, Carl. *On Becoming a Person*. London: Constable, 1961.

Rogers, Jeff. "Outsider quick to judge." *Oregonian*, pg. A7, December 18, 2007.

Rojas-Burke, Joe. "Women's suicide risk rises sharply after military service," *Oregonian*, December 2, 2010.

Rollins, Michael. "So much depends on officer's focus." *Oregonian*, pg. B1, January 9, 2008.

Ross, Darrell. "What Promotes Peak Performance in Lethal-Force Conflicts?" *Force Science News*, #75, June 2007. www.ForceScienceNews (accessed September 24, 2007).

Rouches, Michael, Lieutenant. "Teflon Character: Dealing with Criticism," *Hillsboro Police Training Bulletin #5-2007*, Hillsboro Police Department, Oregon, January 2007.

Rouches, Michael, Lieutenant. "Communication and Combat Verbalization," *Hillsboro Police Training Bulletin #6-2007*, Hillsboro Police Department, Oregon, January 2007.

Rubin, Joel and Richard Winton. "Federal court restricts Taser use by police," *Los Angeles Times*, December 30, 2009.

Saville, Gregory. "Emotional Intelligence in Policing," *The Police Chief*, pp. 38-41, 2006.

Schuler, D. "Counseling Suicide Survivors: Issues and Answers," *Omega*, Vol. IV, 1973.

Schumpert, Phillip. "Quick Ice-Breakers." *Force Science News*, #81, September 2007. www.ForceScienceNews (accessed September 26, 2007).

Schwartz, S.L. "A Review of Crisis Intervention Programs." Paper delivered at the *First Annual Postgraduate Seminar, American Psychiatric Association*. Glen Falls, New York, 1971.

Science Daily. "Faulty brain connections may be responsible for social impairments in Autism," June 12, 2008.

Scott, Richard. "Raising a Voice for Mental Illness." *Case in Point*, pp. 24-27, January 2008.

Scott, Richard. "Awake at Night; The Ill Effects of Poor Sleep and Sleep Disorders." *Case in Point*, pp. 29-31, January 2008.

Shusta, Robert M., Deena R. Levine, Herbert Z. Wong, Aaron T. Olson, and Philip R. Harris. "Language Barriers and Law Enforcement," *Multicultural Law Enforcement: Strategies for Peacekeeping in a Diverse Society*, 4th Edition, New Jersey: Pearson Education, Inc., 2007.

Smith, Jill. "Conquering Conflict," *Oregonian*, pp. 10-13, August. 24, 2006.

Snider, Julie. "Military alcohol dependency on rise," USA Today, March 31, 2009.

Stomps v. City of Gresham. U.S. District Court for Oregon, May 15, 1985.

Strentz, T. "Thirteen Indicators of Volatile Negotiations," *Law and Order*, pp. 135-139, September 1991.

Strentz, T. "The Cycle Crisis Negotiations Time Line," *Law and Order*, pp. 73-76, March 1995.

"Suicide Assessment and Intervention." *FBI National Crisis Negotiation Course*, Quantico, Virginia, June 2006.

J.L. Sumpter. "The art of conversation," *Law & Order*, pp. 14-15, July 2008a.

J.L. Sumpter. "Nonverbal signs of deception," *Law & Order*, pp. 14-15, Sept. 2008b

Taylor, Jo Anne, R.N. *"Unpublished interview regarding conscious and unconscious hospital patients."* Hillsboro, Oregon, March 31, 2011.

Tennessee v. Garner, 471 U.S. (1985).

Terry v. Ohio, 392 U.S. 1 (1968).

Thompson, George and Jerry Jenkins. *Verbal Judo: The Gentle Art of Persuasion.* New York: William Morrow & Co., 1993.

Thompson, Michael, Officer, ed. "Excited Delirium; The Law Enforcement Role in Effectively Dealing with Mentally Ill Persons and Reducing In-Custody Deaths and Injuries," *Hillsboro Police Training Bulletin #3-2007*, Hillsboro Police Department, Oregon, January 2007.

Thompson, Michael, Officer, ed. "Suicide by Cop; Valuable Information to Foster Understanding," *Hillsboro Police Training Bulleting #4-2007*, Hillsboro Police Department, Oregon, January 2007.

Vance, Ed, Detective, ed. "Snakes Without Venom; Suicide Assessment and Intervention," *FBI National Crisis Negotiation Course*, Quantico, Virginia, June 2006.

Vance, Ed, Detective, and Ronald J. Louie, Chief, eds. "Suicide Assessment and Intervention," *FBI National Crisis Intervention Course*, FBI Academy, Quantico, Virginia, June 2007.

Verbaljudo.org; 217 Hart Ave, Staten Island, New York, 10310, (2007). www.Verbaljudo.org (accessed December 1, 2007).

Vets News. "Combat, Suicide Related." *Oregon Department of Veterans' Affairs.* January/February 2008.

Walker v. City of New York, 974 F. 2nd 293; 1992 US App. (2nd Cir. 1992).

Wallace, Samuel E. *After Suicide.* New York: Wiley, 1973.

Ward v. County of San Diego, 791 F. 2nd 1329 (9th Cir. 1986).

Whitaker, Brian. "Religious police told to smile," *The Guardian*, June 10, 2003.

Wikipedia. "Post Traumatic Stress Disorder," Wikipedia.com, (accessed December 12, 2010).

Williams, Patti. "Police and Mediation: Win-Win Partnership," *The Oregon Police Chief*, pp. 24-26, Fall, 1997.

Wiselogle, Andy. "Hillsboro Police Mediation Training," *East Metro Mediation*, Feb. 23-26, 2010.

Yahoo News. "Police academy class slogan: Cause PTSD," yahoonews.com_academy_slogan, (Accessed December 25, 2007).

Zacker, J. and M. Bard. "Adaptive Resistance to Change in a Community," *American Journal of Community Psychology*, Vol. 1, 1973, pp. 44-49.

Zinkin, Mary. Negotiation and Mediation Training Syllabus. *Center for Conflict Studies,* Portland, Oregon, September 2000.

Zoroya, Gregg. "360,000 Veterans may have brain injuries," *USA Today*, March 4, 2009a.

Zoroya, Gregg. "Alcohol treatment programs for military rise," *USA Today*, June 1, 2009b, p. A1.

Zoroya, Gregg. "Narcotic pain-relief prescriptions on rise for Military," *USA Today*, June 23, 2010.

Chief Ron Louie receives his retirement sword, Hillsboro Police Department, Oregon, June 30, 2007

Get *Force Science© News* transmissions sent directly to your e-mail address...free!

Force Science© News is a free e-newsletter provided twice a month by *The Force Science© Institute*. The publication reports on groundbreaking use-of-force findings from the Institute's Force Science© Research Center, as well as other important issues related to the use of force in law enforcement.

Just a few of the more than 100 articles that have been sent:

- New findings on shell ejection patterns help clear officer on trial for murder.
- "Scan Patterns" next breakthrough in survival training?
- Will traumatic stress sharpen your memory... or sabotage it?
- Latest findings and recommendations about traumatic stress.
- Distractions and aggressive subjects- what a new study and past experience tell us.
- Can you really prevent unintentional discharges?
- Was suspect's shooting a "police execution?"
  Detailed findings from *Force Science© Research Center* help Federal jury decide.
- New study may "radically alter" how police deadly force is viewed.
- Low-cost training in crisis decision-making that still "makes 'em sweat."
- Ongoing survey seeks consensus on what's "reasonable" use of force.
- "Canadian Response" technique brings quick restraint of combative, super-strong subjects, FSRC advisor tells excited delirium conference.
- "Lethality Assessment" helps gauge danger from domestic disputes.

You can register for your free subscription to *Force Science© News*:

- ✓ On the Web: visit www.forcesciencenews.com and click on the "sign up" button.
- ✓ By e-mail: Send your name, rank and agency (if applicable), and phone numbers for info@forcescience.org.
- ✓ By fax: Send the above information plus your e-mail address to: 773-913-6205.

For further information on *The Force Science© Institute* and its research and training programs visit www.forcescience.org or call 507-387-1290